D0856686

THE INTRICATE KNOT:

Black Figures in American Literature, 1776-1863

he has plundered our seas, ravaged our coasts, burnt our towns & destroyed

lives of our people:

Scotch and other

he is at this time transporting large armies of foreign mercenaries to comp-

the works of death, desolation & tyranny, already begun with circumstances

scarcely paralleled in the most barbarous ages, and totally

of cruelty & perfidy unworthy the head of a civilized nation:

he has ... excited domestic insurrections amongst us and has

he has endeavored to bring on the inhabitants of our frontiers the merciless Ind-

savages, whose known rule of warfare is an undistinguished destruction

all ages, sexes, & conditions [of existence:]

[he has incited treasonable insurrections of our fellow-citizens, with the

he has constrained others ... on the high seas to bear arms against their country ... to become the executioners of their friends & brethren, or to

allurements of forfeiture & confiscation of our property:

he has waged cruel war against human nature itself, violating it's most

-cred rights of life & liberty in the persons of a distant people who never of-

-fended him, captivating & carrying them into slavery in another hemi-

-sphere, or to incur miserable death in their transportation thither. this

piratical warfare, the opprobrium of infidel powers, is the warfare of the

Christian king of Great Britain. determined to keep open a market

where MEN should be bought & sold, he has prostituted his negative

for suppressing every legislative attempt to prohibit or to restrain this

determining to keep open a market where MEN should be bought & sold:

execrable commerce: and that this assemblage of horrors might want no

of distinguished die, he is now exciting those very people to rise in arms

among us, and to purchase that liberty of which he has deprived them,

by murdering the people upon whom he also obtruded them: thus paying

off former crimes committed against the liberties of one people, with crimes

which he urges them to commit against the lives of another.]

in every stage of these oppressions we have petitioned for redress in the most humble

only

terms; our repeated petitions have been answered by repeated injuries. a prince

whose character is thus marked by every act which may define a tyrant, is un-

+ Dr. Franklin

Thomas Jefferson condemned slavery in this rough draft of the Declaration
of Independence. The pertinent section, in brackets, was not incorporated
into the final text.

THE INTRICATE KNOT:

Black Figures in American Literature, 1776-1863

JEAN FAGAN YELLIN

NEW YORK UNIVERSITY PRESS

NEW YORK   1972

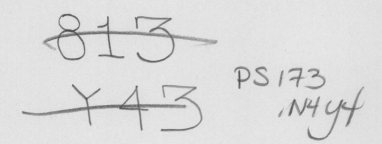

Acknowledgments

Introduction, by Jean Fagan Yellin, to CLOTEL, OR THE PRESIDENT'S DAUGHTER. Arno Press, 1969. Reprinted by permission of Arno Press.

"Black Masks: Melville's *Benito Cereno*," by Jean Fagan Yellin. *American Quarterly*, Vol. 22, No. 3, pp. 678-79. Copyright 1970, Trustees of the University of Pennsylvania. Reprinted by permission of *American Quarterly*.

Frontispiece courtesy of the Manuscript Division of the Library of Congress. Illustrations courtesy of The New York Public Library, Astor, Lenox and Tilden Foundations: p. 14, Prints Division; p. 82, Shomburg Collection; p. 182, Rare Books Division.

For Ed (without whom, not)
and for Pete, Lisa, and Mike (with whom, barely)

PREFACE

The major Afro-American writers have said that the black
man in America is unnamed and unseen. Yet his dark figure is
ubiquitous in our fiction; the American imagination was as
obsessed in the nineteenth century by the black as it is today.
In this book I examine views of black people in American prose
from the time of the Declaration of Independence to the Emancipation Proclamation. Because of the complex interrelationship
between ideas about blacks and attitudes toward slavery, I also
explore discussions of chattel slavery.

Modern literary portraits of black people have been shaped
by the black figures which were outlined by Thomas Jefferson
in the late eighteenth century and filled in by plantation, abolitionist, and insurrectionist novelists and fugitive and rebel
slaves during the next generation. The logic of plantation fiction,
in which the premise that black people are less than human
leads directly to the conclusion that slavery is beneficial to superior whites and inferior blacks, underlies current portrayals
which dramatize an identical view but repress their premises and
leave implicit their conclusion that Afro-Americans should be
content with less than full citizenship. The outrage in the often
deeply ironic autobiographies of fugitive slaves, which reveal the
black faces displayed in plantation fiction to be masks hiding

angry features, is echoed in the harsh tones of black writers today. Antislavery novels, which use both the simple Sambo images of the plantation novels and the ironic double views of the narratives, are mirrored in modern characterizations portraying black people as passive victims. Although the shadow of the black terrorist, glimpsed in plantation and abolitionist fiction and seen in the background of the narratives, darkens both our classical literature and our current perceptions and politics, he remains an enigmatic threat in nineteenth-century fiction and today. "Benito Cereno," written a half-century after Jefferson had projected his conflicting views of black people, like all great art dramatizes the inadequacy of partial visions. Melville's tale, a profound criticism of the characterizations of the black figures in pre-Civil War fiction, points toward the fuller portraits only now being realized.

My method is selective rather than exhaustive and thematic rather than historical. Through the use of nonliterary materials —such as travellers' accounts, polemics, and autobiographies—I have tried to suggest social contexts which will illuminate the literary texts examined. A chart mapping temporal relations between the works discussed and some of the relevant political and social events can be found at the end of the book. Because until recently black materials were systematically excluded from standard discussions of American literature, many have been difficult to locate. Consequently I have made my notes and bibliography rather full in an effort to aid the reader.

For my purposes it has been adequate to identify fictional characters as "black," or "white," or as "mulatto" (signifying any mixture) despite the fact that throughout the period studied racial makeup was more precisely designated. I use the term "racist" to signify one who assigns value on the basis of race. I find it suggestive that our language includes no positive term— only the negation "antiracist"—to indicate one who does not.

I want here to record my great debt to my friend and teacher, Sherman Paul, although I know I can repay him only by offering my students the help he has so freely given me. I also want to thank Dorothy Sterling for graciously sharing with me her materials on Martin Robinson Delany. Like all other studies in this field, my book is built on the work of Sterling A. Brown. I owe thanks to a number of librarians; of great help were Dr. Theodore Grieder and Mr. Max Bissainthe of the Fales Collection, and the Director and staff of the other New York University libraries; and Mr. Henry Birnbaum, Mr. Bruce Bergman, and the staff of the Pace College library. I am deeply indebted to Mrs. Jean Blackwell Hutson, Director, Mr. Ernest Kaiser, and the staff of the Schomburg Collection of the New York Public Library. Without their expert advice and generous aid, this study would have been substantially poorer. I would also like to express my gratitude to the American Association of University Women, whose grant enabled me to spend a year writing this book, and to the Scholarly Research Committee of Pace College, whose award aided me in preparing the manuscript for publication. In addition, I wish to thank Robert Corrigan, of the American Civilization Program and the Committee on Afro-American Affairs at the University of Iowa, for inviting me to present a part of this study as a lecture; and the editors of *American Quarterly* and Arno Press for permission to reprint the portions of this manuscript which first appeared in their pages. The dedication names my deepest debt.

Jean Fagan Yellin
New Rochelle, New York

CONTENTS

Part One:

The Problem

The effect of the Negro's presence in this country has been about as marked as the admittedly great and transforming influence of America upon the Negro. There is this double strand running through the whole scheme....

Alain Locke,
"The Negro in America"

For intricacy, such a knot he had never seen. . . . The knot seemed a combination of double-bowline-knot, treble-crown-knot, back-handed-well-knot, knot-in-and-out-knot, and jamming-knot.

Herman Melville, "Benito Cereno"

Chapter I

JEFFERSON'S *NOTES*

A study of the characterization of black figures in American literature might be begun with Jefferson's *Notes on Virginia*. This essay, written in 1781, is an attempt by the best mind of the Revolutionary generation to interpret life in the new world; in it Jefferson has much to say about chattel slavery and black people.[1] He hypothesizes black inferiority and describes the stereotyped Negro who will recur in plantation fiction; but, arguing for the abolition of slavery, sees the black as oppressed and sounds the note of wrath that will become characteristic of the abolitionists. Significantly, Jefferson begins his discussion with the confession that he does not possess final knowledge about the black man. In his image of the black wearing his dark skin like a veil masking truth, Jefferson hints at the violent disjunction between appearance and reality revealed by the slave narrators.

The *Notes* consistently urge an end to slavery, which is seen as essentially immoral, as a violation of natural law. This position was not new to Jefferson: As early as 1770, arguing on behalf of a mulatto who sued for his freedom, he voiced the theory of natural rights:

Under the law of nature all men are born free. . . . This is
what is called personal liberty, and is given . . . by the
author of nature, because necessary for . . . sustenance.
The reducing of the mother to servitude was a violation
of the law of nature: surely then the same law cannot pre-
scribe a continuance of the violation to her issue, and that
too without end. . . .[2]

Six years later he gave this doctrine its classic form in the Declaration of Independence.[3] Although slavery is denounced as an evil
in *Notes on Virginia,* it is seen as an evil for which Americans are
not responsible—a point of view that Jefferson had already articu-
lated in *A Summary View* and in the antislavery passage expunged
from the Declaration. In the *Notes,* slavery is regarded as the consequence of Royal British inhumanity and greed, as yet another
curse inflicted on the innocent suffering colonists by an usurping
tyrant.

One of Jefferson's moral arguments for the abolition of
slavery rests in his awareness that the core of the servile relationship is not love, but hate, and that it yields "Deep-rooted prejudices entertained by the whites; ten thousand recollections, by
the blacks, of the injuries they have sustained . . ." (XIV). Reflect-
ing on these bitter fruits, he sounds an apocalyptic note:

[L]iberties are . . . the gift of God . . . not to be vio-
lated but with his wrath. . . . Indeed I tremble for my
country when I reflect that God is just; that his justice
cannot sleep forever. . . . The Almighty has no attribute
which can take side with us in such a contest! (XVIII)

He strikes this prophetic tone again—a note which will echo and
re-echo in antislavery writings for years to come—in a letter
written in 1786:

When the measure of their tears shall be full, when their groans shall have involved heaven itself in darkness, doubtless a God of Justice will awaken to their distress, and in diffusing light and liberality among their oppressors, or at length by his exterminating thunder, manifest his attention to the things of this world, and that they are not left to the guidance of a blind fatality.[4]

In addition to expressing ethical criticisms, Jefferson attacks the social consequences of chattel slavery. Despite his disapproval of gambling, dancing, and cards, in many respects Jefferson is a model of the master of the Revolutionary generation who would be drawn repeatedly in our fiction. Like many gentlemen in plantation novels, Jefferson, at one time second largest slave-holder of Albemarle County, suffered considerable loss of property at the hands of the British who carried off thirty of his chattels personal; he was remembered by one of his old slaves as a good master, and by his former overseer as imprudently generous; and he died in debt, land-poor, freeing a few personal servants in his will.[5] Like many masters in abolitionist novels (he is openly named in one) Jefferson may have had a slave mistress and children.[6] Jefferson was sharply aware of the moral climate of a slave society, and in *Notes on Virginia* he argues that both master and slave are deformed by the social roles they play. He does not dwell here—or elsewhere—on the utterly blasted life of the enslaved; but he comments on the pernicious consequences of mastery on the developing character of the young slave owner, and also voices his concern that the industrious nature of Americans might be destroyed (XVIII).

The *Notes* assert that in addition to engendering private and public immorality, the institution of chattel slavery threatens the public safety. Reasoning that a slave cannot feel patriotism for the land of his bondage, and hence by implication is a potential enemy to that nation, Jefferson briefly suggests the possibility of servile insurrection: "[C]onsidering numbers, . . . a revolution of the wheel of fortune, an exchange of situation is among possible events" (XVIII). His muted warning was prophetic. Eight years later, in August of 1791, the revolutionary winds that swept across France spread to the island of St. Domingue in the French Caribbean, with a population of 30,000 whites, 24,000 mulattoes and free blacks, and 452,000 black slaves. When it became apparent that the whites did not intend to extend to their slaves the rights they demanded for themselves, the blacks arose. Aften ten bloody years of civil war, the black republic of Haiti was secured, and slavery was abolished for the first time in a small section of the new world.[7] Most of the whites were killed or had fled: more than ten thousand to the United States, spreading panic with their accounts of the Black Terror.[8] In 1800, during Jefferson's presidency, the apprehensive South realized its worst fears: A massive plot involving several thousand slaves was discovered at Richmond, Virginia. Although the leader, Gabriel, and thirty-six other slaves were executed, the white South was never thereafter free of the fear of servile insurrection which Jefferson had so guardedly hinted at a generation earlier in the *Notes*.[9]

All of his moral arguments to the effect that slavery is a violation of natural law, and an essentially destructive relation; the fear of God's retributive justice; and all practical considerations of the disastrous social consequences and the inevitable danger of insurrection point to one conclusion. Slavery must be abolished. Despite Jefferson's denial that Americans were responsible for this evil, he argues that Americans must act to rectify it. In the *Notes* Jefferson outlines the plan for gradual emancipation which he had framed with Wythe and Mason for consideration by the Virginia Assembly in 1777, but never presented. Almost two decades later, when this proposal was reformulated and commended to the legislature for consideration by St. George Tucker, the House of Delegates refused even to discuss it.[10] Almost forty years after first framing this scheme for the gradual abolition of slavery, Jefferson wrote that it was "the only practicable plan I could ever devise . . . and it is still the one most sound in my judgment." [11] But by then he had given it up.

The optimism which Jefferson felt in 1781 over the likelihood slavery would be abolished rings in the sentences climaxing and concluding his discussion on slavery in the *Notes:*

I think a change already perceptible, since the origin of the present revolution. The spirit of the master is abating, that of the slave rising from the dust, his condition mollifying, the way I hope preparing, under the auspices of heaven, for a total emancipation. . . . (XVIII)

More than a generation later, his labored phrases sound the note of resignation:

Some progress is sensibly made in it; yet not so much as I had hoped and expected. But it will yield in time to temperate and steady pursuit, to the enlargement of the human mind, and its advancement in science. We are not in a world ungoverned by the laws and the power of a superior agent. Our efforts are in his hand, and directed by it, and he will give them their effect in his own time.[12]

Racism is the rock on which Jefferson's emancipation plan foundered. The problem was not slavery, but the black man. As formulated in the *Notes,* Jefferson's original amendment proposing the abolition of chattel slavery in Virginia advocated within a single sentence both emancipation and colonization:

[A]n amendment containing it [proposal for emancipation] was prepared, to be offered to the legislature whenever the bill should be taken up, and farther directing, that they [the slaves] should continue with their parents to a certain age, then to be brought up, at the public expense, to tillage, arts, or sciences, according to their geniuses, till the females should be eighteen, and the males twenty-one years of age, when they should be colonized to such place as the circumstances of the time should render most proper . . . (XIV)

Jefferson initiates his discussion of race in the *Notes* with an admission of a lack of knowledge. His apprehension that the true emotions of the black were concealed behind an "immovable veil" hints at the revelation of deliberate role-playing in the slave narratives that would follow. But though he begins and ends his conjectures with an assertion of ignorance and a plea for knowledge, the modern reader, encountering Query XIV, experiences the same shock he feels when he turns from Locke's ranging speculations on the limits of knowledge to his comments on witches:

> To our reproach it must be said, that though for a century and a half we have had under our eyes the races of black and of red men, they have never yet been viewed by us as subjects of natural history. I advance it, therefore, as a suspicion only, that the blacks, whether originally a distinct race, or made distinct by time and circumstances, are inferior to the whites in the endowments both of body and mind. (XIV)

Using the white man as the norm, Jefferson assigns a series of attributes to the black: By virtue of his color, hair and form, he is less beautiful than the white; he has less body hair, sweats more, and smells; he is more tolerant of heat, and less of cold; he needs less sleep, but sleeps when at rest; he lacks forethought and hence often appears brave; he is "more ardent," but his love is composed of desire, not sentiment; his grief is quickly forgotten. In general terms common to the eighteenth century, the black man, in contrast to the white man, is found to be given more to sensation and less to reflection. Although apparently equal in memory, his reason is "much inferior," and his imagination "dull, tasteless, and anomalous." When contrasted with the Roman slave, the black slave is seen to be inferior, although his burden is lighter. He can, however, be improved by intermixture with the whites. On the more positive side, he has a talent for music and religion, and is benevolent, grateful, and loyal. All in all, the black man Jefferson describes in the *Notes on Virginia* in 1781 is the Compleat Plantation Stereotype.[13]

It is very difficult to determine whether Jefferson ever rejected this view of black people to any great extent, although it has often been assumed that his letter to Benjamin Banneker, written ten years after the publication of the *Notes,* represents a basic change. In 1791 Banneker, a free Afro-American, sent Jefferson the manuscript and calculations for the first edition of his *Almanac,* along with a letter appealing to Jefferson's fairness. He urged Jefferson to "embrace every opportunity, to eradicate that train of absurd and false ideas and opinions, which so generally prevails with respect to us." His most telling passage centers on the disparity between Jefferson's authorship of the Declaration of Independence and his role as slaveholder:

. . . but, Sir, how pitiable is it to reflect, that although you were so fully convinced of the benevolence of the Father of Mankind, and of his equal and impartial distribution of these rights and privileges, which he hath conferred upon them, that you should at the same time counteract his mercies, in detaining by fraud and violence so numerous a part of my brethren, under groaning captivity, and cruel oppression, that you should at the same time be found guilty of that most criminal act, which you professedly detested in others, with respect to yourselves.[14]

Jefferson's response, dated August 30, 1791, asserts that

No body wishes more than I do to see such proofs as you exhibit, that nature has given to our black brethren, talents equal to those of the other colors of men, and that the appearance of a want of them is owing merely to the degraded condition of their existence, both in Africa & America.

In a letter written the same day, Jefferson informed the Marquis de Condorcet of Banneker's mathematical accomplishments, adding:

> I shall be delighted to see these instances of moral emi-
> nence so multiplied as to prove that the want of talents
> observed in them is merely the effect of their degraded
> condition, and not proceeding from any difference in the
> structure of the parts on which intellect depends.[15]

Years later, Jefferson reiterated this attitude in a letter to Henri Grégoire, who had sent him a copy of his *Littérature des Nègres:*

> Be assured that no person living wishes more sincerely
> than I do, to see a complete refutation of the doubts I
> have myself entertained, and expressed on the grade of
> understanding alloted to them [blacks] by nature, and to
> find that in this respect they are on a par with ourselves.
> My doubts were the result of personal observation on the
> limited sphere of my own State, where the opportunities
> for the development of their genius were not favorable,
> and those of exercising it still less so.[16]

But that these statements do not constitute a rejection of the racism expressed in *Notes on Virginia* is evident in light of the following, written at the same time as the note to Grégoire:

> I have a long letter from Banneker, which shows him to
> have a mind of very common stature indeed. As to Bishop
> Gregoire, I wrote him a very soft answer. It was impossible
> for doubt to have been more tenderly, or hesitatingly
> expressed than that was in Notes of Virginia, and nothing
> was or is farther from my intentions, than to enlist myself

the champion of a fixed opinion, where I have only expressed a doubt. St. Domingo will, in time, throw light on
the question.[17]

Given his commitment to the abolition of slavery and his
recurrent belief in black inferiority, Jefferson's insistence on
colonization was made inevitable. In a letter written in 1811, he
rehearses his many proposals to deport the blacks, and affirms his
continued support of the idea:

Having long ago made up my mind on this subject, I have
no hesitation in saying that I have ever thought it the
most desirable measure which could be adopted, for gradually drawing off this part of our population, most advan-
tageously for themselves as well as for us.[18]

But Jefferson's critics have pointed out that for a society like Virginia, in which the entire economy was based on black slave
labor, to make emancipation contingent on the removal of the
black population was to make emancipation impossible.[19]

Jefferson posed the questions of the nature of the black man
and of the role of slavery in a democracy during the Revolutionary period. His answers tentatively hypothesize black inferiority and the necessity for political action to end slavery,
notions which in the next half-century come to dominate American writing on these subjects. In *Notes on Virginia* he embraced
both abolition and white supremacy, although he disclaimed
certain knowledge of the black man. His *Notes* thus embodies
both an assertion of human liberty, and a classic statement of the
racism which has prevented its realization in America.

NOTES—CHAPTER I

1. *Notes on Virginia* was first published at Paris, 1784, dated 1782. It can be found in *The Works of Thomas Jefferson* . . . , ed. Paul Leicester Ford, Federal edition, 12 vols. (New York and London, 1904-05), III, 347-517; IV, 3-119. Because so many editions are available, I have cited query numbers. For an illuminating discussion of the *Notes* as an expression of the pastoral, see Leo Marx, *The Machine in the Garden* (New York, 1964), pp. 73-144.
2. "Case of Howell vs. Netherland," *Works*, I, 274-75.
3. The question of the inclusiveness of the statement of natural rights in the preamble of the Declaration was debated until the Emancipation Proclamation was signed. For generations the abolitionists argued that "all men" meant all men regardless of color; the proslavery spokesmen pointed out that the passage condemning the Crown for its role in inaugurating slavery and the slave trade was excluded from the final draft. In the 1820s when the Missouri Compromise was debated, proslavery Congressmen cited the Declaration to argue that political compacts could not forever bind posterity and thus concluded that slavery could not permanently be prohibited north of 36°30′. See Philip F. Detweiler, "Congressional Debate on Slavery and the Declaration of Independence, 1819-1821," *American Historical Review*, LXIII (April 1958), 598-616. For a discussion of Southern renunciation of the Declaration of Independence in the nineteenth century, see Clement Eaton, *The Freedom-of-Thought Struggle in the Old South*, rev. ed. (New York, 1964).
4. "Additional Questions of M. de Meusnier, and Answers," *Works*, V, 73.
5. Letter to Dr. William Gordon July 16, 1788, *Works*, V, 417. *Memoirs of a Monticello Slave: as Dictated to Charles Campbell in the 1840's by Isaac, One of Thomas Jefferson's Slaves*, ed. Rayford W. Logan (Charlottesville, 1951), p. 75. Interview with Edmund Bacon, first published in Rev. Hamilton W. Pierson, *Jefferson at Monticello* (New York, 1862). Reprinted in *The Jefferson Reader*, ed. Francis Coleman Rosenberger (New York, 1953), p. 70. "Jefferson's Will," *Works*, XII, 478-83.
6. Gossip about Jefferson's black family was first published by James T. Callender in the Richmond *Recorder* in 1802. It is mentioned, among other places, in Mrs. Frances Trollope, *Domestic Manners of the Americans*, 2 vols. (London, 1832). An abolitionist writer who made use of this was William Wells Brown in *Clotel, or, the President's Daughter* (London, 1853), discussed in Chapter VIII. The allegations have recently been discussed by W. Edward Farrison, *William Wells Brown, Author and Reformer* (Chicago, 1969); and Pearl M. Graham, "Thomas Jefferson and Sally Hemings," *Journal of Negro History*, XLIV (1961),

89-103. An interesting assessment is included in Winthrop D. Jordan, *White Over Black,* Chapel Hill, 1968, pp. 461-75.

7. John Hope Franklin, *From Slavery to Freedom,* 2nd ed. (New York, 1967), pp. 339-41; Hubert Herring, *A History of Latin America* (New York, 1955), pp. 148-51.

8. Eaton, pp. 89-90.

9. *A Documentary History of the Negro People in the United States,* ed. Herbert Aptheker (New York, 1962), I, 45-58. In a letter dated July 13, 1802 addressed to Rufus King, Jefferson sketches a picture of the revolt in Santo Domingo, relates it to the Gabriel Conspiracy, then explores the possibility of deporting the insurgents. *Works,* IX, 383-86. Also see V, 146; IX, 317; and *The Adams-Jefferson Letters,* ed. Lester J. Cappon (Chapel Hill, 1959), I, 570. The two events are linked by Benjamin Quarles, *The Negro in the Making of America* (New York, 1967), p. 81; and by Eaton, p. 90.

10. For the fate of Jefferson's amendment, see the *Autobiography, Works,* I, 76-77. For Tucker's proposal, see *A Dissertation on Slavery with a Proposal for the Gradual Abolition of It in the State of Virginia* (Philadelphia, 1796). This provided for gradual abolition and increasingly stringent laws in Virginia designed to induce freedmen to leave and take up lands in the West. For a cogent discussion, see Robert McColley, *Slavery and Jeffersonian Virginia* (Urbana, 1964), pp. 132-35.

11. Letter to David Barrow, May 1, 1815, *Works,* IX, 515-16.

12. *Ibid.*

13. Frederick Douglass comments on Jefferson's racist theories and his "amalgamationist" practice in "Thomas Jefferson and Slavery," *Frederick Douglass' Paper,* April 1, 1852.

14. Letter to Thomas Jefferson, in Aptheker, I, 23-26.

15. *Works,* VI, 309-11.

16. *Works,* XI, 100.

17. Letter to Joel Barlow, October 8, 1809, *Works,* XI, 120. For a compilation of most of the pertinent material on this question, see "Jefferson's Thoughts on the Negro," *Journal of Negro History,* III (1918), 58-89. The author (Carter G. Woodson?) speculates that at one point Jefferson tentatively rejected the racist position espoused in the *Notes,* but that subsequently he retreated to his original belief in black inferiority.

18. Letter to John Lynch, January 21, 1811, *Works,* XI, 178.

19. McColley, p. 130. For some of the complexities of Jefferson's attitudes and actions, see William Cohen, "Thomas Jefferson and the Problem of Slavery," *Journal of American History,* LVI (1969), 503-26.

An idyllic view of plantation life is shown in this nineteenth-century wood engraving by the American artist Alexander Anderson.

Part Two:
Plantation Visions and Revisions

> "But it is to Babo here to whom, under God, I owe not only my own preservation, but likewise to him, chiefly, the merit is due, of pacifying his more ignorant brethren, when at intervals tempted to murmurings."
>
> "Ah, master," sighed the black, bowing his face, "don't speak of me; Babo is nothing; what Babo has done was but his duty."
>
> "Faithful fellow!" cried Captain Delano. "Don Benito, I envy you such a friend; slave I cannot call him."
>
> As master and man stood before him, the black upholding the white, Captain Delano could not but bethink him of the beauty of that relationship which could present such a spectacle of fidelity on the one hand and confidence on the other.
>
> Herman Melville, "Benito Cereno"

In 1781, when Jefferson wrote his *Notes,* black slavery had been in existence in Virginia for more than six generations. His hypothesis, that "the blacks are . . . inferior to the whites in the endowments both of body and mind," provided a theoretical basis for his sketch of the sweating, dull, loyal, musical, religious black man: the "Sambo" stereotype that existed in American culture before there was a native literature. The plantation novels which authors began to write in America in the next generation included this conventional figure and treated him without any variation at all. The black man was presented in minor roles for the next eighty years, providing humor and local color, the only development being an increasing insistence on his grotesqueness, his hilarity, and his love of servitude.

The first two novels considered here, *The Valley of Shenandoah* and *Westward Ho!,* are not properly a part of the genre. Tucker's book, though proslavery, does not present black men in terms of the stereotypes found in the other novels. But, in line with its proslavery bias, it shows them as content. Critics who have excluded *The Valley* from the plantation canon claim that it lacks the retrospective glow present in more typical examples of the genre; but Tucker's theme—the decline of the civilization in the South—is at the center of the tradition; and his mood, the sense of loss suffered with the passing of the old ways, is precisely the distinctive tone of the plantation tradition. It is suggested that he is somehow a "realist" where others are "romantic" because he describes a slave auction. But later novelists (Paulding, Kennedy, Simms) center their works on the threat to the old plantation; and in Paulding and Simms, slaves are sold or mortgaged—though behind the scenes. Perhaps the glow that critics find characteristic of the genre is not golden but lily-white; perhaps the element Tucker lacks, an essential element in the plantation tradition, is the stock racist view of the black man.

Paulding's *Westward Ho!* is excluded on other grounds: Its treatment of the black man is utterly stereotyped, but it dramatizes the purple dream of a slave empire, while the plantation tradition idealized slavery in the South. Paulding's novel, a peculiar instance of the Western as Southern, embodies an imaginative conception that died aborning.

The traditional plantation view of black people is found in Kennedy's *Swallow Barn*, a sketch of the mythic South of the declining present (1830s) and in Simms' *Woodcraft*, which depicts the mythic South of the heroic past. Despite disturbing hints, the overt portrayal of the black as a racial inferior happy in bondage, and of slavery as a beneficent relationship, is consistent in both works.

All of these novels include polemics espousing slavery. Tucker and Kennedy first present formal disclaimers, made by the proponents of slavery, before they advance arguments which convince skeptical Northerners of the excellence of the slave system. Paulding and Simms never show critics questioning the system of slavery; slaves themselves demonstrate their love of servitude by refusing to accept their freedom.

It is commonly stated that plantation fiction is significant because it represents one of the roots of our national literature. Such an assertion is revealing. In these novels, slavery is celebrated as The American Way; racism is the mode of American thought.

CHAPTER II

GEORGE TUCKER

In 1816, a tiny book, purportedly written by a young Royalist traveler, appeared anonymously. *Letters from Virginia, Translated from the French* is now generally attributed to George Tucker, author of the early Virginia novel *The Valley of Shenandoah*.[1] The volume includes a lengthy criticism of the racism in Jefferson's *Notes* and an emotional plea against the evils of slavery.

In 1795, the year before St. George Tucker published his abolitionist *Dissertation on Slavery*, his nephew George had emigrated from Bermuda to Williamsburg to read law. The young man moved to Richmond in 1800, the year of the Gabriel Conspiracy. He wrote his first published work, a pamphlet proposing an end to slavery and colonization of the blacks, as a result of Gabriel's aborted servile insurrection against the city. Though George Tucker was to publish fictional, sociological, historical, political, and economic accounts dealing with slavery throughout his long life, this tract, written when he was twenty-six, contained his only proposal for abolition.[2]

Tucker's first wife died in 1799, and during the fifteen years between *Letter . . . on . . . the Late Conspiracy of the Slaves* and *Letters from Virginia,* he married Maria Carter, a member of the Washington family, was accepted into William Wirt's literary circle, and wrote polite essays for the Richmond *Enquirer.*

Though for a time Tucker served as Commissioner of Bankruptcy, he failed at the law despite his social and literary position in Richmond. The life he led was unexemplary: Involved in gambling and speculations, he was the center of a financial scandal involving Richmond Academy, which he served as trustee. In 1806, deeply in debt, Tucker left the city and, with his wife and children, moved to the plantation of his wife's parents, the Carters, in the Shenandoah Valley. Two years later he purchased land and slaves and moved his growing family to Woodbridge in Pittsylvania County. Shortly thereafter, Carter was forced to sell the Shenandoah Valley plantation at a loss, and when unable to meet the payments on his new estate, he contemplated moving west to Kentucky with his slaves. To avoid this, Tucker, who had recently bought an additional "parcel of negroes" for himself, purchased twelve of his father-in-law's field slaves at auction and conveyed them to him in trust, redeemed some of his property, and settled Carter at nearby Deerwood, to run the plantation for their joint profit. Tucker began to work at the law and became active in politics while at Pittsfield. He also wrote polite essays,[3] and—if his biographer is correct—*Letters from Virginia*.

The slim volume includes twenty-three short essays, ranging from descriptions of Virginia cities to characterizations of the Yankee and the Southren, comments on Virginia eloquence and letters, and discussions of Virginia manners. Letter XI is a critique of the racist arguments in *Notes on Virginia*. Commenting on Jefferson's initial disclaimer that he lacks positive knowledge about the black, Tucker says that "this indirect apology, is hardly sufficient to excuse him . . . for this libel upon so large a portion of his fellow-creatures" (74). Tucker admits that he, too, finds the white more beautiful than the black. But after alluding to Jefferson's notorious relations with his slave women, he questions the use of white characteristics as "the standard of taste for all the world" (75). He points out that beauty is not a criterion of genius, and characterizes as "frivolous" Jefferson's enumeration of alleged physical differences between black and white; "They only prove that the blacks are different, not that they are inferior" (77).

Point by point Tucker argues Jefferson's assertions. He rebuts Jefferson's claim that black people need less sleep: "Like ourselves, they have a quick and lively relish for the pleasures of social intercourse. Is it wonderful then, that they seize the only moments in their power, to indulge this propensity of nature?" He disputes the notion that they are more ardent than whites; if so, he says, this is caused by "the fewer restraints which their manners, morals, and mode of living impose upon the violence of their passions rather than . . . any constitutional difference of nature." He questions the notion that they easily forget sorrow: "It is indeed, very true, that these poor blacks exhibit great patience, and even cheerfulness, under the handicaps of their condition. . . . But, after all, is their apathy quite as great as is supposed? If it is, why this feverish solicitude of the laws to guard against the spirit of insurrection and revenge? (79, 83, 84). All in all, Tucker finds their servile environment sufficient cause for the seeming inferiority of the blacks.

To make his point more strongly, he contrasts the behavior of young children who have not yet learned their social roles, and finds that despite attempts by "the little imitative tyrants of the nursery" to dominate "their sable subjects," the black children do not exhibit less "spirit, invention, or genius" than the white. He concludes that no racial inferiority is evident among small children (98-99). Then, in a remarkable passage, Tucker describes the blighting effects of slavery:

For my own part, I think there is not in nature a more melancholy picture than that of a little black when he first discovers that he is a slave. When the poor boy is taken from the street to be disciplined for the house, he is welcomed with smiles. . . . A new livery is put upon him, which he views again and again with delight, because he is yet to learn that it is the badge of sorrow and disgrace. . . . By and by however, the novelty of the scene wears off. . . . This is the time of transition from happy ignorance to painful knowledge. His carelessness and neglect of duty must be punished with the whip. With the first stroke the

whole illusion of liberty vanishes never to return. The
marks on his body are soon effaced; but what time can
obliterate the lashes from his mind? He is now a slave, and
he feels that he is one. His mind soon sinks to the level of
his condition, from which nothing, not even liberty at a
subsequent period, shall ever raise it again. After this, let
no man tell me that "it is nature, and not their condition,"
which has made the blacks inferior to the whites. (99-101)

This unusual egalitarian view can perhaps be traced to an incident of his very early childhood which Tucker, writing his autobiography in 1858 at the age of eighty-three, still recalled:

When I was too young to be left to myself I was attended by a colored boy several years older than myself.
This boy taught me to count, and to multiply as far as 12
by 12. How he acquired this knowledge, I never knew, nor
in fact ever inquired—but at the first school I was at after
I left my hornbook seminary, seeing the larger boys standing up to be examined in the multiplication table, . . . I
stood up with them and to the surprise of all, answered
every question readily and correctly. . . . From this incident, . . . I have always had doubts about the inferiority
of the intellect of the coloured race, tho' I admit that the
arguments in support of that hypothesis are very strong.[4]

Letter V strikes the exclamatory, emotional note that would
come to characterize antislavery writings. Tucker expresses horror
at encountering a group of shackled slaves being driven to Carolina after their sale at the courthouse, and includes a pathetic
sketch of the chattel, "some of them loaded with chains to prevent
their escape; while others had hold of each other's hands, strongly
grasped, as if to support themselves in their affliction." It describes "a poor mother, with an infant sucking at her breast as
she walked along, while two small children had hold of her apron

on either side, almost running to keep up with the rest," and the sound of their voices as they sang "a little wild hymn of sweet and mournful melody . . ." (30). Repelled by the scene, the traveler is further appalled when he learns that their sale is not the consequence of any crime they have committed, but of the "sordid avarice" of their masters, and he passionately argues against the callousness of slavery:

> There are those indeed who calmly tell us, that negroes have no feelings. What then: are they not human beings? Have they no heart? Do they not love their wives, their children, their homes, as well as their masters? The charge is a libel upon human nature, I had almost said, upon the Creator. The truth is, they feel, and exquisitely too. They weep with bitterness at these cruel separations. The sentence of banishment strikes them like the message of death. I have myself heard, with shuddering, their wild and frantic shrieks on these occasions, and my heart still trembles at the recollection. I must pity from my heart, that deplorable want of virtuous feeling, which makes man indifferent to the miseries of his fellow, a stranger to his own flesh, beholding his tears with levity or insult, for all the different complexions of his skin. (34)

Although for forty years Tucker maintained this position, he did not again condemn slavery.

Four years later, while debating the Missouri Question in Congress, Tucker opposed federal restrictions to the extension of slavery, justifying his stand that the government should not intervene by predicting that slavery would die out from economic reasons: positions he would continue to hold throughout his long life. While Professor of Moral Philosophy and Political Economy at the University of Virginia from 1825 to 1845, Tucker wrote a series of scholarly treatises defending the institution of chattel slavery, and after he retired he became even more insistent in his support of it.[5] In *History of the United States* (1856) Tucker again

criticizes Jefferson's *Notes on Virginia;* but, although forty years
earlier he had found the racism in error, he now feels that the
abolitionism is ill-founded. Here he argues that slavery is not
detrimental to manners; on the contrary, mastery fosters "habits
of forbearance and self-restraint." [6] Tucker expands on the beneficial effects of slavery in *Political Economy for the People,* published the following year, praising the character formed by "the
habit of command," and noting the happiness of slaves who are
treated with "familiarity and kindness" by Southern gentlemen.[7]
Tucker had moved far indeed from the nursery tyrants and the
hopeless slaveboy he had envisioned four decades earlier in
Letters from Virginia.

After his third term in Congress, Tucker made an unsuccess-
ful attempt to establish himself as a novelist in order to avoid an
academic career. He drew on much of his Virginia experience in
writing *The Valley of Shenandoah*—the youthful profligacy and
debt; his work in bankruptcy courts; the two-year residence with
the Carters; their ruin and anticipated flight to Kentucky; his
experiences running a plantation; even the recent sorrow of his
wife's death.[8] One of the earliest novelists to use a plantation
setting, in *The Valley* Tucker dramatizes the effects of economic
change on Virginia life. Although he wrote his book during the
summer of 1824, Tucker places the action in 1795, the year he
came to Virginia, during the period of the Santo Domingo
uprising.

The story begins after Colonel Grayson's death has forced his
widow and children to move from their estate on the James to
Beechwood, their plantation in the Shenandoah Valley. The
novel shows the last stages in the decline of the Grayson family:
They are driven to sell their land and their slaves and to retreat
to a small house on the Oppeccan; young Louisa, seduced by a
fast-talking New Yorker, wastes away and dies; and her brother
Edward is fatally stabbed after attempting to defend her name.
The happy past—here located in the Revolutionary era—is
warmly recalled by aged slaves. It is everywhere contrasted with
the mean present, a time during which mercenary men in both
the North and South profit while the improvident aristocracy,

represented at best in the present generation by victimized Louisa
and Edward, and at worst by their profligate and romantic cousins,
declines. Thus the neighboring Fawkners, always on the lookout
for bargains "in land, or negroes, or bonds," who are descended
from a former Grayson overseer, do not want their daughter to
marry Edward because he is now poor; and the seducer's father,
a New York merchant, will not permit his son to marry Louisa
for the same reason. (Southern greed proves less pernicious than
Northern, however, for the Fawkners become reconciled to the
marriage while the New Yorker does not.) The novel dramatizes
the decline of the Old South not only by sketching the growing
ascendancy of the North and the rise of the *nouveau riche* at
home, but also by including the presence of German and Scotch-
Irish immigrants in the Ancient Dominion; by suggesting the
decay of the Tidewater region and the push toward new lands in
Kentucky; and—though it is mentioned only once—by referring
to the slave insurrection at Santo Domingo, which is shown as
having warned white Virginians of the dangers of slavery but as
having had no effect at all on their happy slaves.

The Valley of Shenandoah includes a lengthy apology for
slavery. Discussing the peculiar institution with his Northern
guest, Edward Grayson remarks on the radical inconsistency between liberty and chattel slavery which Banneker had earlier
pointed out. Although he finds slavery evil, he denies any responsibility for it, as did Jefferson. Further, he asserts that emancipation would result in another Santo Domingo, that colonization
is impractical, and that therefore the problem cannot be solved.
Thus, he argues, slavery should not be criticized, although he
glibly proclaims that it "checks the growth of our wealth—is
repugnant to its justice—inconsistent with its principles—in-
jurious to its morale—and dangerous to its peace" (I. 61-62). In
a later passage he justifies slavery only because it is expedient:
When an attorney quotes the Declaration and asserts the equality
of mankind, the Northerner's cynical whisper, " 'Except negroes' "
is rebuked by a Virginian, who answers, " 'And they, too, by
nature, . . . but not by the law of the land, nor yet by the great
law of necessity' " (I. 235).

In sharp contrast to the description of the blighting effects of slavery in the *Letters,* what we are shown in *The Valley* encourages us to agree with the tractable Northerner that "whatever might be the condition of other slaves, the bonds of Beechwood sat lightly upon them" (I. 65). Indeed, Tucker reveals that the "chief mischief" resulting from the slave system is not its consequences for the blacks, but for the whites. In contrast to Tucker in the *Letters,* in his *Notes* Jefferson had also stressed the evil results of slavery on the slave owner. But where both *Letters* and *Notes* show mastery to breed tyranny, in *The Valley* Edward Grayson explains that this charge is unfounded; he finds its worst consequence—not at all insurmountable—to be the encouragement of idleness among the master class.

In *The Valley of Shenandoah* Tucker portrays happy slaves at work in the fields (they are fed whiskey during the harvest), in the stables, in the big house, and in the quarter. The only discontent is expressed by a houseboy who, as punishment for having fathered the child of a thirteen-year-old favorite housemaid, has been sent to the fields. Chagrined at having displeased his master, he speechlessly clasps his hand in gratitude when forgiven by Edward (I. 66-67).

But the decline of the aristocratic Graysons inevitably involves a change in the life of their slaves. Even before the beginning of the events dramatized in *The Valley,* the family had moved from Easton, their plantation on the James River, leaving an overseer in charge. Edward's visit to the estate reveals many of the evils of absentee ownership. He finds that John Cutchins, the overseer, "a smooth, plausibly voluble man," has not only been cheating the Graysons—he has lined his own pockets enough to buy both land and slaves for himself—but has neglected the welfare of the slaves (II. 33). Edward visits the quarters and finds the people "uncomfortable in clothing. . . . Several were sick with agues; and these were badly nursed, and ill supplied with medicines. . . . Throughout the whole body of them, an air of sadness, and sometimes of sullen discontent, manifested itself . . ." (II. 43-44). His mission is not to remedy their situation, however, but to inventory them for sale.

The Graysons' bankruptcy is complete. Not only the sullen chattel at Easton, but the happy slaves of Beechwood must be sold. In a savagely ironic scene evidently intended to display her beneficence, the virtuous widow Grayson calls the women together one morning and informs them they will be sold in the afternoon. She bestows on them "her old clothes, most of them not past wearing," and permits them to choose whether they will be among the group bought by a Georgia planter, or will be auctioned on the open market in Virginia (II. 201). Although the Graysons are "good masters," they do sell their slaves.

Not only does Tucker show slavery to be a heavier burden for the master than the slave, but even the slave trade causes greater hardship to the seller than the sold. Although he retains some sympathy for the men and women on the block, there is a wide gulf between the moral outrage of Tucker's sketch of the coffle in *Letters* and the flatness of his description of the slave auction in *The Valley:*

A pine table, about four or five feet square, was brought out of the kitchen, and placed on the lawn before the south door, on which these people were made to ascend, one by one, unless there was a family in which case they all stood on the ground. One not accustomed to this spectacle, is extremely shocked to see beings, of the same species with himself, set up for sale to the highest bidder, like horses or cattle; and even to those who have been accustomed to it, it is disagreeable, from their sympathy with the humbled and anxious slave. The weight of his fetters, the negro, who has been born and bred on a well regulated estate, hardly feels. His simple wants are abundantly supplied, and whatever of coercion there is on his will, it is so moderate and reasonable in itself, and, above all, he has been so habituated to it, that it appears to be all right, or rather, he does not feel it to be wrong. He is, in fact, a member of a sort of patriarchial family. But when hoisted up to public sale, where every man has a right to purchase him, and he may be the property of one whom he never saw before, or of the worst man in the community, then the delusion vanishes, and he feels the

bitterness of his lot, and his utter insignificance as a
member of civilized society. (II. 207)

Despite Tucker's minutely detailed description of the Graysons' successful efforts to arange that none of their slaves suffers
in consequence of the sale, it seems clear that their condition will
worsen, for while the Graysons evidently do not practice slave-
breeding, neglect the sick, or prostitute their slave women, others
do. The men who bid for the Grayson slaves are descendants of
overseers like Fawkner, whose father once received two young
black girls from old master Grayson in exchange for a pair of
horses, and then used them to breed thirty slaves; or like the
overseer Cutchins, who denied the Easton slaves adequate medical care; or, though he was not permitted to buy the Graysons'
"likely" mulatto, the trader who bid up her price to "forty or
fifty dollars more than she was worth" because "slaves of this description often . . . happen to suit the tastes of some of the liber-
tines of the French or Spanish settlements . . ." (I. 292-93; II. 40;
II. 208-09). After seeing these prospective purchasers, it is not re-
assuring to learn that the man buying most of the Beechwood
slaves for his Georgia plantation is the son of an overseer who
had once worked for Mrs. Grayson's father.

The slaves, however, are all content. Although originally
some had been apprehensive about leaving Virginia, when the
excellent Mrs. Grayson explains to them that in Georgia "peaches,
water melons, and sweet potatoes . . . were better, and more
abundant," they are satisfied to go (II. 198). After they are sold,
they leave their homes saying prayers for " 'my kind mistress
wherever she goes . . .' " (II. 212).

Aside from providing local color, Tucker mainly. uses the
black characters to convey a sense of loss through their recollections of the heroic Revolutionary past; to suggest the aura of decay he found already present in Virginia society in 1795. In *The
Valley of Shenandoah,* Tucker sees life in retrospect. He envisions an idyllic past pushed back in time beyond the complexity
of the narrative present, which itself is located in the past. The
task of testifying to this edenic past is, paradoxically, assigned to

the slaves. Although they actually have the smallest share in the benefits of society, they attest both to its past glories and its present delights. Tucker depicts them as the least stable element in the population, completely at the mercies of chance, but uses them dramatically to create an atmosphere of stability and continuity.

Tucker justifies slavery on political and economic grounds, not on the basis of racial inferiority. Surprisingly, he does not use stock racial stereotypes; but although he individualizes them, he depicts the black characters—like Granny Mott, the garrulous old crone whose portrait is more carefully drawn than the others, and like Phill the coachman, and Uncle Bristow at Easton—as content with their lot and as unfalteringly faithful to the Graysons. It is true that, like the narrator's comment on the slave mounting the block, Edward Grayson's assertion that the black slaves are oblivious to the hardships of their situation rests more heavily on environmental adaptation than on race:

> The error of this subject proceeds from a white man's sup-
> posing himself in the situation of a slave, without recol-
> lecting that these people were born slaves, and that there
> is as much difference between their feelings respecting
> their condition, and those of a white man, as is the priva-
> tion of sight to one who is born blind, and one who has
> become so. (I. 64)

But carefully as Tucker maintains this distinction, it finally does not matter. Whether because of race or conditioning, black people are shown to be inferior to their masters—and happy and content in their slavery.

In his novel, Tucker incorporates many contradictory elements: a glorification of the Old South and a basic criticism of plantation society; a nostalgic recollection of the vanished past and a didactic analysis of the weaknesses which have made change necessary and good; a polemic against abolition and an assertion of black humanity. Nevertheless, *The Valley of Shenandoah* remains an apology for slavery.

NOTES—CHAPTER II

1. [George Tucker], *Letters from Virginia, Translated from the French* (Baltimore, 1816). Parenthetical page references in the text are to this edition.

    The biographical information is drawn from "Autobiography of George Tucker," introd. Tipton R. Snavely, *Bermuda Historical Quarterly*, XVIII, Nos. 3, 4 (1961); and from Robert Colin McLean, *George Tucker, Moral Philosopher and Man of Letters* (Chapel Hill, N.C., 1961). McLean, pp. 68, 70, 182, concurs with Jay B. Hubbell, *The South in American Literature, 1607-1900* (Durham, N.C., 1954), p. 250, in attributing *Letters* to Tucker.

2. *Letter to a Member of the General Assembly of Virginia, on the Subject of the Late Conspiracy of the Slaves with a Proposal for their Colonization* (Baltimore, 1801). Citing the inevitability of servile insurrection and the increase in slave population, Tucker argues for abolition; stating that the blacks will not be satisfied without social and political equality which the whites will not permit, he argues for colonization. Tucker finds transporting the slaves to Africa impractical and proposes that they be colonized in the West. See McLean, Chapter 11.

3. "Thoughts of a Hermit" appeared in the Philadelphia *Port Folio*, 1814-15. A few years later, Tucker expanded his work and published *Essays on Various Subjects of Taste, Morals, and National Policy* (Georgetown, D.C., 1822). This volume prompted Tucker's appointment to the faculty of the University of Virginia.

4. "Autobiography of George Tucker," 85-86. Tucker also repeated his belief stated in *Letters from Virginia* that environment, not race, was responsible for the apparent inferiority of the black man, in *America and the West Indies Geographically Described*, ed. George Long, George R. Porter, and George Tucker (London, 1841), pp. 223-24.

5. In *Laws of Wages, Profits, and Rent, Investigated* (1837), he notes the detrimental effect of slavery on the master class but finds the institution generally beneficial, though he foresees its eventual extinction. Six years later, in *Progress of the United States in Population*, he repeats his public prediction of the end of slavery, although in the interim he had written an unpublished novel envisioning slavery still entrenched in 1941, and had continued to lecture to his classes about the benefits of utilizing slave labor in southern factories. See McLean, pp. 197-98.

6. *History of the United States from their Colonization to the End of the Twenty-Sixth Congress, in 1841*, 4 vols. (Philadelphia, 1856-58), I, 98.

7. *Political Economy for the People* (Philadelphia, 1859), pp. 86-87. Al-

though before moving to Philadelphia upon his retirement Tucker had freed five house slaves, by 1858 he questioned the wisdom of this manumission: Two had died; the third was afraid that he would be forced to leave Williamsburg and his enslaved wife and children because of Virginia restrictions against free black people; and the two others, who had agreed to accompany Tucker to Philadelphia to work for wages, "incited by some black abolitionists . . . betook themselves to New York. . . ." "Autobiography," 156. Three years later, Tucker died while touring the South.

8. *The Valley of Shenandoah: or, Memoirs of the Graysons,* 2 vols. (New York, 1824). Parenthetical references in the text to page numbers are to this edition. Using the pseudonym Joseph Atterley, he published a second novel, the fantasy *Voyage to the Moon* (New York, 1827).

CHAPTER III

JAMES KIRKE PAULDING

In 1817, a year after Tucker's *Letters from Virginia* appeared, James Kirke Paulding published two small volumes with a similar form and title, *Letters from the South*. Purportedly addressed to a Philadelphia college chum by a Northerner traveling in Virginia, the essays discuss the Old Dominion in the polite manner of the eighteenth century.[1] In his closing lines Paulding expresses the patriotic impulse behind the work:

> The more I see of my country and my countrymen, the more I love them; and I am satisfied, that nothing but ignorance of each other, causes those stupid misconceptions, unfounded aspersions, and ridiculous antipathies, that still subsist between the different extremes in our country. A little social intercourse would do away [sic] all these, by showing distinctly to all, that there may be a difference in people, without any inferiority on either part; and that in every class and every climate, there is enough of a family likeness to demonstrate us to be one people. (II. 260)

This positive assertion of Americanism is characteristic of Paulding. Born during the Revolution behind Yankee lines where his patriot family had fled for safety, the son of a Dutchman who served as Colonel in the New York Militia, Paulding's nationalism was bred in the bone.[2] He experienced great poverty in his childhood: His father had gone into debt procuring supplies for the rebels, but when independence was secured, he was not reimbursed by Congress. He suffered bankruptcy, and in 1785 was arrested for debt and imprisoned at White Plains. Paulding later recalled that as a boy of seven, he rode a borrowed horse every Saturday the six miles from Tarrytown to the jail, carrying food and clothing to prison. Although his father was soon free— he simply walked home when the log jail burnt down—he was a broken man, and only his mother's courage and industry held the family together. The boy, their eighth child, had little schooling; most of his time was spent in desultory farming, fishing, and hunting. At the age of about eighteen Paulding changed his life dramatically, when he left Tarrytown for a job in New York City.

While he stayed with his sister, who had married William Irving, brother to Washington Irving, he wrote some short pieces for Peter Irving's *Morning Chronicle.* He then collaborated with William and Washington Irving in writing *Salmagundi,* the series of satirical poems and letters modeled on the *Spectator* which became the talk of New York. During the War of 1812, Paulding expressed his nationalism and Anglophobia in a political satire, *The Diverting History of John Bull and Brother Jonathan,* and in a poetic parody, *The Lay of the Scottish Fiddle.* In 1815 he wrote the patriotic *United States and England,* which attracted the attention of President Madison, and won him a position as secretary of the Board of Navy Commissioners—the first of a series of governmental posts which he would fill for the next forty-three years, climaxing in his appointment by Van Buren in 1838 as Secretary of the Navy and culminating with his retirement in 1841.

Young Paulding moved to the still-unfinished capital in 1815, and the following July accompanied the Commissioners on a survey of Chesapeake Bay. He left the official party at Norfolk

for reasons of health, and traveled throughout Virginia the rest
of the summer, visiting the Springs and returning to Washington
in late fall. *Letters from the South* is a result of this excursion.

In his book, Paulding notes the decay of the ancient planta-
tions that Tucker had dramatized with such mixed feelings in
The Valley. Although Tucker had seen the twilight of the Old
South in the emigration from the Tidewater, the young New
Yorker viewed the movement West as the dawn of a glorious day
for the Republic.

Letters from the South deals with both Eastern Virginia
planters and Western farmers and is particularly interesting because of the range of its comments on slavery and on black
people. In the third letter, Paulding describes a visit to a large
plantation and includes an idyllic sketch of the happy slaves.
Their comfortable quarters, "with each a little garden," are
bright and clean; field hands working at harvest enjoy a "whole-
some dinner"; old slaves—the narrator notes one aristocratic
"patriarch" whose body is "bent in a curve" and whose laugh
carries a half-mile—lead "a life of perfect ease." The narrator
repeats the formula used by Jefferson and Tucker: Noting that
most of the slave masters "lament" chattel slavery, and expressing
his own concern about the institution which "appears as a stain
on the lustre of . . . freedom," he asserts that America is not responsible for the evil because slavery was instituted by the English
over the protest of the colonials; the present generation is not
responsible because it merely inherited the system and immediate
emancipation is impossible. Hence the problem of slavery is dis-
missed with the pious hope that the lot of the slave would be
"mitigated by kindness and plenty." Paulding buttresses his
routine apologia by racist assumptions: Fortunately, black men
possess an "unreflecting gaiety" which can "perhaps make them
some amends for the loss of freedom" (I. 24). The New Yorker
seems ill at ease with this, however, and in Letter Ten observes
that his pleasure in the country west of the Blue Ridge is en-
hanced by the relative absence of slaves (I. 110).

In Letter Eleven, after again running through the stereotype

—black people are "a gay, harmless, and unthinking race" who
laugh, sing, dance, and are happy, happy, happy in bondage—the
narrator expresses his sharp awareness of the contradiction between American political philosophy and slavery (I. 118). He
then quickly falls back, however, on racist premises and the weak
hope that the black is well-treated and happy:

> Don't mistake, and suppose that I am the advocate of
> slavery; for I hate it: and wish most sincerely and ardently,
> that there was not a man in our country that could stand
> up, and with his black finger point to the preamble of our
> constitution, which declares—all men are born free and
> equal—and swear it was not true. But yet I am gratified
> when I can persuade myself, that a race of men which is
> found in this situation in almost every Christian land, is
> not without some little enjoyments, that sweeten the bitter
> draught of slavery. . . . (I. 119-20)

He explains that this outburst is the result of an encounter with
a slave trader, "an ill-looking, hard-featured, pock-marked, black-
bearded fellow," and recounts the "catiff's" tales of slave-buying
expeditions (I. 121). These tales present a different view of
slavery and the black: "When he had got some half a dozen of
these poor creatures, he tied their hands behind their backs, and
drove them three or four hundred miles, or more, bare-headed,
and half-naked, through the burning southern sun" (I. 122).
Afraid that "even southern humanity would revolt at such an ex-
hibition of human misery, and human barbarity, he gave out
that they were runaway slaves"; when one slave woman told the
truth, he beat her " 'till her back was white' " (I. 122-23). The
trader freely admits that he routinely separates parents from children and husbands from wives, forcing them to accept new mates;
he tells of a mulatto slave girl who committed suicide after being
separated from her master, and of a blind slave who was beaten
until he obeyed as well as if he had had his sight. Filled with re-

vulsion for the trader and with sympathy for the slaves, the young
traveler in a unique passage momentarily repudiates the racism
used to justify slavery:

> There is something of the true pathetic in all this, were
> these people not negroes. This spoils all; for we have got
> such an inveterate habit of divesting them of all the best
> attributes of humanity, in order to justify our oppressions,
> that the idea of connecting feeling or sentiment with a
> slave actually makes us laugh. (I. 127)

Leaving the tavern, he encounters a slave coffle:

> First, a little cart, drawn by one horse, in which five or six
> half naked black children were tumbled, like pigs, to-
> gether. The cart had no covering—and they seemed to have
> been actually broiled to sleep. Behind the cart marched
> three black women, with head, neck, and breasts un-
> covered, and without shoes or stockings: next came three
> men, bare-headed, half naked, and chained together with
> an ox-chain. Last of all came a white man . . . on horse-
> back, carrying pistols in his belt, and who, as we passed
> him, had the impudence to look us in the face without
> blushing. I should like to have seen him hunted by blood-
> hounds. At a house where we stopped a little further on,
> we learned, that he had bought these miserable beings in
> Maryland, and was marching them in this manner to some
> one of the more southern States. Shame on the State of
> Maryland! I say,—and shame on the State of Virginia!
> (I. 128-29)

But having emotionally denounced the abuses of slavery, he again
resorts to the formula: The evil slave trader was (thank God) not

an American; Americans did not inaugurate chattel slavery; Americans "cannot get rid of it"; given a slave economy, the slave trade "cannot be avoided."

The essay ends in confusion. Taking all sides of the question, the narrator first chastizes those who criticize the South: "It is easy for people who have no slaves to talk about emancipation, as it is easy to be benevolent at the expense of others"; and then asserts that "such flagrant and indecent outrages on humanity as that I have just described" are a disgrace to the nation. His conclusion is ludicrous: "If they must be transported, in this inhumane and indecent manner,—let it be in the night-time, and when there is no moon or stars.—Let not the blessed sun see it,—or the traveller carry the news to distant countries." He expresses the belief that once he has pointed it out, the Southerners will "wipe away this one stain"—but we are uncertain just what will be eradicated (I. 129-31). Not slavery, surely? Nor the slave trade? Perhaps daytime slave coffles? Or accounts of them?

In Letter Thirty-four Paulding offers a third view of black slavery. On the banks of the Shenandoah in the West, the travelers stumble on a happy valley where the quiet is broken only by the pastoral sounds of the tinkling cowbell and—incredibly—"the negro's sonorous and resounding laugh, which waked the mountain echo." Here they meet a hard-working German settler who recounts his version of the American Success Story: married at twenty-seven, he owned only £328 "and a negro man"; he, his wife, and his slave worked hard in the fields; prospered; his wife bore him children; he built a house; and now "I am forty-three years old, I have twelve hundred acres of as fine bottom as any in Virginia,—a good grist and saw-mill, and tolerable good wife . . . a decent home over my head; and I owe no man a shilling except Tom, who by now and then raising a little grain, shooting a deer, and waiting on travellers, has in my hands enough to buy his freedom. But he is free already, for that matter, and knows he can go, where he pleases" (II. 164-65). This episode, meant to illustrate agrarian virtue, presents a peculiar vision of the Western yeoman as slaveholder, and of the black as enslaved by choice—a vision Paulding would later dramatize in *Westward Ho!* [3]

Paulding drew on his Southern excursion to write poetry and drama, and on the early Dutch environment for his fiction, before putting his Virginia experiences to use in a novel.[4] A strange composite of plantation fiction, Western, and Gothic psychological thriller, *Westward Ho!* includes black characters who resemble two of the types Paulding had described in the *Letters:* the grotesque old aristocrat of the quarter, and Tom, the Western slave. None of the individuals or incidents reflects the victimized slave, the third characterization he had included. We hear of no beaten blind men and no mulatto suicides and are shown no slave traders or chained men and brutalized women and children.

The first section of the story is located in the recent past, and dramatizes Tucker's theme, the disintegration of the Tidewater civilization; but while this brought dishonor and death to the Graysons, it results in regeneration in the West for Paulding's Dangerfields. Most of the action is set in the prosperous Kentucky settlement of Dangerfieldsville nine years after their trek West. The plot of this second section is psychological, and concerns a romance between Rainsford, a blighted young man who, believing himself cursed by hereditary madness, falls prey to religious fanaticism, and Dangerfield's daughter Virginia, the prairie flower whose love restores him to health.

The plantation section of *Westward Ho!* dramatizes the attempt of prodigal Colonel Cuthbert Dangerfield to rid himself of debt by betting everything on his racehorse—who loses. His ancient slave Pompey, the black character most fully described, is a comic figure defined by physical grotesqueness: his limbs resemble "a pair of little bandy drumsticks, by the aid of which he waddled along" and hence he is called Pompey Ducklegs); by snobbishness (once the property of Lord Dunmore, he is assigned the incongruous role of upholding aristocracy); by loyalty to his master (he ties up and whips his grandson Little Pompey for losing the horserace and thus disgracing the family); and by constant happiness (I. 28-29). Although the point is made that Pompey's personal relationship with the Colonel is unusual—Dangerfield confesses to his creditor that he does not even know how many slaves he owns—Paulding defines the servile relation in terms of the conventional roles of pampered servant and indulgent master. In a scene that will later be repeated *ad nauseam* in plantation fiction, the black himself chooses slavery. When Little Pompey, who was to have been freed if he had won the horserace, is gallantly offered his liberty despite failure, he refuses freedom, saying, " 'Only don't leave me behind, massa; dat all nigger want' " (I. 58).

Slavery is justified by black inferiority, and Paulding dramatizes the notion that black men are incompetent to care for themselves when he depicts Pompey, tempted to assert his liberty while traveling in Philadelphia, seeing the depraved condition of free blacks in the city and then running to his master to beg him to buy them all into slavery. Similarly, Paulding portrays the simpleminded happiness of the black even in the face of the slave trade, which was one of the most criticized aspects of the peculiar institution. Like Tucker, Paulding describes weeping slaves begging their mistress not to sell them; then shows them distracted by a banjo-tune: "At that irresistible signal, the light-hearted slaves, the very prototypes of children in their joys, their sorrows, their forgetfulness of the past, their indifference to the future, listened, dried their tears, and soon they were dancing . . ." (I. 58).

In the second section of the novel, set in Kentucky nine years later, Paulding neglects most of these conventional plantation elements to develop familiar Western themes. Double visions of the past reinforce the concept of the regenerative power of the West: In the Virginia section Dangerfield, whose present existence no longer realizes the glorious Southern heritage, envisions an even more glorious future in the West; in the Kentucky section Rainsford, blighted by an hereditary curse pronounced on his Tory grandfather by a Rebel neighbor wounded at his hands, finds that ancient hatreds can be exorcised in the West.[5]

But although it encompasses a number of standard Western elements, Paulding's vision of the frontier seems peculiar to us because it does not depict the West in the familiar terms of the freesoil North, but in terms of the slaveholding South—an imaginative construct that was destroyed at Appomattox.[6] The West is seen not only in terms of renewal, but in terms of racial supremacy; the continent will be tamed by "the irresistible influence of the 'wise white man,' who, wheresoever he goes, to whatever region of the earth, whether east or west, north, or south, carries with him his destiny, which is to civilize the world, and rule it afterwards" (I. 94). In subduing the land, he will establish slavery in the wilderness. The Western version of the servile relation is dramatized in the novel by the frontiersman Bushfield and his slave, Mammy Phillis. Bushfield is described as a mountain man: "The forest supplied him with food. . . . the skins of the deer and the bear furnished him with bed and clothing; his rifle was his purse; his powder and shot his ready cash" (I. 178). Mammy Phillis, his old black woman, is glimpsed only a few times, at work in the kitchen. Her master explains her presence by saying that after a bout of illness he tried to buy a slave boy as a nurse but, having no money, took her. He complains loudly that he lost his freedom in acquiring his slave, whom he calls "Old Snowball." She calls him Massa. Nothing further is revealed about the nature of the relationship between the backwoodsman and the enslaved woman.

As prototypical Westerner, Bushfield loudly voices the doctrine of freedom, but his racism insists on a double standard: slavery for the black man, freedom for the white. His concern is not slavery, but white servility, and he finally is moved to push westward when he meets a white man with a white servant:

> " 'What!' says I, 'one white man be a servant to another! Make a nigger of himself! Come, that's too bad!' and I began to feel a litle savage. I asked one if he wasn't ashamed to make a slave of a feller-cretur, and the other if he wasn't ashamed to make a nigger of himself; and they got rather obsterpolous. I don't know exactly how it came about, but we got into a fight, and I lick'd them both. . . . Well, what do you think? Instead of settling the thing like a gentleman, the feller that had a white man for his nigger . . . sent a constable after me. Well, I made short work of it, and licked him too, anyhow. But I can't stand it here any longer. . . . I must look out for some place where a

man can live independent, where there's no law but
gentleman's law, and no niggers but black ones."
(II. 182-83)

Bushfield's hands are Natty Bumppo's, but his voice is Pap
Finn's.[7]

Paulding published a second edition of the *Letters* in 1835.[8]
His revisions of the manuscript, first published eighteen years
earlier, are significant. Paulding does not change the portrayal of
the happy slaves on the Tidewater plantation or the sketch of the
willing Western slave, but the description of the slavetrader and
coffle—indeed, all of the criticisms of slavery, including nine pages
of Letter Eleven—have been expunged. A year earlier Paulding
had published a satirical fantasy which included an attack on
abolitionists,[9] and he now inserts a new passage in Letter Nineteen harshly critical of the "advocates of emancipation," whose
"misguided, or wilfully malignant zeal" has mounted "a crusade
against the constitutional rights of the slave owners, by sending
among them fanatical agents, and fanatical tracts, calculated to
render the slave disaffected, and the situation of the master and
his family dangerous"; who have appealed, "under the sanction
of religion, to the passions of these ignorant and easily excited
blacks" in such a way as "to rouse their worst and most dangerous
passions" and to endanger the lives of their masters; who have
formed organizations "for the avowed purpose of virtually de-
stroying the value of this principal item in the property of a
southern planter [that is, slaves]"; and who have influenced the
government to a point where it is questionable "whether the
rights of the master over his slave shall be any longer recognized
or maintained." Letter Nineteen now warns that abolition is a
present threat to the nation; when the South recognizes that
"nothing will preserve them but secession," they will leave the
Union ([1835] I. 172-73). Paulding also includes in this edition
the fable of the "Isles of Engines," an anti-industrial fantasy. In
addition, he inserts admiring character sketches of two types of

the Virginia slaveholder: the moderate Washington, whose biography he had just written, and the intemperate Randolph. Both Paulding's deletions and his additions result in a book significantly more sympathetic and less critical toward the South than the first edition.

Paulding published a two-volume defense of chattel slavery the following year.[10] At first glance, *Slavery in the United States* appears to be a defense of the Union, seen as threatened by the attacks of abolitionists; but it rapidly reveals itself as a full-dress argument in support of human slavery. In a letter to Van Buren dated December 16, 1835, Paulding asserts that "[A]lmost every argument in mitigation of the atrocity of slavery—if there be any atrocity in it,—goes directly in the teeth of the fundamental principles of our government. I have endeavoured however to get over this difficulty. . . ." [11] The uncertainty expressed here contrasts with the harshly positive tone of *Slavery in the United States.* In his book Paulding expounds the proslavery argument based on the Bible and cites passages from both Old and New Testaments to demonstrate that neither rejects slavery. He then attempts to reconcile slavery with American democracy, proclaiming that "The government of the United States belongs of right wholly and exclusively to the white man." Citing the probable consequences of emancipation, he asserts that the "debauchery" of Santo Domingo is prophetic. He discusses "amalgamation" as "a project for debasing whites by a mixture of that blood which, wherever it flows, carries with it the seeds of deterioration." Analyzing the possible social and political relations between blacks and whites in the event of emancipation, Paulding predicts that a power struggle will take place, resulting in black despotism and the degradation of civilization. He defends property in slaves, chastizes the North for interfering in Southern affairs, and attacks industrial labor conditions. He discusses the effect of slavery on the American image abroad, denouncing abolitionists as divisive cats-paws of England, the ancient enemy. After praising the Virginia slave code and approving the life of the black slave, he attacks abolitionists as fanatics.

Throughout, Paulding justifies slavery on racist grounds:

> [T]he distinction of colour, . . . cannot be mistaken. It is a
> natural distinction. . . . The contrast of colour, to say
> nothing of the hair, the odour, and other distinguishing
> peculiarities of the African mark him out wheresoever he
> goes. . . . The physical disparities, setting aside all others,
> between the two races, are equivalent to those which sep-
> arate various species of animals. . . . The white and black
> races of men are probably the nearest to each other of all
> these varieties; but they are not homogeneous, any more
> than the orang-outang, the ape, the baboon, and the
> monkey. (270-71)

. . .

> It is . . . not without ample reason that anatomists and
> physiologists have classed the negro as the lowest in the
> scale of rational beings. (280)

The most that can be done for these inferior creatures is to enslave them: "to treat them with patriarchal kindness . . . making
due allowances for their ignorance, and for the peculiarity of
their tempers and disposition . . . interchanging with them all
those kind offices not incompatible with the relations that subsist
between the master and slave . . ." (75-76). When enslaved thus,
as in the South, black people exhibit a "uniform hilarity and
cheerfulness"; indeed, "Of all the varieties of the human race
and of human condition that have ever fallen under observation,
the African slave best realizes the idea of happiness, . . . for he is
. . . the most light-hearted, sportive, dancing, laughing being in
the world" (176).

In his zeal to defend chattel slavery against abolitionist
charges of brutality, Paulding goes so far as to repudiate his own
writings. In *Slavery in the United States* he flatly denies he knows
of conditions such as those he had described twenty years earlier
in *Letters from the South:*

In a residence of several years within the District of Columbia, and in a pretty extensive course of travel in some
of the southern states, we never saw or heard of any such
instances of cruelty. We saw no chains and heard no
stripes. (166-67)

Poe, whose review of the tract descants on the beautiful
moral relation between master and slave, announced that *Slavery
in the United States* would enhance Paulding's reputation "as a
writer of pure and vigorous English, as a clear thinker, as a patriot, and as a man." [12] He was wrong. Whether it is true, as has
been charged, that Paulding shamefully expunged his writings of
antislavery matter to gain political place or, more mercifully,
that his memory and perception of reality shifted with his position, his stature dwindles with his mutilation and repudiation of
Letters from the South.[13]

Paulding's last novel, *The Puritan and His Daughter*, written ten years later, reflects the hardening of his position. The
book deals with religious fanaticism, a problem Paulding had
touched in his characterization of Rainsford in *Westward Ho!*
and had polemicized against in his attacks on abolitionists in the
second edition of *Letters* and in *Slavery in the United States*.
The story is dreary, predictable, and long. Harold Habingdon, a
Puritan in Carolinian England, immigrates to Virginia, where his
daughter Miriam falls in love with Langley, son of a neighboring
Royalist, who heroically saves the Crop-ears from the attacking
Indians. The lovers are separated when Habingdon moves his
family to New England. The Habingdons lead an idyllic life in a
pioneer settlement. After her parents' deaths, however, Miriam
is accused of witchcraft by a jealous suitor who is a fanatical Puritan. She is rescued with great difficulty after Langley fortuitously
appears, and at the end of Volume II, the betrothed descendants
of Puritan and Cavalier flee to Virginia.
    Despite its historical setting and the patriotic theme of rec-
onciliation in the New World, and although it never mentions
the question of slavery (black slaves are almost entirely absent

from the more than two hundred pages of action set in colonial
Virginia), *The Puritan and His Daughter* speaks directly to the
growing schism between North and South in 1849. The haven
for hero and heroine, once the entire New World, is now "the
Sunny South" (II. 268). The villains are the hypocritical fanatics:
in the seventeenth century, Puritans; in the nineteenth,
abolitionists.

A year later, in an article entitled "The Conspiracy of Fanaticism," Paulding crudely vented his racism and his hatred of
abolitionists: "all their five senses are devoted to the descendants
of Africa. Their eyes dwell with unceasing delight on wooly heads,
flat noses, thick lips, crooked legs and cucumber-shins . . ." and
concluded, "The real foes to the Union are not in the South, but
the North. The North is the aggressor, and will justly be held
responsible for ALL the consequences, be they what they may." [14]
In 1851, Paulding wrote a letter allying himself with the South
Carolina fire-eaters; still insisting on his love for the Union, he
asserted the right of secession and the defense of Southern honor.
His letter was published as a secessionist pamphlet in 1860, the
year of his death.[15]

The literary patriot had come full circle. Although once, as
a young man, he had questioned chattel slavery and the racist assumptions with which it was buttressed, he later purged such
matter from his writings and published a defense of the peculiar
institution. His novel *Westward Ho!* has significance today only
as a curiosity: an early, brief example of the plantation tradition,
and a relic of the Southern dream of a slave West.

NOTES—CHAPTER III

1. [James Kirke Paulding], *Letters from the South, Written during an
Excursion in the Summer of 1816. By the Author of John Bull and
Brother Jonathan, &.&.,* 2 vols. (New York, 1817). Parenthetical volume
and page numbers in my text refer to this edition.
2. Biographical material was drawn from the following sources: William
I. Paulding, *Literary Life of James K. Paulding* (New York, 1867);

Amos L. Herold, *James Kirke Paulding, Versatile American* (New York
1926); James Kirke Paulding, *The Letters of James Kirke Paulding,*
ed. Ralph M. Alderman (Madison, 1962).

3. James Kirke Paulding, *Westward Ho!* 2 vols. (New York, 1832).
4. The narrative poem "The Backwoodsman" appeared in 1818, and his
    play *The Lion of the West* in 1830. *The Dutchman's Fireside,* perhaps
    Paulding's best novel, was published in 1831. During this period,
    Paulding also wrote *Koningsmarke,* a novel; revived *Salmagundi;* and
    published several volumes of tales.

    For discussions of the literary origins of *Westward Ho!* see Ralph
    M. Aderman, "James Kirke Paulding on Literature and the West,"
    American Literature, XXVII (1955), 97-101; and Arlin Turner, "James
    K. Paulding and Timothy Flint," *Mississippi Valley Historical Review,*
    XXXIV (June 1947), 97-101.
5. The fate of Rainsford's Rebel neighbor had actually been suffered by
    Paulding's grandfather who was cut across the head by British soldiers
    because he refused to shout "God save the King!" He suffered perma-
    nent partial derangement, and Paulding recalled him as a pathetic
    old man walking along Tarrytown beach picking up sticks. See Herold,
    p. 14.
6. The classic analysis of the development of the Western myth is Henry
    Nash Smith, *Virgin Land* (Cambridge, Mass., 1950). In particular, see
    Chapter XIII, "The South and the Myth of the Garden," a discussion
    of the contrast between the myth of the plantation, and that of the
    West.
7. The notion of democracy for the master race and tyranny for their
    subordinates is discussed in George M. Frederickson, *The Black Image
    in the White Mind* (New York, 1971). Frederickson's conclusions,
    reached through an historical approach, are often in agreement with
    those I have come to in this literary study.
8. *Letters from the South by a Northern Man,* 2nd ed. (New York, 1835).
    Parenthetical references to this edition in my text are labelled 1835 ed.
9. James Kirke Paulding, "Journal of a Late Traveller to the Moon,"
    The New-York Mirror, Saturday, June 7, 1834, pp. 389-90.
10. James Kirke Paulding, *Slavery in the United States* (New York, 1836).
    Parenthetical references to page numbers in my text refer to this edi-
    tion. Material quoted in this paragraph is taken from pp. 42, 55, 61.
11. *Letters,* p. 172.
12. [Edgar Allen Poe], Review of Paulding, *Slavery in the United States,
    Southern Literary Messenger,* II (April 1836), 336. Jay B. Hubbell, *The
    South in American Literature, 1607-1900* (Durham, N.C., 1954), p. 536
    assigns this review to Beverly Tucker. But Paulding's most recent
    biographer, Floyd C. Watkins, *James Kirke Paulding: Humorist and
    Critic of American Life* (Nashville, 1951), p. 6, following standard
    practice, attributes it to Poe, who edited the *Southern Literary Mes-
    senger.*
13. Paulding's biographers and critics have generally ignored this, although
    it was deplored by abolitionists in the American Anti-Slavery Society's

American Slavery As It Is: Testimony of a Thousand Witnesses (New York, 1839) and, at Paulding's death, by Theodore Tilton in "James Kirke Paulding, His Expurgation of his Writings Against Slavery," *National Anti-Slavery Standard,* April 21, 1860.

William I. Paulding makes little of his father's writings on slavery. He neglects the antislavery indignation in the first edition of *Letters* and does not note its later deletion. He briefly treats *Slavery in the United States* as a Unionist book.

Herold characterizes the 1816 edition of *Letters* as balanced. He does not mention the expurgations in the second edition, or the discrepancy between the first edition of *Letters* and *Slavery in the United States.*

Lorenzo Turner, *Anti-Slavery Sentiment in American Literature prior to 1865* (Washington, D.C., 1929), p. 40, refers to Tilton's article in a note. He is attacked for this by Floyd C. Watkins, who in "James Kirke Paulding and the South," *American Quarterly,* V (1953), 219-30, minimizes the differences between the first and second edition of *Letters,* apologizes for Paulding's deletions by asserting that "One could not print such stories after 1830 without being branded an abolitionist" (226), and ignores Paulding's claim in *Slavery* that he never saw scenes such as those he had described in the first edition of *Letters.* Watkins complains that Tilton—and Turner, in mentioning his article—is unfair in implying that Paulding turned his coat for political preferment.

Hubbell, 203-04, does not mention the expunged second edition of *Letters,* and ignores the discrepancy between the first edition of *Letters,* and *Slavery in the United States.*

William R. Taylor, *Cavalier and Yankee* (New York, 1961), pp. 228-34, discusses the second edition of *Letters.* He comments perceptively on the inclusion of the characters of Washington and Randolph and the sketch of the Engine Isles but does not mention the discussions of black slavery in either edition, although he correctly characterizes *Slavery in the United States* as "a detailed and virtually unqualified defense of Negro slavery."

Ralph M. Aderman does not mention the second edition of *Letters,* and finds little difference in attitude between the 1817 text of *Letters* and *Slavery in the United States,* in his edition of *The Letters of James Kirke Paulding.* In an article, "James Kirke Paulding as Social Critic," *Papers on English Language and Literature,* I (1965), 217-29, Aderman finds the second edition of Paulding's *Letters* "more moderate and more palatable to his Southern friends," but ignores the discrepancy between the first and second editions. He consistently characterizes Paulding as a moderate, but explains that this became "a moderation which enabled Southerners to preserve slavery."

14. James Kirke Paulding, *The Puritan and his Daughter* (New York, 1849). Before this appeared, Paulding published *The Old Continental,* a novel he reworked from earlier manuscripts.

15. James Kirke Paulding, "The Conspiracy of Fanaticism," *Democratic Review,* XXVI (1850), 385-400. For a discussion of anti-abolitionism in

the North, see Lorman Ratner, *Powder Keg: Northern Opposition to the Antislavery Movement* (New York, 1968).

16. Letter addressed to F. D. Richardson, H. H. Raymond, and W. H. Peronneau, dated September 6, 1851, *Letters*, pp. 521-27; published as a pamphlet by William D. Porter, entitled *State Sovereignty and the Doctrine of Coercion together with a Letter from J. K. Paulding* (Charleston, 1860).

Chapter IV

JOHN PENDLETON KENNEDY

On the night of August 31, 1831, an apparently docile slave owned by "a kind master" led a band of blacks through Southampton County, Virginia, killing men, women, children—everyone they encountered with a white skin except the members of one family who owned no slaves. The leader, "Prophet" Nat Turner, was a religious mystic who bore stigmata and heard voices. There is conjecture that he planned to locate the insurrection at the county seat of Jerusalem in accordance with a Biblical passage; certainly he set the date by reading a solar eclipse as a heavenly sign. Within twenty-four hours his rebel band swelled from seven to seventy, and fifty-five whites were dead. In retaliation, three thousand armed white men converged on Southampton County. When they were done, they had massacred at least fifty slaves, and tried and hanged sixteen more. According to a Richmond editor, "Men were tortured to death, burned, maimed and subjected to nameless atrocities. The overseers were called upon to point out any slaves whom they distrusted; and if any tried to escape they were shot." They stuck the slaves' heads on pikes and displayed them in savage warning against further revolt. With the entire South in panic, Turner hid out in woods and swamps for almost two months. He was captured, tried, and hanged at Jerusalem on November 11, 1831. The Southampton

Insurrection was the bloodiest slave revolt in American history, and the South never forgot it.[1]

That winter the General Assembly of Virginia publicly debated slavery. Their discussion—a last echo of the antislavery ideology of Jefferson's generation and a first rehearsal of the arguments of Lincoln's—ended in the defeat of abolition by a vote of 68 to 65.[2] Further debate over slave labor in the South was stopped by the new economics that made cotton king.

In Boston on New Year's Day, William Lloyd Garrison had proclaimed his determination to end chattel slavery. He backed up his words by inviting legal prosecution, republishing in the first issue of *The Liberator* the denunciations of a slave trader which had already caused him to be jailed for libel in Baltimore.[3]

During the last days of 1831 a young Baltimore attorney, John Pendleton Kennedy, expressed his conflicting attitudes toward slavery in his journal. Vowing never to own another black, he wrote that although he had planned to educate and free his young slave, instead he had sent the boy to Virginia to be sold because he had found him to be "a liar, thief and rascal." [4] A few days later he made another note: He had completed his first novel, *Swallow Barn*,[5] a pastoral idyll. Perhaps the most interesting thing about the novel is that it does not deal with any of these events in the growing crisis over slavery, although Kennedy wrote it while they were shaking the nation and placed his story in contemporary Virginia, the heart of the storm.

Kennedy's choice of setting was natural. His mother was a Virginia Pendleton, and although he had been born in Baltimore, the first son of an immigrant from Ireland, he had spent his childhood summers at family plantations in the Shenandoah Valley. He made a leisurely visit to the Tidewater in 1819; the following year his parents and three brothers moved to a Pendleton farm near Charles Town, Virginia, and in 1825 to Adams Bower, his favorite childhood retreat. He visited them and his numerous relatives in Jefferson and Berkeley counties faithfully each August, and while writing his book, toured with a friend throughout the state. Thus, although all of his life John Pendleton Kennedy was to identify himself with "the progress"—a

Southern Whig and a Unionist, he represented Baltimore's manufacturing and financial interests both in the Maryland legislature and in Congress—he was well equipped to write his pastoral
elegy, which he subtitled "A Sojourn in the Old Dominion."

Kennedy's role as both participant in and visiting observer
of Virginia life is reflected in the epistolary structure and in the
tone of *Swallow Barn,* a curious blend of satire and sentiment.
The story—which he suggests is not properly a novel, perhaps
more accurately "a book of episodes"—is narrated by Mark
Littleton, a young New Yorker visiting his Virginia relations
(I. viii). In an "Introductory Epistle" he writes to a New York
friend that he will "set down, in a random way, all that interests
me during my present visit . . ." (I. 16-17). Kennedy uses the
epistolary form only sporadically, however. The beginning section is a series of set pieces, introducing the people and scenes,
and showing glimpses of the charming country life at Swallow
Barn. Kennedy sets the plantation in the eastern Tidewater area
of Virginia, although he portrays the life he knew in the western
part of the state. We are given the conventional characters of
Frank Meriwether, country squire and master of the plantation;
Cousin Lucretia, his capable wife; their beautiful daughters and
impish son; Cousin Ned Hazard, Southern cavalier; and a host of
typical hangers-on. At the neighboring plantation, The Brakes,
we are acquainted with the testy old aristocrat Isaac Tracy; his
daughter, the high-spirited belle (indeed, she is named Bel); and
his awkward son. Two plot lines are then introduced. The first,
involving an old legal dispute between the Hazards and the
Tracys over title to some worthless marshland, is resolved at the
end of Book I. The second, concerning a love affair between Ned
and Bel, is intermittently developed throughout both volumes,
and finally completed in a postscript. More important than these
story lines are the affectionate sketches of Virginia plantation
life: visits to neighboring plantations, to the stables, accounts of
amateur theatricals, of a fourth of July celebration, dinner
parties, possum hunts, all-night card sessions—and a description
of the slave quarters. Three independent narratives are inserted
into this mixed context: the story of Mike Brown, a vernacular

devil-tale; a narrative of Abe, an heroic black slave; and a history of Captain John Smith.

Despite its dominant mood of easy good nature, there is a mocking undercurrent in *Swallow Barn* which was immediately perceived by the reviewer for the New England Magazine who, in addition to seeing in the novel the charming reflections of Irving which everyone identified, also recognized the harsh outlines of Swift. He characterized the book as "A gentle satire on the pride, aristocratic feeling, and ignorance of a certain class, rather numerous in the south," and concluded that the main characters were displayed "in a ridiculous light." [6] It is precisely this doubleness of tone—at once sentimental and satiric—that modern critics have found significant in *Swallow Barn.*[7]

Unlike the contrast drawn in *The Valley of Shenandoah* between a glorious revolutionary past and a declining present, or that in *Westward Ho!* between a declining past and a glorious present, *Swallow Barn* views both present and past with a mixed attitude. The narrator is charmed by life on the plantation, but at the same time is critical of its provincialism. The conflict in the love plot hinges on Bel's foolish romanticism, which temporarily frustrates Ned's successful courtship. Infatuated by notions of chivalry she has gleaned from Scott's novels, she tames and splendidly outfits a marshhawk in imitation of medieval falconry, but does not train him to obey her command to return—so he flies away. She dresses up an itinerant old fiddler as a minstrel so he will carol romantic lays—and he sings the local ballad "The Yarmouth Tragedy." Straightforward Ned finally wins his lady after agreeing to conform to her notions of gentility—to behave like "an ass of the first water" (II. 157). In addition to this burlesque of the aristocratic pretensions of provincial gentry, Jemmy Smith's trial and the fistfight at the crossroads give us glimpses of the more sordid side of Virginia society. The mindlessness of Southern political thought is satirized in a discussion at the July Fourth celebration at the Landing in which "states' rights" is defined as "a sort of law . . . against cotton and wool." Kennedy burlesques both Virginia rhetoric and the dominance of the planter aristocracy in a vignette in which Frank Meriwether warns a group of his neighbors that "the sovereignty of this

Union will be as the rod of Aaron;—it will turn into a serpent,
and swallow up all that struggle with it," and then listens with
pleasure as the schoolmaster mimics his phrasing in the classroom,
the overseer repeats it to some poor whites, and an old slave is
overheard mumbling, "Look out . . . Aaron's rod a black snake in
Old Virginny!" (I. 81).

Kennedy portrays not only the present, but the past with this
mixture of sentiment and satire, daring even to ridicule Southern
valor in the Revolutionary War (II. 93-100). This is perhaps
most clearly seen in the second plot concerning the lawsuit.
About 1750, Edward Hazard had decided to build a flour mill by
damming up Apple-pie Creek, which marked the boundary between Swallow Barn and The Brakes. He sent off to England for
the machinery, put his slaves to work damming the stream, hired
a miller, and informed his neighbors that they would soon be
able to utilize the results of his industry and resourcefulness. The
mill was opened with great fanfare, but ran for only two hours
because there was no more water in the millpond. Of course it
fell into disuse and disrepair, and finally the dam wore away and
the creek resumed its course. Eventually the title to the land
Hazard had obtained for the millpond came into question. In the
present generation, this lawsuit over useless marshland has become an obsession with old Isaac Tracy, and when it is resolved—
he is made to win his claim by trickery—his zest for life is gone.
The story is significant because of the attitude it displays toward
the South. One feels that if a similar history had been included
in a novel about a Yankee family, the ending would have been
completely different: Their initiative and inventive genius would
have made them all rich. Instead, *Swallow Barn* demonstrates the
impracticality and mechanical incompetence of the Virginians in
the past, and their litigiousness in the present.

Despite the satirical tone Kennedy uses in describing much
of Virginia life, he does not handle the Southern "peculiar institution" ironically. Although Littleton makes his visit to his Virginia cousins in part to test "some unseemly prejudices against
Old Dominion"—one may perhaps assume that they are related
to chattel slavery—halfway through his book he finds himself

thinking that if he had only "a thousand acres of good land, an old manor-house, on a pleasant site, [and] a hundred negroes" he would be a happy man (II. 60).

With the exception of a few brief sketches, the slaves merely provide a background in *Swallow Barn,* but near the end of the second volume, Meriwether and his guests tour the stable and the slave quarter. After spending a full chapter discussing his horses, when the master finally turns his attention to his slaves, they are found to be undeviatingly happy. Adequately housed and well fed—each of the picturesque cabins has a pretty little garden complete with roosting chickens—they are fond of their considerate master, and look forward to his regular visits, confident that he will redress their small grievances or grant some favor. Impressed by what he has seen on the plantation, Littleton decides that the blacks are "a comparatively comfortable and contented race of people, with much less of the care and vexation of life than I have often observed in other classes of society" (II. 227). Upon communicating his conclusions to Meriwether, Littleton is subjected to a proslavery diatribe as was the Northern visitor in *The Valley.* Though Frank Meriwether has been satirized consistently throughout both volumes, his views on this subject— which begin with the familiar abolitionist disclaimers and move on to the familiar apologist conclusions—are introduced as the ideas of "an intelligent slave-holder" (II. 227).

While Meriwether admits that slavery is "theoretically and morally wrong," he claims that Americans are not responsible for it. Since he believes that "a violent removal" or "a general emancipation" would threaten the public safety and be detrimental to the black people themselves, he concludes that the duty of Americans is simply to treat the slaves "kindly and justly" until such time as they can be freed "on terms easy to ourselves and to them." The Virginian reminds his New York guest that slavery is not the business of the North. Whenever abolition is achieved, he asserts, it will be done by "the slave-holding states themselves, as they are the only persons in this country who are able to deal with the subject"; everyone else is "deluded" by "a feeling of unmitigated abhorrence" aroused by "the abstract question of slavery." He urges that it is most important for the "real friends of humanity and justice" to try to avoid any controversy over slavery, to "allay the ferments of the country on this question, and, especially, to soothe the mind of the slave himself" so that he is reconciled to his "destiny." Meriwether runs through the familiar arguments: The master suffers more from slavery than the slave; little work is required of the blacks; they are better off than "the tillers of the soil of other nations"; stories about their mistreatment are not true. He admits that it would be desirable, however, for the legislature to pass laws regulating the treatment of slaves, though he is confident that the instances in which such legislation is needed are very rare.

Having outlined his position, Meriwether confides to his guest that he has a pet project—he would like to inaugurate a kind of feudal system whereby the "most deserving" black men over the age of forty-five could become tenant farmers. He believes that this would not only serve as an incentive for "good conduct" among the slaves and, by permitting these privileged serfs to administer justice to others, do away with the charge of cruel treatment, but points out—straight-faced—that it would also be an economic measure, since it would release the master from any obligation to support "a surplus slave population" (that is, worked-out old slaves).

The racism in *Swallow Barn* is as consistent and as straightforward as the defense of chattel slavery. It is perhaps most compactly expressed in a description of the servants at a dinner party:

> A bevy of domestics, in every stage of training, attended upon the table, presenting a lively type of the progress of civilization, or the march of intellect; the veteran waiting-man being well-contrasted with the rude half-monkey, half-boy, who seemed to have been for the first time admitted to the parlor; whilst, between these two, were exhibited the successive degrees that mark the advance from the young savage to the sedate and sophisticated image of the old-fashioned negro nobility. It was equal to a gallery of caricatures, a sort of scenic satire upon man in his various stages. . . . (II. 78)

Old Carey, the most carefully drawn black man, is characterized as a dog. A stableman conventionally labelled by critics as a "pampered servant," he is affectionately referred to as an "old mastiff" by his master, who explains that he is "a faithful old cur, too, that licks my hand out of pure honesty" (I. 32). Later, when Old Carey is crossed, Littleton describes him as being "angry as a vexed bull-dog" (II. 221).

The only black child individualized is Beelzebub, "a little ape-faced negro" who is young master Rip's personal slave (I. 116). In a short sketch describing the two boys, fishing lines in the water, uproariously catching frogs on the shores of Apple-pie Creek, we recognize an early version of an American pastoral convention Twain was to turn to brilliant account.

Like young Rip's slave, the other black children are described as animals—"untamed monkeys," "baboons," "ducks," and "terrapins"—and as imps and devils. This strange blending of metaphors, each of which insists on inhumanity and grotesqueness and hints at danger, is illustrated by the sketch in which Master Ned encounters a group of children, most wearing only long shirts, but one dressed in cut-down trousers held up by a piece of rope. Seeking diversion from his boredom, he orders them to run a footrace, with a coin for prize:

> At the word, away went the bevy, accompanied by every dog of the pack, the negroes shouting and the dogs yelling in unison. The *shirts* ran with prodigious vehemence, their speed exposing their bare, black, and meager shanks, to the scandal of all beholders; and the strange baboon in trowsers struggled close in their rear, with ludicrous earnestness, holding up his redundant and troublesome apparel with his hand. In a moment they reached the brook with unchecked speed; and, as the banks were muddy, and the dogs had become tangled with the racers in their path, two or three were precipitated into the water. This only increased the merriment, and they continued the contest in this new element, by floundering, kicking, and splashing about, like a young brood of ducks in their first descent

upon a pool. These young negroes have wonderfully flat noses, and the most oddly disproportioned mouths, which were now opened to their full dimensions, so as to display their white teeth in striking contrast with their complexions. They are a strange pack of antic and careless animals, and furnish the liveliest picture that is to be found in nature, of that race of swart fairies which, in the old time, were supposed to play their pranks in the forest at moonlight. Ned stood by, enjoying this scene like an amateur; encouraging the negroes in their gambols, and halloing to the dogs, that by a kindred instinct entered simultaneously into the sport and kept up the confusion. It was difficult to decide the contest. So the money was thrown into the air, and as it fell to the ground, there was another rush. . . . (II. 57-58)

More than a century later, Ralph Ellison would describe a modern version of this pastoral entertainment in a harrowing scene depicting frightened adolescent boys scrambling for coins on an electrified floor for the amusement of the whites.

Each of the three tales Kennedy introduces into the narrative of *Swallow Barn* contrasts dramatically with the easy, familiar tone of the novel. Taken together, they dramatize a darker side of life in the South, undercut the characterization of the black man as happy inferior, and provide a norm against which the quality of plantation life can be measured.

The first, the story of Mike Brown, is narrated by an itinerant Revolutionary veteran. The rough folk quality of this vernacular devil tale of a hard-drinking blacksmith who matches wits with Satan contrasts sharply with the genteel literary tone of the novel. Perhaps more important, it gives us another view of the countryside: Bordering thrice-blessed sunny Swallow Barn plantation is a dark impenetrable swamp. In this swamp—within the recollection of living men—Mike Brown gamely fought the devil. The image is suggestive. There was indeed someone lurking in Southern swamps in the 1830s—perhaps not Mike Brown's Old

Nick, but an escaped slave—perhaps Old Nat Turner himself.

The second tale concerns the slave Abe, and, like the devil yarn, describes a darker past than that revealed through the sketches in *Swallow Barn*. This pathetic story not only represents another abrupt shift in tone, its characterizations of black people contradict the pictures of happy inferior slaves that are otherwise consistently maintained throughout the novel. The story, told to Littleton by Frank Meriwether, is prefaced by their visit to the slave hut of Old Lucy, a madwoman. It begins during the Revolution, with the exploits of Captain Walter Hazard and his faithful slave, Luke. After descanting on the testimonial to slavery implied in such service, the narrator says that Hazard offered Luke his freedom in recognition of his fidelity, but that the slave declined. Instead he was given a cabin and some land at Swallow Barn, and in time grew old and died, leaving his wife Lucy and her youngest child, Abe. In contrast to the rest of their children, all of whom were industrious and docile, recalcitrant Abe ominously resembled "the negroes of the West Indies" (II. 239). While in his teens, he developed wild habits, and finally ran off to join a band of outlaw slaves living in the swamps. When he was captured and brought back to Swallow Barn, old Lucy, distraught with worry, implored her master to save her son from the authorities. Accordingly, Meriwether—ever the kind master—arranged to send Abe away to be a sailor. The description of the separation between Mammy Lucy and her child is sentimental in the extreme. The young man refused her gift of a few coins, and disclaiming any wish either for money or for freedom, asked only for his mother's kerchief as a memento. As time passed, Abe developed into an excellent seaman. Despite Lucy's loneliness, he was not brought back to the plantation because he himself preferred his new life. About four years before Littleton's visit, Abe and four other black sailors were lost at sea while heroically trying to save a crippled brig stricken in a storm. His old mother, refusing to believe him dead, went mad from loneliness and grief. She now sits in her cabin at Swallow Barn, muttering and fingering a handkerchief they told her was taken from her son's body.

In the third interpolation Kennedy reached back to the seventeenth century to chronicle the exploits of John Smith. Although the long section dealing with Smith was excised from the second edition, and only a short chapter remains, his heroism is the standard against which life at Swallow Barn is measured: Bel's literary notions of chivalry and Ned's fist-fight, like Uncle Edward Hazard's attempts to tame nature and Philly Wart's ludicrous Revolutionary campaign, are properly seen as ridiculous in contrast to the achievements of that *"chevalier très hardi"* who planted colonies in the wilderness. The life John Smith led makes life at Swallow Barn appear truly "grotesque, peculiar, and amusing," and gives the Abe narrative added significance (I. viii). It is strange that in the first important book to celebrate the antebellum South, the closest approximation to a true hero is a rebellious slave.

When Kennedy revised his novel for a new edition in 1851, he felt that the modes of life he had sketched in *Swallow Barn* were already vanishing, victims of the "uniformity" of manners that inevitably accompanied "the progress." [8] His revisions reflect both his sense of loss and the morning's newspaper headlines: The second edition, which is more sentimental and less satiric than the original, was justified by its author as "an antidote to this abolition mischief." [9]

Kennedy extensively reworked the chapter entitled "The Quarter," and inserted a three-hundred word proslavery racist essay in which the Northern narrator claims that he has observed the condition of the slaves and that "the contrast between my preconceptions of their condition and the reality which I have witnessed, has brought me a most agreeable surprise" (452). He flatly asserts their happiness, and after speculating briefly on the possibility that slavery is merely a temporary state in the development of black people from "barbarism to civilization," presents a racist diatribe: The black man is "in his moral constitution, a dependant upon the white race"; he is helpless as a child and needs constant supervision; he is "parasitical"; "extravagantly imitative"; fond of music and dancing, gay at heart—"In short, . . . the most good-natured, careless, light-hearted, and happily-constructed human being I have ever seen" (454-55). Consequently, to free the slaves would be "most cruel . . . an act of legislation in comparison with which the revocation of the edict of Nantes would be entitled to be ranked among political benefactions." The narrator asserts that slavery is the business of the South alone even more strongly than he did in the earlier edition, although, significantly, he now suggests reforms in the slave code to permit marriage among slaves, and to prohibit the separation of husband and wife, and of young children from their mothers, two of the outrages that the abolitionists had most publicized.

Swallow Barn is generally characterized as the book which first embodied the pattern of the plantation novel.[10] Tucker's *The Valley,* though in part a celebration of a past civilization, lacks its elegaic mood; Paulding's *Westward Ho!* envisions a slave West, and is only partially concerned with life in the South. Although his view of the plantation, like Tucker's, is mixed, Kennedy consistently reveals a racist, proslavery bias which envisions the black as happy inferior and chattel slavery as beneficent. He counters this view somewhat in his imagery and in the Abe episode but insists upon it even more strongly in the revised edition. *Swallow Barn* has been praised for more than a hundred years as an accurate portrayal of antebellum Southern life.[11] But, set in contemporary Virginia and written during the legislative debate on abolition and the Nat Turner revolt, what is impressive is not its realism, but the extent to which it succeeds in ignoring reality. A modern novel showing contented black men on the streets of Detroit in the summer of 1967 would be analogous. What is important here is not fact, but fantasy. Kennedy's statement of the American myth of the black on the Old Plantation is classic.

NOTES—CHAPTER IV

1. The description of Joseph Travis is from *The Confessions of Nat Turner, the Leader of the Late Insurrection in Southampton, Va.; As Fully and Voluntarily Made to Thomas R. Gray* . . . (Baltimore, 1831), an appendix in Herbert Aptheker, *Nat Turner's Slave Rebellion* (New York, 1966), p. 138. The editor's statement appears in Lerone Bennett,

Jr., *Before the Mayflower: A History of the Negro in America 1619-1964*, rev. ed. (Baltimore, 1966), p. 124. Commentators disagree as to the number of whites killed by the insurrectionists, the number of blacks killed by troops, or the number of slaves punished. The figures given here are among those commonly cited. For additional discussions of the revolt, see Herbert Aptheker, "The Turner Cataclysm and Some Repercussions," *American Negro Slave Revolts* (New York, 1943); William Sidney Drewry, *Slave Insurrections in Virginia (1830-1865)* (Washington, 1900); F. Roy Johnson, *The Nat Turner Slave Insurrection* (Murfreesboro, N.C., 1966); *The Nat Turner Rebellion: The Historical Event and the Modern Controversy*, ed. John B. Duff and Peter M. Mitchell (New York, 1971); and the *Southampton Revolt of 1831: A Compilation of Source Materials*, ed. Henry I. Tragle (Amherst, 1971). For more on Turner, see Chaper IX.

2. Richard Beale Davis, *Intellectual Life in Jefferson's Virginia 1790-1830* (Chapel Hill, N.C., 1964), p. 416. Aptheker, *American Negro Slave Revolts*, pp. 316 f., asserts that the defeated measure was not a bill for abolition but for colonization.

3. *Documents of Upheaval: Selections from William Lloyd Garrison's The Liberator, 1831-1865*, ed. Truman Nelson (New York, 1966), pp. 1-3. *The Liberator* was not the first abolitionist newspaper in America. For a discussion of the antislavery press, see W. Sherman Savage, *The Controversy Over the Distribution of Abolitionist Literature 1830-1860* (Washington, D.C., 1938).

4. Charles H. Bohner, *John Pendleton Kennedy, Gentleman from Baltimore* (Baltimore, 1961), p. 169. Biographical materials used in this chapter were drawn from Bohner; from J. V. Ridgeley, *John Pendleton Kennedy* (New York, 1966); and from Henry T. Tuckerman, *The Life of John Pendleton Kennedy* (New York, 1871).

5. [John Pendleton Kennedy], *Swallow Barn, or a Sojourn in the Old Dominion*, 2 vols. (Philadelphia, 1832). Parenthetical volume and page numbers in my text refer to this edition.

6. *New England Magazine*, III (July 1832), 76-79.

7. See, for example, William R. Taylor, *Cavalier and Yankee* (Garden City, N.Y., 1961), pp. 156-67; and Ridgeley, pp. 36-64.

8. John Pendleton Kennedy, *Swallow Barn, or a Sojourn in the Old Dominion*, rev. ed. (New York, 1851). See "A Word from the Author to the Reader." Parenthetical page references in my text refer to this edition. In the interim since the first edition, Kennedy had published historical romances, a political satire, and Wirt's memoirs.

9. For a characteristic instance of the shift in tone, contrast the description of Swallow Barn, 1832 edition, pp. 19-20, in which it is seen as unfinished, awkward, dilapidated and odd, with the revised passage in the 1852 edition, pp. 27-28, where it is seen as quaint and charming. For the significance of the plantation home in Southern fiction, see Guy A. Cardwell, "The Plantation House: An Analogical Image," *Southern Literary Journal*, 2 (Fall 1969), 3-21.

The quotation is from a letter to William Gilmore Simms dated

March 8, 1851, cited by Bohner, p. 187. In an influential series of articles which appeared in the *National Intelligencer* during the Civil War, republished as *Mr. Ambrose's Letters on the Rebellion* (New York, 1865), Kennedy asserts that the crucial issue is not slavery, but the Union, and condemns Northern and Southern "fanatics" who would destroy it.

10. For example, see Francis Pendleton Gaines, *The Southern Plantation: A Study in the Development and the Accuracy of a Tradition* (New York, 1925), p. 22.

11. Voicing the standard critical approach, Jay B. Hubbell, *The South in American Literature, 1607-1900* (Durham, N.C., 1954), p. 492, contrasts Kennedy's sketches of Virginia life with those of Caruthers, Cooke, and Page, whom he criticizes for having glamorized their materials.

CHAPTER V

WILLIAM GILMORE SIMMS

William Gilmore Simms hailed Kennedy's dramatization of the plantation myth as "the most conclusive answer to the abolitionists that could be made." [1] Coming from the central figure in the literature of the Old South, the man who spent years constructing an historical past for the plantation fantasy, this was high praise.

Both Simms himself and his biographers, no matter how much they dispute the effects of his environment, agree that the determining factor in his development as a writer was his intimate connection with his native city of Charleston, South Carolina.[2] He was born in 1806 of an Irish immigrant father and a mother whose family had moved from Virginia to South Carolina before the Revolution. Simms' great grandfather was one of the prominent Charlestonians held hostage during the British occupation of the city; his grandfather fought with Marion's Brigade, and his maternal grandmother, who raised him, filled the boy's head with the tales of this revolutionary heritage which he would later use in his fiction. An equally significant influence on his mature thought was the material legacy left him by his mother, who died when he was an infant: two Charleston houses and "about twenty-five slaves." When his father, despondent at the loss of his wife and two children, left Charleston to go west to

Mississippi, Gilmore, an imaginative, bookish boy, chose to remain with his grandmother in Charleston. He received casual schooling until his twelfth year, when he was apprenticed to an apothecary. At eighteen he visited his father, and spent many months in the Southwest touring Indian territory and frontier settlements, absorbing more of the matter he would later use in his writing. On his return to Charleston, the young man produced the first of his eighty-two volumes of fiction, poetry, drama, and criticism. He also became involved with the publication of *The Album,* the earliest of a long series of periodicals in which he attempted to establish a Southern literary culture. In 1830, while editing the Charleston City *Gazette,* Simms took the unpopular Unionist position and opposed Nullification. As a consequence, he was attacked by a mob. Distressed by the recent death of his young wife, and alarmed by the incendiary spirit of the people of South Carolina—which in later years he would help fan into flame—the young man decided to sell his paper and leave the state. In the summer of 1832, Simms undertook the first of the series of trips North during which he became acquainted with Paulding's Knickerbocker Circle. Though still threatening to move West, he returned to Charleston with the manuscript of a novel he had written while visiting in New Haven. Entitled *Martin Faber,* it was published in 1833, and in the same year Simms brought out *The Book of My Lady,* a collection of short stories and sketches. These two volumes established him as a professional author. The following year, he first used his native South as a setting for his fiction. In *Guy Rivers,* a border romance, Simms sketched the low Southern characters he would develop in his later novels: squatters, frontiersmen, and faithful slaves.

Simms published *The Yemassee,* the first of his colonial romances in 1835.[3] The view of the American past presented here fits a tight formula: The history of the settlement of the continent is seen as the history of superior whites conquering inferior Indians with the aid of inferior blacks. The central action dramatizes the successful defense of an English colony in Carolina against an Indian attack in 1712. Simms' choice of situation is suggestive: After the Nat Turner revolt of 1830, narratives of attempts to massacre whites, even when conventionally dramatized with Indians cast as the villains, perhaps were weighted with added significance. In a brief passage, one of Simms' white characters makes explicit the implied connection between demonic red and black men when he curses his Indian torturers as "ye monkeys, and ye allegators, and ye red nagers" (260).[4] The romantic plot, which involves a genteel hero and heroine (the mysterious Harrison, who is at last revealed to be the legendary Governor Craven, and Bess, the flower of the forest) raises the theme Paulding was to use later of Cavalier versus Puritan in the New World, and reveals Simms' bias for the former. A subplot deals with a noble Indian chief Sauntee, his dissolute son Occonestoga, and the Indian mother torn between loyalty to her people and love for her worthless child. As in all his work, Simms crams his pages with vital, picaresque characters.

The problems of race and of slavery lie at the heart of *The Yemassee:* Simms portrays the Indian uprising as a desperate act by a doomed people, a vain attempt by the Indians to ward off the inevitable advance of the whites.[5] Thus the chief, who recognizes that "the superior must necessarily be the ruin of the race which is inferior," and that color differences must result in "the formation of castes" because inferiors "tacitly become subjects if not bondmen," plans to exterminate the whites in a desperate attempt to save his nation from slavery (22). The chief's debauched son exemplifies the inevitable depravity of inferiors when in contact with the master race. He hunts escaped slaves for the English in return for whiskey and is contemptuously described by his father as a slave himself (18). While the Indians are motivated by their hopeless wish to escape slavery, Chorley, the low English villain who precipitates the attack by cementing ties between the Yemassees and Spain, is motivated by the desire to own slaves. If the attack is successful, he will be rewarded with the chattel of the English massacred by the Indians. Impatient for mastery, Chorley prematurely kidnaps a slave and thus divulges the plot against the colony.

The most significant dramatization of slavery is the portrayal of the relationship between the hero Harrison and Hector, his devoted slave. Critics have characterized Hector as heroic.[6] Actually, he is no more a hero than is Harrison's other faithful chattel, the dog Dugdale; both of them repeatedly save their master's life. (Dugdale is of a breed trained in the Caribbean to hunt men —Simms mentions that such dogs were used in Santo Domingo to capture insurrectionist slaves—and is thus tremendously helpful against the Indians.) Hector's role is most clearly defined in the passage in which he begs to be allowed to join Dugdale in search of his master, who has not returned after reconnoitering the Indian camp:

> "I must go see a'ter 'em. Dugdale gone 'ready—Dugdale no better sarbant dan Hector . . . I hab hand and foot —I hab knife—I hab eye for see—I hab teet for bite—I 'trong, missis, and I must go look for maussa."

Then, as a significant afterthought, the faithful slave calls back,

> "—but 'member—if maussa come back and Hector loss— 'member, I say, I no runway—'member dat. I scalp—I drown—I dead—ebbery ting happen to me—but I no runway." (312-13)

The message is clear: the black man identifies with the brute and is utterly loyal to his superior master, for whom he would fight and die. Thus at the end of the romance, slaves are armed (though with clubs, not guns) and permitted to indulge their bestiality in the mopping-up campaign against the Indians.

It is not surprising, then, that Hector rejects his freedom when it is offered in reward for his having saved his master's life. Simms gives race relations under slavery their classic form in plantation fiction in the dramatic passage in which Hector, the human chattel, desperately refuses to relinquish the chain with which he holds Dugdale, the canine chattel, while he roars his love of slavery: " 'I d-n to h-ll, maussa, ef I guine to be free! . . .

I cant' loss you company, and who de debble Dugdale guine let feed him like Hector? . . . No maussa—you and Dugdale berry good company for Hector. I tank God he so good—I no want any better' " (392). The reviewer for the *American Quarterly* instantly recognized the significance of this scene, and commented that "A better argument in favour of the continuance of slavery, after it has become a habit, has rarely been made." [7]

Two years later, Simms reformulated into a reasoned argument the racist, proslavery attitudes dramatized in *The Yemassee*. In the interval, he had married Chevillette Roach and had moved to Woodlands, one of her father's plantations on the Edisto River. Here he wrote his review of Harriet Martineau's *Society in America*.[8]

Miss Martineau had published her study of American political, economic, and social institutions in 1837, following a two-year visit to the United States. In her Introduction the British authoress proposes to compare American practice with American principle, and to recount her experiences so that the reader can evaluate her conclusions for himself. This framework places her at the center of the contradiction between the doctrine of natural rights and the institution of chattel slavery. Like Jefferson, she finds political democracy inconsistent with a slave economy, and uses her book to argue against slavery; but because she does not assume the inferiority of black people ("Happily, . . . the coloured race is not cursed by God, as it is by some factions of his children"), she does not founder on the shoal of colonization, as he had (I. 197). After answering a series of arguments in favor of colonization, she points out the economic impossibility of removing the labor force of the South, and concludes that colonization is a false solution and that emancipation is inevitable.

While Miss Martineau's description of slavery on the Kentucky frontier is reminiscent of Paulding's *Letters from the South*, and her report of a Georgia slave coffle is more moderate than those of Tucker and Paulding in their early writings, her impression of slave quarters in Alabama as "something between a haunt of monkeys and a dwelling-place of human beings . . . small, dingy, untidy houses . . . children crouching round the fire" has

little in common with Kennedy's sunny sketch in *Swallow Barn*
(I. 302). Her horror at the plight of the slave is reminiscent of
the early Tucker: "It is usual to call the most depressed of them
brutish in appearance. In some sense they are so; but I never saw
in any brute an expression of countenance so low, so lost, as in
the most degraded class of negroes"(I. 291). In contrast to the
plantation writers, Miss Martineau includes anecdotes of slaves
struggling for freedom. Like Jefferson, she asserts that hatred, not
love, is at the center of the servile relationship:

>As long as the slave remains ignorant, docile, and con-
>tented, he is taken good care of, humoured, and spoken of
>with a contemptuous, compassionate kindness. But, from
>the moment he exhibits the attributes of a rational being,
>—from the moment his intellect seems likely to come into
>the most distant competition with that of whites, the most
>deadly hatred springs up;—not in the black, but in his
>oppressors. It is a very old truth that we hate those whom
>we have injured. (II. 152-53)

Almost as if directly referring to Simms' symbolic tableau of
hound and slave held by a single chain, she comments that "the
'endearing relation' subsisting between master and slaves . . . appeared to me the same 'endearing relation' which subsists between
a man and his horse, between a lady and her dog" (II. 152).

In a section entitled "The Morals of Slavery" Miss Martineau addresses the problem of whether the morality of a master
class in a slave society is consistent with a democratic morality.
While, like the later Tucker, she asserts that mastery can foster
some good, such as mercy, indulgence, and patience, she finds, as
did Jefferson, that its negative effects of tyranny, vice, and violence far outweigh any possible virtues. She concludes that the
slave society of the American South suffers from an immorality
of which it is largely unaware, and that the fundamental denial
of human rights inherent in this slave society is destructive of
democracy in America.

Simms had reviewed Mrs. Trollope's *Domestic Manners of the Americans* five years earlier, and although he had found the comments on slavery uninformed, had not discussed them because "the topic is an irksome and ungracious one, in many sections of the country." [9] Instead he had patriotically protested against female English travelers publishing impressions of the United States. His mood was very different in 1837, when he wrote his critique of Harriet Martineau's *Society in America.*[10]

In his review Simms resolves the contradiction between democratic theory and American practice by repudiating the theory. His article, which runs to seventeen closely printed pages, begins with the familiar attack against English critics and ends with a flippant dismissal of the Declaration of Independence and an enthusiastic endorsement of human slavery. After harshly ridiculing Miss Martineau's age and her deafness, characterizing her attitude toward slavery as "biassed and bigoted," and correcting various errors of fact, Simms confidently asserts that in the South black people are indeed loved and that race hatred exists only in the North where the inferior black competes with his white superiors; that the slaves are happy, slavery is good for the black, and abolitionists are stirring up all the trouble; and that perhaps the absence of black lunatics in Southern asylums can be explained by the mental inferiority of black people. Simms' tone changes when he deals with Miss Martineau's chapter "The Morals of Slavery." He finds the section "painful, because it is full of truth," and discussing what he calls the abuses of slavery—Miss Martineau had found these evils inherent in a slave system—Simms answers her charges of Southern tyranny, vice, and violence by citing restraints imposed by enlightened Southern opinion, by pointing to prostitution in the North, and by referring to the general lawlessness on any frontier (647). In a peculiar aside, Simms deplores all prostitution, but he suggests that in the South, where the prostitutes are black slaves, it has one positive consequence: a generation of mulattoes racially superior to their mothers. He hints that perhaps in time, "that, which would otherwise forever prove a separating wall between the white and the black,—the color of the latter,—will be effectually removed" (647). But having raised this remarkable apology for prostitution and "amalgamation," he immediately drops the subject. Simms cites the loyalty of slaves to their masters during the Revolution—a theme he will develop in his Revolutionary romances—and, in a discussion of the Seminole War, reiterates the ideas about the Indians he had dramatized in *The Yemasee:* The consequlence of their contact with whites must be either "their subjection as inferiors, or their extermination" (650).

Jefferson had been aware of the impossibility of reconciling the theory of natural rights with the institution of chattel slavery and had repudiated slavery. Simms, equally aware of the dichotomy, scraps Jefferson's Declaration, commenting that "Our forefathers, when they declared this truth to be self-evident, were not in the best mood to be philosophers . . ." (652). In its stead, he embraces the hierarchical doctrine he finds propounded by Ulysses in Shakespeare's *Troilus and Cressida,* and arrives at a series of definitions:

> [T]rue liberty is, the undisturbed possession of that place in society to which our moral and intellectual merits entitle us. He is a free-man, whatever his condition, who fills his proper place. He is a slave only, who is forced into a position in society below the claims of his intellect. He cannot but be a tyrant who is found in a position for which his mind is unprepared, and to which it is inferior. (653)

Thus black people, whose inferiority fits them for servitude, are not slaves. Nonetheless, Simms, sounding the doctrine of progress, asserts that "The time will come, I doubt not, when the negro slave of Carolina will be raised to a condition, which will enable him to go forth out of bondage." But of course this can only happen in a period "very far remote" (656).

Simms declares that man's rights, rather than inhering in his nature, derive from his obedience to laws and his fulfillment of duties. From this, he devises a proslavery version of Ben Franklin's philosophy: Man must labor to gain property, the basis of

society; advanced propertied peoples subjugate backward peoples
and by warring against them and enslaving them, raise their level;
thus slavery is a blessing to the inferior race, and mastery a moral
responsibility of the master race. "[T]he slaveholders of the
south, having the moral and animal guardianship of an ignorant
and irresponsible people under their control, are the great moral
conservators, in one powerful interest, of the entire world"
(657).[11]

Between 1835 and 1856, Simms produced his seven Revolutionary romances. The role of South Carolina in the Revolution
had long been disputed, and Simms' books are of particular interest as a revelation of some of the ways in which South Carolina
viewed her national origins as she prepared to secede from the
Union.[12] Taken together, the novels embody a myth of the
Southern past. Simms set the romances within the frame of the
history of the Revolution in South Carolina between June, 1780,
and January, 1783. The earliest, *The Partisan* (1835), opens after
the surrender of Charleston to the British, and sketches the beginnings of armed resistance against the occupation; *Mellichampe*
(1836) concerns British attempts to wipe out Marion's forces;
Katherine Walton (1851) depicts occupied Charleston after the
battle at Camden; *The Scout* (1841) deals with warfare in the
highlands at the same time; *The Forayers* (1856) shows the raids
on British communications lines; and *The Sword and the Distaff*
(1852)—later renamed *Woodcraft*—begins with the triumphant
American return to Charleston in 1782, and dramatizes the establishment of the Southern Way of Life after Independence.

The opening scenes of *Woodcraft* show the successful attempts of the widow Everleigh to recover slaves taken from her
and her patriot neighbor Captain Porgy by the British.[13] The
central action of the romance concerns Porgy's attempt to re-
establish himself on his plantation at Glen-Eberley and—in the
face of British occupation, outlawery, and native governmental
interference—to secure the Southern Civilization.[14] Porgy's plantation and his slaves are jeopardized repeatedly by external
threats. When returned by the British, his slaves are kidnapped
by ruffians, and he regains them by his skill at arms. After he is

established on the plantation, the sheriff attempts to foreclose land and slaves in payment of old debts, but Porgy temporarily staves off his enemies. At the end, his creditor is revealed to be a traitor, and both plantation and slaves are secured.

The plot of *Woodcraft* embodies Simms' view of history and of politics in 1852. The achievement of American political independence is considered a necessary prelude to the establishment of an American civilization, which is consistently envisioned in terms of the Southern slave society.[15] Long before he wrote *Woodcraft,* Simms had concluded that this culture was endangered by the external threat of abolitionism, and as early as 1850, had argued that South Carolina must secede from the Union to protect her institutions.[16]

Simms' concern with external threats and apparent obliviousness to dangers within the South itself seems remarkable in light of the fact that, while a young apothecary's apprentice in Charleston, he had lived through the terror arising from the Denmark Vesey affair. Vesey was a free literate black man who had been captured in Africa and transported to America as a boy. He reportedly was conversant with abolitionist speeches on the Missouri Compromise, was in touch with the rebels of Santo Domingo, and read Scripture to his followers to inspire them to strike for their liberty. His conspiracy evidently involved many thousands of slaves, and was to have culminated in a multiple attack on the city of Charleston on the second Sunday in July, 1822. Two of his fellow conspirators were betrayed by an informer but, deceived by the slaves' "composure and coolness," authorities freed them late in May. Aware that the plot had been discovered, Vesey advanced the date a month; but after a second betrayal, the conspiracy was completely exposed. In Charleston, the trials dragged on all summer: Four white men were fined and imprisoned for encouraging the conspirators; one hundred thirty-one blacks were arrested; forty-seven were condemned; thirty-five were hanged. No one knows the number actually involved in the plot. Most of the slaves followed the advice of a leader, Peter Poyas, to "Die silent, as you shall see me do." Despite the suppression of news of the event in the local papers, the sixteen-year-old Simms could hardly have been impervious to the fear that gripped the city, and could hardly have missed seeing the Federal troops sent to prevent possible uprisings during the executions.[17]

Nevertheless—perhaps because his theories of racial inferiority did not permit him to conceive that slaves could threaten Southern society, or perhaps because he wanted to show that society as monolithic—Simms does not even hint at the possibility of black terror in his romance. Throughout the novel, the black man is consistently seen as a passive inferior. His role, made explicit in a conversation between the overseer Millhouse and Porgy, is identical with that Simms had assigned him in the review of Harriet Martineau's book:

> "The difference between a white man and a nigger, or an Ingin, is that a white man was made to gather substance about him, and a nigger and an Ingin was made to waste it. That's the whole. The Ingin was born to clear the woods of the varmits for us; and the nigger to clean up after we've eaten. That's the philosophy."
>
> "And a very sensible philosophy too, Millhouse."
> (191)

Nor is slavery at issue—strangely, in terms of historical accuracy, for there was a great deal of disagreement in the South about slavery during the period dramatized in *Woodcraft*. But by 1852 Simms was evidently no longer interested in addressing himself to the critics of slavery, and he includes no discussion of the merits of the peculiar institution. He consistently shows the slaves to be obedient and content. Most of them quietly allow themselves to be taken by the outlaws but are pleased when retaken by their master; those who do attempt escape run to find someone to return them to their master; the slaves who avoided British capture by hiding in the swamp are so anxious for servitude that they go back to the plantation immediately upon learning of their master's return; when the sheriff threatens their master, they passively permit themselves to be herded back to the swamp to await the outcome.[18] All in all, they are shown as "glad once

more to find themselves in possession of a homestead, certain provisions, and the protection of a white man . . ." (367).

In addition to sharing basic assumptions about race and servitude, all of the characters in *Woodcraft* have common goals:
They agree that the Good Life is life on the old plantation, although for a moment, early in the book, an alternative life style
is fleetingly mentioned. Porgy, believing himself impoverished,
recalls an old French squatter who lived by hunting whatever
small creatures he could shoot and by cultivating a couple of
acres of vegetables, and who amused himself by dipping snuff
and playing the violin. Charmed, Porgy briefly dreams of realizing this vision of a Gallic Walden, but dismisses these fancies
when land and slaves are restored to him. Aside from this single
lapse, no diversity of goals is suggested. The major distinction between the heroes and villains in *Woodcraft* concerns means, not
ends. Thus the romance recounts Porgy's successful recovery of
Glen-Eberly; the ambition of the villain M'Kewn, his creditor,
is to own a fine plantation; and even M'Kewn's tool, the evil
squatter Bostwick, hopes to buy his daughter slaves to make her
a lady.

The ordering of social relationships is equally simplified.
Consistent with Simms' static concept of degree outlined in reply
to Harriet Martineau, problems arise in *Woodcraft* when a low
individual attempts to rise above his capacity (M'Kewn and Bostwick) or when an aristocrat is demeaned (Porgy). The model
social structure is feudal and is exemplified on all its levels by
the relations between the planter aristocrat Captain Porgy; his
freeholding faithful follower Lieutenant Lance; his faithful poor
white overseer Sargeant Millhouse; and his faithful black slave
Tom. The perversion of this society is demonstrated by the relation between the upstart aristocrat M'Kewn and squatter Bostwick, his criminal tool.

Racial superiority, slavery, social goals and social structure
are not at issue. What is disputed is the precise nature of the
ordered good life on the plantation, and Simms presents two
major attitudes, which apparently are reconciled in a series of
discussions and incidents contrasting the view of the aristocrat
Porgy, who represents some sort of humanism, and the overseer

Millhouse, who expounds utilitarianism. (Simms has made the overseer's name a double pun. "Millhouse" not only refers to John Stewart Mill's utilitarianism, but suggests that the sargeant would run a house like a mill; that is, would transform the home into a factory.)

The divergent ideas Porgy and Millhouse hold can clearly be seen in their attitudes toward the black slaves. When Porgy's old nurse Maum Sappho appears at Glen-Eberley and announces that she and her family, who had hidden from the Redcoats in the swamps, will return to the plantation, Porgy is genuinely happy to see her and is anxious for news of the people; but Millhouse's response is to add the unexpected newcomers to his labor force and to plan a bigger crop. The implication that Porgy's relationship with the slaves involves something more than Millhouse's crass economics is underscored by a series of details: Millhouse opposes permitting the slaves to attend coon hunts and weddings because the loss of sleep will impair their efficiency in the fields, and forbids them to own dogs because the animals will inevitably attack livestock. But despite the fact that Porgy is a patriarchal master and is aware of Millhouse's lack of humane impulse and of his proclivity to violence, he agrees to make Millhouse his overseer and gives him complete control over the slaves and the crop.

Later the impoverished Porgy mortgages all these faithful slaves, with the exception of Tom, a special favorite. His relationship with Tom merits special consideration. A note of hysteria has crept into Simms' description: In *The Partisan* (1835) Porgy's attachment to his slave is so great that he will not permit anyone else to kick him; in *Woodcraft* (1852) he is willing to kill Tom before he will allow him to belong to another man, reasoning that "Tom . . . would rather die my slave, than live a thousand years under another owner" (113). When he informs Tom of his determination and suggests that, if he does not have time for the bloody deed, Tom commit suicide, Porgy appears shocked at the slave's reluctance: "Is it possible that you could wish to live, if separated from me? Impossible, Tom! I will never believe it. No, boy, you shall never leave me. We shall never part. You shall be my cook, after death, in future worlds, even as you are here . . ."

76 The Intricate Knot

(185). (It is, however, possible that the author intended that this episode be humorous. At times it is difficult to determine what to take seriously here.) When faced with the sheriff's warrant, Porgy tells Tom he would rather see him dead than slave to M'Kewn, the villainous creditor; finally he sells him to the widow Eveleigh and then hires him back immediately, thus technically keeping his vow not to sell Tom to another man. When Porgy's debts are cancelled and he offers the slave his liberty, Tom, of course, refuses it. With less vehemence—but not less sincerity— than Pompey in *The Yemassee,* the black man tells his master " 'You b'longs to me Tom, jes' as much as me Tom b'long to you; and you nebber guine get you free paper from me long as you lib' " (509).

But although Porgy's humanism is superior to Millhouse's utilitarianism, it is not seen as economically feasible. In fact, Porgy's lack of concern with economic considerations has resulted in the debt that represents the only internal threat to Glen-Eberley. Evidently the way to run a plantation is Millhouse's way. Thus Simms presents as necessary the compromise whereby Porgy limits himself to some vague higher pursuit and gives Millhouse total control of the economy and a free hand with both land and slaves. The Southern Way of Life envisioned in *Woodcraft* is a strange combination of the mercenary business practices the South generally characterized as Yankee and the aristocratic high culture it delighted to claim as its own—though it is odd to see the Falstaffian, belly-bound Porgy cast as its representative.[19]

Both Simms' Porgy and Thomas Jefferson emerged from their years of Revolutionary service laden with debts—they had had slaves stolen by the British, and came home to estates encumbered in consequence of the master's insistence on his pleasures—and both had visions of the new life they would establish. However, despite their agreement that the black is an inferior, there is a startling contrast between Simms' fantasies of Southern culture, projected backward from 1852 to 1782, then presented as a view of the future, and Jefferson's vision, partially embodied in his *Notes* in 1781. Though Jefferson's thought was rooted in Virginia, its scope was national; it embraced the development of a vital democratic culture, and recognized that a slave economy was destructive of this. Simms' view is local, and his concern, finally, is with the establishment of a stable aristocratic culture buttressed by slavery. This divergence is reflected in the literary modes used to embody their visions: Jefferson chose an open form, susceptible to endless improvisations; Simms, the conventional historical romance.

Throughout 1852, Simms' novel appeared semi-monthly as a supplement to the *Southern Literary Gazette;* the sensational *Uncle Tom's Cabin* had run in the *National Era* from June, 1851, to April, 1852. In a letter to James Hammond, written in December of 1852, Simms characterized his romance as "probably as good an answer to Mrs. Stowe as has been published." [20] Though only one teasing phrase in his book refers to Mrs. Stowe's novel—Tom's gruff response, " 'Don uncle me, you chuckle-head' " when another slave addresses him as Uncle Tom—Simms was probably right (179). That same year he published another indirect answer to Mrs. Stowe. *The Pro-Slavery Argument,* which became the standard defense of the Southern peculiar institution, is composed of four essays.[21] Simms' contribution, "The Morals of Slavery," is an expanded version of the review of Harriet Martineau's book that he had written many years earlier.

In a new introduction, Simms asserts that in the 1830s, when the essay was originally published, slavery was generally defended on grounds of expediency; but that now, in the 1850s, slavery is correctly seen as moral; as essential to "the progress of civilization"; as "under the immediate sanction of Heaven" and part of the "divine plan" (178). Evidently with Harriet Beecher Stowe in mind, Simms justifies republication of his old work on the grounds that her British namesake, to whom it was originally addressed, is representative of "that tribe whose restless eagerness, morbid self-esteem, and complacent philanthropy . . . are at the bottom of all the dangers which threaten the existing civilization and safety of mankind" (180). Only with great reluctance can Simms bring himself even to address the critics of slavery: "Why should we account to these people? What are they that they should subject us to the question?" (183). He attacks as hypocrites both British abolitionists, whose nation planted slavery in

America, and New England abolitionists, whose forefathers
fattened on the sale of slaves to the South. *Uncle Tom's Cabin* is
mentioned only in a short passage charging that the horrors it
reveals are incidental to, not inherent in, a slave society. Simms'
revised text does not include his original argument mitigating
the evils of black prostitution; he now asserts that black whore-
dom is superior to white because it cannot corrupt the already
degenerate black woman. Although Simms makes one veiled reference to the Denmark Vesey conspiracy, which he characterizes
as the unique scheme of "an imported mulatto," he persists in
identifying the danger to the South as external—as the work of
evil abolitionists. He intensifies his attack on Jefferson and the
theory of natural rights. Simms' racism has hardened, and rather
than envision any possibility of the black man advancing from
slavery, he writes: "I do not believe that he ever will be other
than a slave, or that he was made to be otherwise; but that he is
designed as an implement in the hands of civilization always"
(270). The tone of the essay, originally harsh, is now proud, hos-
tile, belligerent. His letters soon would become hysterical.[22]

William Gilmore Simms was crushed by the collapse of the
slave society he had apotheosized. He lived until 1870, grinding
out romances, reviews, and articles in a ceaseless attempt to finance the re-establishment of plantation life at Woodlands after
Lee's surrender. His realities contrasted sharply with the vision of
the heroic planting of Southern civilization he had celebrated in
Woodcraft.

NOTES—CHAPTER V

1. Letter to John Pendleton Kennedy May 12, 1851, in *The Letters of
   William Gilmore Simms,* ed. Mary C. Simms Oliphant, Alfred T. Odell,
   and T. C. Duncan Eaves, 5 vols. (Columbia, S.C., 1952-56), III, 122.
2. Biographical information in this chapter is based on materials in the
   Letters, and in William P. Trent, *William Gilmore Simms,* American
   Men of Letters Series (Boston and New York, 1892); J. V. Ridgeley,
   William Gilmore Simms (New York, 1962); Alexander S. Salley, "Bio-
   graphical Sketch of Simms," *Letters,* I, lix-xc.

Trent, asserting that a slave society cannot produce high culture, concludes that Simms was "sadly hampered by his environment," p. 325. Vernon L. Parrington, *Main Currents in American Thought,* 3 vols. (New York, 1927, 1930, 1954), II, 119-30, argues that aristocratic Charleston stunted the plebian Simms. Salley and Ridgely, Simms' modern biographers, pointing to his best fiction, which is deeply rooted in Southern history and culture, and to his most astute criticism, which espouses a national literature based in the local, suggest that Simms' environment was his source of strength.

3. William Gilmore Simms, *The Yemassee,* 2 vols. (New York, 1835). The standard edition is *Works of William Gilmore Simms,* 20 vols. (New York, 1853-66), XV; because this has not been available to me, my citations refer to an edition edited by Alexander Cowie, American Fiction Series (New York and Cincinnati, 1937), which follows the revised 1853 text. I have checked quoted passages from the Cowie edition against the 1835 text, to determine whether Simms' racism and pro-slavery attitudes were included in the first editions. They were.

4. For a discussion of suppressed diabolism, see Alan Henry Rose, "The Image of the Negro in the Pre-Civil War Novels of John Pendleton Kennedy and William Gilmore Simms," *Journal of American Studies,* 4 (February 1971), 217-26.

5. For a somewhat blurred discussion on this point, see Alexander Cowie, "Introduction," to Simms, *The Yemassee* (New York and Cincinnati, 1937), pp. xxvii-xxviii.

6. See, for example, Charles E. Burch, "Negro Characters in the Novels of William Gilmore Simms," *The Southern Workman,* LII (April 1923), 192-95; or Sterling Brown, *The Negro in American Fiction,* Bronze Booklet No. 6 (Washington, D.C., 1937), p. 9. For the opposite interpretation, see Austin J. Shelton, "African Realistic Commentary on Culture Hierarchy and Racistic Sentimentalism in *The Yemassee,*" *Phylon,* XXV (Spring 1964), 72-78.

7. *American Quarterly Review,* XVII (June 1835), 545-48.

8. Some critics claim that Simms' attitudes changed dramatically after his entrance into the planter class. See, for example, Parrington, II, 120; and John W. Higham, "The Changing Loyalties of William Gilmore Simms," *Journal of Southern History,* IX (May 1943), 210-23. But an examination of *The Yemassee* shows that Simms was overtly sectional, racist, and proslavery as early as 1835.

Harriet Martineau, *Society in America,* 3 vols. (London, 1837). Quoted material in the text refers to this edition.

9. *American Quarterly Review,* XII (September 1832), 109-33.

10. A South Carolinian [William Gilmore Simms], "Miss Martineau on Slavery," *Southern Literary Messenger,* III November 1837), 641-57. Page numbers in my text refer to this edition. The review was republished as a pamphlet in 1838.

11. It seems remarkable that one of Simms' best critics, Donald Davidson, "Introduction," William Gilmore Simms, *Letters,* I, xxxvi, in 1952 argued that Simms' work can be examined freshly because "the social

and political questions that befogged Trent [see n. 1 above] are no longer live issues at least in their old form."

12. The psychology of South Carolinians during the period from 1836 to 1866 is discussed in Steven A. Channing, *Crisis of Fear: Secession in South Carolina* (New York, 1970). For the problem of the role of South Carolina in the Revolution, see Herbert Aptheker, *American Negro Slave Revolts* (New York, 1943, 1963), p. 22. The most recent historical treatments can be found in the series of Tricentennial Booklets (Columbia, S.C., 1970).

    One school of critics praises Simms as a realist; for discussions of the Revolutionary romances as myth, see William R. Taylor, *Cavalier and Yankee* (New York, 1961), and Ridgely. Also see C. Hugh Holman's interesting article, "William Gilmore Simms' Picture of the Revolution as a Civil Conflict," *Journal of Southern History*, XV (1949), 441-62.

13. William Gilmore Simms, *The Sword and the Distaff* (Charleston, 1852); revised and republished as *Woodcraft* (New York, 1854). I have been unable to examine the standard edition, *Works*, V. The 1854 text and title are retained in the edition I have used, published in New York, 1961, with an introduction by Richmond C. Beatty. Parenthetical page references in my text refer to this edition.

14. Cecil L. Moffit, "Simms's Porgy as National Hero," *American Literature*, XXVI (1965), 475-84, envisions Porgy as a representative American, and his establishment of Glen-Eberley as the planting of American culture. But Simms' vision, in *Woodcraft*, is narrower: the romance is not national, but regional. The community that Captain Porgy, the representative Southron, establishes, is the slave society of the South. As Taylor points out, what Simms writes is the mythic past of the slavocracy.

15. Simms' critical writings are pertinent here. C. Hugh Holman, "Introduction," to Simms, *Views and Reviews in American Literature, History, and Fiction,* First Series (Cambridge, Mass., 1962), discussing Simms' theory of national literature, argues persuasively that the defensive provincialism characteristic of Simms in the 1850s and 1860s was not present in the 1840s, when he argued for a democratic native literature. Holman's claim, however, in "William Gilmore Simms' Picture of the Revolution as a Civil Conflict," that Simms' view of national literature as sectional anticipates modern theories, must be examined in light of the fact that Simms conceived of the South as a nation. See, for example, *Letters*, III, 518. For further discussion of Simms' criticism, see Edd Winfield Parks, *William Gilmore Simms as Literary Critic* (Athens, Ga., 1961).

16. Salley, p. lxxxvi, implies that although Simms propagandized for secession for a full decade before Sumter, he is somehow a moderate because he argued that South Carolina should convince her sister slave states to leave the Union with her, rather than to secede alone.

17. For the Vesey affair, see *The Trial Record of Denmark Vesey*, ed. John Oliver Killens (Boston, 1969); Aptheker, *American Negro Slave Revolts*, pp. 267-76; Herbert Aptheker, *A Documentary History of the*

Negro People in the United States (New York, 1962), I, 74-76; and Clement Eaton, *The Freedom-of-Thought Struggle in the Old South,* rev. ed. (New York, 1964), pp. 90-91.

18. As outlaws who prey on chattel, in Southern fiction slave-thieves play a role analogous to that of cattle-rustlers in the Western. During the generation preceding Emancipation, abolitionists called slave owners "man-stealers"; slave owners called the operations of the Underground Railroad "slave stealing."

19. As this discussion indicates, the stereotype of Simms as uncritical of the South is false. For more on this point, see John R. Walsh, "William Gilmore Simms, Critic of the South," *Journal of Southern History,* XXVI (1960), 201-14.

20. *Letters,* III, 218-23. See S. P. C. Duvall, "William Gilmore Simms's Review of Mrs. Stowe," *American Literature,* XXX (1958), 107-17; and J. V. Ridgeley, "*Woodcraft:* Simms's First Answer to *Uncle Tom's Cabin,*" *American Literature,* XXXI (1960), 421-33. Jeanette Reid Tandy, "Pro-Slavery Propaganda in American Fiction of the Fifties," *South Atlantic Quarterly,* XXI (1922), 41-50, 170-78, points out that in the two years following the publication of *Uncle Tom's Cabin,* fourteen proslavery novels were published.

21. Chancellor Harper, Gov. Hammond, Dr. Simms and Professor Dew, *The Pro-Slavery Argument* (Charleston, 1852). Parenthetical page referecenes in my text are to this edition.

22. See, for example, *Letters,* IV, 264-66.

The antislavery emblem of the victimized slave, here used on a broadside, was painted on teacups and worked into embroideries sold to raise funds for abolitionism.

Part Three:
Abolitionist Views

"Ah, when will master get better from his sickness; only the sour heart that sour sickness breeds made him serve Babo so; cutting Babo with the razor, because, only by accident, Babo had given master one little scratch; and for the first time in so many a day, too. Ah, ah, ah," holding his hand to his face.

Is it possible, thought Captain Delano; was it to wreak in private his Spanish spite against this poor friend of his, that Don Benito, by his sullen manner, impelled me to withdraw? Ah, this slavery breeds ugly passions in man—poor fellow!

Herman Melville, "Benito Cereno"

Jefferson displayed multiple visions of the black man in
Notes on Virginia. Just as plantation fiction embodies his notion
of black inferiority, so the abolitionist novels that soon followed
reflect his denunciations of black slavery. These books are not
easy to characterize. It is not true that they can be distinguished
from the plantation tradition by their inclusion of polemic;
even the early Virginia novels included debate. It is not even
true that they can be identified by their inclusion of abolitionist
propaganda; *Uncle Tom's Cabin,* the most famous of them all,
proposes colonization as a solution to the American race problem—and this, twenty years after Garrison had attacked the
American Colonization Society as a major obstacle to immediate
emancipation.

What most clearly characterizes these books is a special perspective and tone. In contrast to the nostalgia of plantation
fiction, the abolitionist novels confront the perilous present.
Characters must act under threat of immanent cataclysm, the result of God's wrath or historical inevitability. But despite this
mood of apocalypse, these novels end on an optimistic note:
Slaves are manumitted; fugitives escape; lovers, parents, and children are reunited. In the few instances where virtue is not rewarded on earth, it is utterly triumphant in heaven, and the
reader is made to understand that this is what is really important.

The writers of these books gave the slaves more important
roles in the plots and criticize the system of slavery more severely
than the plantation novelists. But racist stereotypes of the black
man are not consistently rejected—Mrs. Stowe's books alone include more stock black characters than Tucker's or even Kennedy's—and the servile relation is often shown as beneficent.
Frequently what appears to be a fresh characterization of the
black man is in reality the vision of a new figure: the mulatto.
Nonexistent in plantation fiction, the mulatto is ever present in
antislavery novels. In order to understand the portrayal of blacks
and mulattoes in abolitionist fiction, in addition to examining
views of slavery as in plantation literature, it is necessary to look
at the variations in character in relation to the variations in skin
color. When the mulatto is consistently seen as different from his

darker brother, it is important to note whether these differences
are presented as the consequences of environment or of race.

Many of the abolitionist novels are based on slave narratives,
which present a vision of the black man and of chattel slavery
antithetical to that found in plantation fiction. These autobiographies, written by fugitives who escaped from slavery, display
the underside of the plantation tradition. Here the hero, inevitably successful (he could not have written his story otherwise), is
the slave; the action describes his struggle to be free. Despite all
their differences, each of the narrators studied—Josiah Henson,
Lewis and Milton Clarke, William and Ellen Craft, William
Wells Brown, Frederick Douglass—reveals that slavery meant
war, and that in his battle against enslavement he masked his
true face. Thus the black figures displayed in even the crudest of
these books show an ironic complexity impossible in the most
sophisticated of the plantation novels. These early narratives
sound the militant accents of the first black voices raised in our
literature; their tone and message accurately presage today's
dark anger.

The abolitionist novels run the gamut from portrayals of
the angry ironist of the slave narratives to depictions of the loving black simpleton of the plantation novels. The earliest,
Richard Hildreth's *Archy Moore,* first appeared anonymously as
a slave narrative and successfully combines the militancy of the
slave autobiographies with the structure of the sentimental novel.
The only other antislavery novel with comparable force is *Uncle
Tom's Cabin.* While ostensibly based on the narratives, which by
midcentury had appeared in large numbers, Mrs. Stowe's book
derives its power by dramatizing not a slave's struggle for mundane freedom, but a martyr's spiritual triumph. The synthesis of
sentimental novel and slave autobiography that Hildreth had
achieved was not repeated even by William Wells Brown, a fugitive slave and the first Afro-American novelist. Although in
Clotel Brown introduced characters and incidents from his own
experience, his succeeding versions of the book became increasingly sensational, sentimental, and genteel.

The standard critical complaint about white abolitionist

writers is that, because they were unfamiliar with slavery and
black people, they depicted black chattel responding as they
thought they themselves would respond if enslaved. But this was
rarely true. The stock abolitionist characterization of the black
as passive victim reveals the inability of these writers to conceive
of black men acting as effective agents in their own lives. One
indication of the significance of race in the American imagination
is the fact that we have produced few writers capable of creating
a character with a skin color different from, and a humanity
identical with, their own.

CHAPTER VI

RICHARD HILDRETH

They will not suffer us to meet together to worship the God who made us—they brand us with hot iron—they cram bolts of fire down our throats—they cut us as they do horses, bulls, or hogs—they crop our ears and sometimes cut off bits of our tongues—they chain and handcuff us, and while in that miserable and wretched condition, beat us with cow-hides and clubs—they keep us half naked and starve us sometimes nearly to death under their infernal whips or lashes (which some of them shall have enough of yet).—They put on us fifty-sizes and chains, and make us work in that situation, and in sickness, under lashes to support them and their families.—They keep us in the most death-like ignorance by keeping us from all sources of information, and call us, who are free men and next to the Angels of God, their property!!!!!! They make us fight and murder each other, many of us being ignorant, not knowing any better.—They take us (being ignorant) and put us as drivers one over the other, and make us afflict each other as bad as they themselves afflict us—and to crown the whole of this catalogue of cruelties, they tell us that we the (blacks) are an inferior race of beings! [1]

On this subject I do not wish to think, or speak, or write, with moderation. No! no! Tell a man whose house is on fire to give a moderate alarm; tell him to moderately rescue his wife from the hands of the ravisher; tell the mother to gradually extricate her babe from the fire into which it has fallen;—but urge me not to use moderation in a cause like the present.[2]

Ye who would know what evils man can inflict upon his fellow without reluctance, hesitation, or regret; ye who would learn the limit of human endurance, and with what bitter anguish and indignant hate the heart may swell, and yet not burst,—peruse these Memoirs!

Mine are no silken sorrows, nor sentimental sufferings, but . . . [the] . . . stern reality of actual woe. . . .[3]

These passages, published in Boston between 1829 and 1836, sound a new, urgent note in our national letters. The first is taken from a pamphlet written by David Walker, a free black man, and was thought to have incited Nat Turner to insurrection. The second is William Lloyd Garrison's announcement of his determination to dedicate his life to the abolition of slavery and was published in the first issue of *The Liberator*. The third is the opening paragraph of a novel in which Richard Hildreth, a white lawyer-turned-newspaperman, attempted imaginatively to transform himself into Archy Moore, the slave. His remarkable success is suggestive of Garrison: Just as in the early years the editor of *The Liberator* was thought to be a black man, so it was assumed that the author of *Archy Moore* was indeed a slave.

It is fascinating to speculate on the origins of Hildreth's remarkable imaginative feat.[4] His early life followed a pattern typical of his generation. Born in 1805 of old New England forebears, Richard was trained at Exeter, where his minister father taught, and at Harvard, where he studied the classics and read poetry. He wrote the customary weekly essays which E. T. Channing rigorously excised, training him in the straightforward style which our ears approve but which dismayed his reviewers, who preferred the flowing prose of Parkman and Bancroft. Upon graduation in 1826, Hildreth taught school for a year before preparing for a legal career. He read law at Newburyport, where he might have met Garrison, and at Boston, where he discovered the English novel and read Smollett, Sterne, Fielding, Austen, and Scott.

An aspiring writer, Hildreth submitted standard literary appreciations of the classics and brief attempts at fiction to the fledgling American journals that began to appear. In his most pretentious essay, "National Literature," Hildreth makes the distinction between "popular" and "permanent" letters, and while not entirely rejecting the "peculiar," "local," and "transient," asserts the need for a "lasting, solid, substantial" national literature, which will express the "universal" and the "beautiful." He strikes a different patriotic note in a later issue when, reviewing Captain Basil Hall's *Travels,* in his haste to defend the United States against "wholesale abuse" by the English he neglects even to mention Hall's criticisms of American slavery.[5]

Hildreth was admitted to the bar, but almost immediately began the newspaper career he was never entirely to abandon. In 1832 he helped found the Boston *Daily Atlas,* a pugnacious Whig sheet, and immersed himself in rough and tumble political journalism and Temperance Whig politics. Within two years his health, never robust, failed; he sold his interest in the paper and went to Florida to recuperate.

It is possible that Hildreth's choice of reading matter during his convalescence was influenced by his having met or heard of the two French prison commissioners who had visited Boston three years earlier—or perhaps his interest in current French letters was instrumental.[6] Whatever the cause, it appears that Hildreth read the newly published *Democracy in America,* Tocqueville's essay on American institutions, and its companion volume *Marie,* Beaumont's novel of American manners.[7] A product of the eighteenth- and nineteenth-century French antislavery literary tradition, *Marie* was the first such novel based on direct observations of American life. It includes both the sentimental romance of an idealistic young Frenchman whose search for liberty in America ends in failure, and a series of provocative essays—some interpolated into the narrative, most gathered into long appendices—commenting on American customs and manners. In these, although Beaumont discusses a number of topics, his major concern is the central theme of his novel: "The Social and Political Condition of . . . Free People of Color."

The romance is largely narrated by a French hermit. At his retreat in the Michigan forest, he tells a young fellow countryman of his quest for self-realization in the New World and of his ill-fated love for Marie, a beautiful girl who has learned that her mother's family "had been soiled by a drop of black blood" (55). After a series of incidents impress upon him "the profound American hatred for the blacks" (74), the hero, pursued by a mob, flees West to the wilderness with Marie. A minor plotline follows Marie's brother who, in contrast to her sad acceptance of the white standards which characterize her as "stained," proudly asserts himself equal to anyone. Embracing his "rightful place . . . among the black men," he participates in a joint insurrection they undertake with the Indians against the whites. In a letter he proclaims that "the hatred between us and our enemies is irreconcilable. . . . This enmity will end only with the extermination of one of the two races" (172). With his note comes news of his heroic death leading the Indians, and of the craven failure of the blacks to rise up. Distressed by her brother's death and ill from her hard journey West, Marie dies murmuring, "accursed race, base blood, inexorable destiny"; her lover remains to mourn near her grave. At the conclusion of the hermit's pathetic story, his young listener, sobered by the gulf between egalitarian theory and racist practice in America, hastily returns to France.

The Southern environment in which Hildreth evidently read *Marie* must have seemed as strange to him as our Eastern cities and Western wilderness had appeared to the French novelist. Hildreth, like his fellow Northerners depicted in the fiction of Tucker and Kennedy, was deeply interested in Southern life. Unlike them, he found Southern slavery as shocking as Beaumont had found Northern prejudice. The plantation where he stayed during his convalescence was owned by aristocratic Virginians, and in the immediate neighborhood were wealthy and poor white newcomers and their black slaves from South Carolina, North Carolina, Georgia, and Kentucky. Hildreth later commented that this contact with masters and slaves influenced him deeply:

> After a time this impression became so strong as to create a desire to communicate to others the new lights and new feelings which he had obtained upon a subject of which till lately, he had been wholly ignorant. To bring about that result, it seemed best to carry the reader through much the same course of facts, and conclusions from those facts, which had operated upon the writer's own mind; and in order to do that, the best way appeared to be to arrange into a coherent narrative, the most striking of those incidents which had come to the writer's knowledge, adopting such an order of arrangement and such modifications as the interest of the story might require—it being plain that any artistic embellishment, or any small narrative skill on the writer's part, would but very feebly compensate for the difference of impression made on the mind by things seen and things merely told. To this story, by way of a complete exhibition of his ideas, the writer proposed to himself to add a formal treatise in which the subject should be handled in a didactic manner.[8]

When Hildreth returned to Boston in April, 1836, he carried with him both a polemic entitled *Despotism in America,* a tough analytical denunciation of chattel slavery evidently written in response to Tocqueville,[9] and a remarkable novel—perhaps inspired by Beaumont—insistently "peculiar" and "local": *Archy Moore.*

Hildreth wrote *Archy Moore* as the autobiography of a fugitive slave, and in it follows his adventures from his early life on a Virginia plantation where he loves and loses his beautiful wife Cassy; south through the slave trade to reformist masters in Middle Virginia and North Carolina where he and Cassy are reunited and again separated after the birth of their son; then further south into slavery on a rice plantation in South Carolina where he and the black slave Thomas rebel, and from which Archy escapes North. After briefly sketching his adventures at sea and years of settlement in England, the book concludes with Archy's resolve to return to America to find and free his wife, their son, and his friend.

The single most remarkable thing about *Archy Moore* is this first person narration: The Boston attorney has assumed the identity of a plantation slave. The book's acceptance as autobiography has been so complete that it has been discredited as a false slave narrative; even twentieth-century critics have felt it necessary to point out that it is fiction.[10]

Like *Marie, Archy Moore* includes both the romance of a beautiful light-skinned heroine, and the tale of a mulatto rebel. But Hildreth's theme is the institution of chattel slavery and its ideology of white racism, not the prejudice that Beaumont had seen as a "secondary consequence" which persisted after its "first cause [slavery] has disappeared" (6). Thus Hildreth changes the focus of Beaumont's vision in a number of ways. He gives the adventures of the rebel precedence over the love story, and instead of portraying the black slaves as passive, he creates Archy's friend Black Thomas, the first black insurrectionist in American fiction.

Archy Moore is not, like *Marie,* a cautionary novel addressed to a European "public which seeks . . . ideas for the intellect and emotions for the heart." Instead, Hildreth's announced audience is the "generous and heroic youth" of America, and his stated purpose is to move them to "break down the ramparts of prejudice . . . snatch the whip from the hand of the master [and] . . . break forever the fetter of the slave!" (6).

The action of *Archy Moore,* located in the South that is described in plantation fiction, does not move like Beaumont's from urban East to frontier West. Instead, Hildreth charts a route south through the slave trade, then north to freedom, as did the writers of the slave narratives. It does not end in defeat and withdrawal, but in partial success and the promise of ultimate victory.

Here tone and voice express neither the resignation of a defeated European idealist as in Beaumont's *Marie,* the detachment of an American observer as in Tucker's or Paulding's *Letters,* nor the nostalgia of a Northerner charmed by the South as in Kennedy's *Swallow Barn,* but the urgent anger of a rebellious native son, his master's mulatto bastard.

The initial section dramatizes Archy's childhood and youth at Spring Meadow, the family plantation in lower Virginia, and describes his aristocratic father, a veteran of the Revolution, his beautiful mother, on one side descended from the Randolphs, and his youthful romance with the lovely Cassy. This appears curiously reminiscent of the views of family life in the plantation novels, but Hildreth's shift in perspective from white to black, from master to slave, transforms the scene. Here the father is master of his lovely mulatto concubine; their son Archy is a slave; Archy's marriage to Cassy (who is also Colonel Moore's child) is first forbidden because the master wants her for himself, then annulled by Archy's sale. Hildreth's radical shift in point of view reveals the perversion and destruction of the family on the old plantation.

All attempts to ameliorate the evils of slavery are seen as futile. Although Major Thornton, one of Archy's reformist masters, forbids whippings to enforce discipline, he uses fear to keep his chattel obedient. While he feeds and clothes his slaves decently, it is for the same reason he rotates his crops—to realize a better return on his investment. Another, Master James Carleton, professes awareness of his responsibility for the souls of his slaves, but preaches to them only "obedience, submission, diligence, and subordination," delegating responsibility for their mundane existence to a brutal overseer—an arrangement much like Porgy's in *Woodcraft.* Cassy's experiences serving both poor whites and the aristocratic Mrs. Montgomery teach the same lesson: The problem is not the abuses of slavery, but the system itself.

Similarly, Archy's sale away from Virginia, the first of a series of episodes dramatizing the slave trade, like the later sketches of auctions and coffles and pens and slaveships, makes the

point that this notorious traffic is not an accidental, but an inevitable part of the slave system.

While at Spring Meadow, Archy's life centers around his
family. On the Thornton and the Carleton plantations, except
for his renewed tie with Cassy and his feelings for their baby, we
see his relationships to his masters. When Archy reaches Loosahachee, General Carter's rice plantation in South Carolina, the
institution of slavery, stripped of paternalism and of reformist
attempts at amelioration, stands naked as a system of forced labor.
Here Archy emerges as a leader of the slave community. He is the
spokesman when his fellows futilely demand salt to flavor their
hominy. He retaliates for a whipping received from a white man
to whom he had refused to doff his cap by informing on the man's
illegal trade with slaves and thus having him sent to jail. Made
driver, he tries to use his position to his fellows' advantage, and
because he will not force ill slaves into the fields during the
"sickly season," he loses his favored post. But though Archy uses
his intelligence and his position as weapons of survival, covertly
helping his fellows when he can, his exploits do not measure up
to those of another slave: Black Thomas is the rebel hero at Loosahachee. Archy is relegated to the role of his faithful friend.

Although "naturally proud and high-spirited," Thomas, a
black man "of unmixed African blood," was a model Christian
until his wife's death following a brutal beating. Then, renounc-
ing his creed of "passive obedience and patient long-suffering,"
he becomes a rebel. When Thomas assumes the leadership of a
band of slave marauders who prey upon the plantations, Archy
joins the gang, and they gradually extend their operations until
one night they are surprised by patrollers. Thomas and Archy
get away but are tracked to Loosahachee. Fearful of capture, a
few days later the friends escape.

In their experiences as fugitives, as on the plantation,
Thomas is the protagonist and Archy his subordinate. Hunted
through the swamps by a posse, Thomas, though unarmed, cap-
tures the overseer who had fatally whipped his wife. When the
man advises them to surrender, Archy wavers, but Thomas has decided to fight for his freedom: " 'I want no such pardon as they
will give. I have been a slave too long already. I am now free;

and when they take me, they are welcome to take my life' " (156).
He has determined to execute him for his wife's murder, and
after informing the man of his decision, Thomas kills him.

During their flight, Archy and Thomas discover a maroon
encampment in the swamps and participate in the guerrilla war
the outlaw society wages against the system—the swamps indeed
contained devils, as Mike Brown had said in *Swallow Barn*. The
quality of the fugitives' life suggests that led by later runaways
who floated down the Mississippi on a raft:

> In the daytime we ate, slept, told stories, and recounted
> our escapes; or employed ourselves in dressing skins, mak-
> ing clothes, and curing provisions, but the night was our
> season of adventure and enterprise. As the autumn was
> coming on, we made frequent visits to the neighbouring
> corn-fields and potato-patches, which we felt no scruples
> whatever in laying under severe contribution. This how-
> ever was only for a month or two. Our regular and certain
> supply was in the herds of half wild cattle, which wander
> through the "piney woods." . . . (180)

After the winter, the fugitives move on. They are surprised
by a posse, and all but Thomas and Archy are killed. The friends
are captured, but their bonds are cut by a little white girl, and
after their escape Thomas tells Archy they must separate. The
black man says that he will return South to lead an outlaw's life,
but urges the light-skinned Archy to try to make his way North,
to freedom.

The rest of the 1836 version rapidly recounts Archy's flight.
He travels to New York City, is seized as a fugitive, and succeeds
in escaping. Thus forcefully made aware of the danger he faces
even in the North, Archy ships out on a vessel bound for France.
On the high seas, filled for the first time with the sensation of
freedom, he expresses his feelings toward America, "Land of the
tyrant and the slave" (174). Although he ultimately achieves
prosperity and success in England, Archy's happiness is marred

by his concern for Cassy and their child, and for Thomas. After recounting a series of attempts to locate them, he ends his narrative with a ringing announcement of his determination to find and free his friend, his wife, and his son. Should he be seized as a fugitive slave, he vows to take his own life: " 'I cannot be a slave the second time' " (182).

Hildreth's treatment of his black characters is complex. He acknowledges the scars left by slavery, and shows whites corrupted by their roles as oppressors, and blacks marked by their oppression.[11] At the same time, he raises basic questions about black appearance and reality, pointing out that as a result of his oppression, the black man has assumed a mask and that the relationship between the face he reveals to the whites—whether docile or degenerate—and the features beneath is radically ambiguous.

The characterizations of the blacks and mulattoes in the novel reflect this. Archy is something of a rogue hero; that is, he drinks, lies, and cheats—though on a much smaller scale than his masters. His education involves learning to live as a slave, and understanding that his interests oppose those of his masters. His mother's snobbery and his own favored position when a child on the home plantation had led him to feel superior to people with dark skins, but his love for Cassy, who is not as light as he, teaches him to reject his masters' ideology of white supremacy. Similarly, when he complains of an unjust beating and is given a second whipping for "insolence," he discovers that their justice does not extend to him. Accepting the conclusion that "fraud is the natural counterpart to tyranny; and cunning is ever the defense of the weak against the oppression of the strong," Archy learns that to oppose the superior force of the slavocracy, he must fight covertly, must wear the mask (50). He plays the fool to win Major Thornton's favor, masquerades as a sycophant to gain Carleton's goodwill, and acts as overseer's stooge at Loosahachee.

Closer to an heroic norm is black Thomas, who is strong, brave, honorable, and unselfish. But although Thomas displays many of the excellences of the romantic outlaw-hero, even he is not idealized. The point is made that, although perhaps morally

justified, his outlawry involves him in theft, arson, and murder.
Only Cassy escapes the almost inevitable brutalization to which
the slave is subjected; she is idealized in terms conventionally
reserved for the Southern white woman.

The depiction of the other slaves bears out Archy's contention that

> [m]en born and bred in slavery, are not men, but children.
> Their faculties are never permitted to unfold themselves;
> and it is the aim of their masters, and the necessary effect
> of their condition, to keep them in a state of perpetual
> imbecility. Tyranny is ever hostile to every species of
> mental development; for a state of ignorance involves of
> necessity a state of degradation and of helplessness. (76-77)

Thus, like the writers of plantation novels, Hildreth often depicts
the slaves as degraded, but he makes it evident that their even
more decadent masters have made this servile degradation inevitable. For example, Archy notes the casual nature of sexual
relationships among the slaves and points out that all servile
relationships were potentially impermanent because marriage between slaves was not recognized by society, and that even when a
slave marriage was solemnized, this did not prevent masters from
separating husbands from wives. Similarly, slaves are shown stealing from each other—they strip Archy's cabin bare while he re-
cuperates from a beating—but he comments that it is absurd to
condemn such servile theft when the slave master has stolen their
labor and their very bodies from them. In addition, the slaves
who are lazy and idle are seen as responding to their condition:
"Labour, in their minds, is indissolubly associated with servitude
and the whip; and *not to work,* they have ever been taught to
look upon as the badge and peculiar distinction of freedom"
(34). Their proverbial drunkenness is also seen as a result of
their servitude: It is encouraged by their masters, and is accepted
by them as an attempt to escape the real, "to find relief in dreams
and illusions. Drunkenness, which degrades the freeman to a level

with the brutes," comments Archy, "raises, or seems to raise the
slave, to the dignity of a man" (66).

In the slave pens at Washington, Archy watches men and
women make temporary sexual alliances; a group of slaves fiddle
and dance in a desperate attempt to forget their sorrow; and a
slave preacher sings, prays, and exhorts his listeners, then climaxes
his performance by sticking his foot through a barrelhead and
taking a pratfall. Archy concludes that, for many of the slaves, the
interval in the pens is "a sort of holiday. They had nothing to do;
and not to be compelled to work seemed, for them, the supreme
ideal of happiness. . . . They seemed anxious to drown all
memory of the past and all dread of the future, and to bask without concern in the sunshine of their present felicity" (77). Similarly, the people in the slave coffle traveling from Carleton Hall
to the Charleston slave market appear happy and content. After
having walked for a few days, the women and children had their
chains removed, and, with shoes to wear and enough food to eat,
many "went along laughing and singing more like men travelling
for pleasure, than like slaves going to be sold." Archy concludes
that "so little accustomed is the slave to kindness or indulgence
of any sort, that the merest trifle is enough to put him into ecstasy.
The gift of a single extra meal is sufficient to make him fall in
love even with a slave-driver" (126). The crucial point here is
that in *Archy Moore* the vices the slaves exhibit arise from their
condition, not from their race.

With a single exception—a brief passage early in the book
in which Archy describes his mother as "contaminated" by her
"African blood" and claims that he inherited his "proud spirit,
sensitive feelings, and ardent temperament" from his father—
racism is explicitly rejected throughout *Archy Moore*.[12] Indeed,
Archy forcefully argues that racism is the main bulwark of slavery
in America. Commenting on his own renunciation of feelings of
caste superiority, he says,

I no longer took sides with our oppressors by joining them
in the false notion of their own natural superiority;—a
notion founded only on the arrogant prejudice of conceited

ignorance, and long since discarded by the liberal and enlightened; but a notion which is still the orthodox creed
of all America, and the principal, I might almost say the
sole foundation, which sustains the iniquitous superstruc-
ture of American slavery. (126-27)

Later, when New Yorkers aid him in escaping from his master,
Archy sharply comments, "When they heard that I was seized as
a fugitive slave, some of them appeared not a little outraged at
the idea that a white man should be subject to such an indignity.
They seemed to think that it was only the black whom it was
lawful to kidnap in that way" (171).

Some of Hildreth's critics appear to suffer from an analogous
failure of sensibility. Because the narrator of *Archy Moore* purports to be a fugitive slave, they have questioned the verisimili-
tude of the novel, charging that the writing is too fluent for this
to be credible.[13] But Hildreth carefully laid the groundwork for
his protagonist's literary proficiency by providing for his early
education. (In a passage remarkably prescient of Tucker's autobiography, written more than twenty years later, Archy relates
that he was taught his letters in order to help his duller half-
brother Master James.) The author then places Archy as secretary
at Carleton Hall, and comments that in this position he had ac-
cess to his master's library of two or three hundred volumes. Once
his hero is free in England, Hildreth describes his undertaking a
wide course of study—he even fashionably condemns fiction and
poetry while indulging his preference for "voyages, travels, his-
tories and narratives of every sort" (179). The literary level of the
memoirs, which are ostensibly written by Archy at middle age, is
thus convincingly rationalized within the text. The critics further
charge that *Archy Moore* is too perceptive to be accepted as the
production of a fugitive slave. This touches the heart of the book:
its assertion that the black slave is a man. Hildreth, answering an
early instance of this criticism, commented that "To have been
bred a slave" was to many "to have grown up destitute of intellect
and feeling. When the book and the criticism were written, there
were yet no Fred. Douglasses. The author foresaw them. . . ."[14]

The assumptions of these critics, however, raise a problem central to *Archy Moore:* Its protagonist is a slave whose basic experience is black, but whose appearance is white. The question must be posed whether, in choosing a mulatto hero and heroine, Hildreth has made his book into a variation of Jefferson's *Notes on Virginia,* which is at once abolitionist and racist, or of Beaumont's *Marie,* which begs the question of race. But white is not right in *Archy Moore.* With the exception of the little girl who frees Archy and Thomas after their capture, all of the whites characterized in the novel—Southern slave masters and poor whites, and Yankees alike—are seen as villainous in consequence of their relationship with the institution of slavery. (In addition to this young girl, Hildreth idealizes Cassy and Thomas' wife Ann; despite their difference in color and caste, all three are seen as feminine victims of slavery.) Furthermore, a quarter of the novel is given over to the exploits of a black hero. Although he is not idealized, both in his role as suffering Christian slave and as outlaw leader, Thomas is repeatedly presented as more admirable than Archy. In making his protagonist a mulatto, Hildeth dramatizes the abolitionist argument against the sexual immorality of the slave society. While there is no question that his white audience identified more readily with the mulatto than with the black man, Hildreth's book, whose mulatto protagonist learns to reject his own belief in white supremacy and to fight with his black brothers against the white master, does not support this racism.[15]

Eighteen thirty-five, which marked Hildreth's conversion to abolitionism, was a year of harsh repression against antislavery men and women both South and North. He had just denounced this outbreak of violence in the treatise written in Florida and he would later dramatize it in a sequel to his novel. But now Hildreth, thwarted by the very repression he deplored, could not find a publisher for either of his books. Always reluctant to bring out abolitionist books which might cost them "the Southern market," publishers were suddenly afraid of being mobbed. Hildreth finally put up the money himself and brought out *Archy Moore* late in 1836. The book appeared anonymously; he later wrote that he felt he, too, was entitled "to the exercise of a little prudence." His old friend John Eastham who put his own name on the title page as printer—the only name to appear anywhere in this edition—thereby lost his contract as official printer for the City of Boston.[16]

The book was noticed by the Boston *Atlas,* with which Hildreth was still connected. But instead of publishing the announcement he had composed, the editors printed a review which, after commenting on its strength, intelligence, and "plain, nervous, and sincere" style, denounced *Archy Moore* on grounds of content: *"We cannot too much deprecate the publication of such works. We are aware of no purpose which they can answer, save that of sustaining and impelling a dangerous excitement."* The Boston *Daily Advocate* predicted that it would cause "more sensation, if it is ever read south of the Potomac, than the massacre at Southampton . . ." (the Nat Turner insurrection). In New York, the *Plain Dealer,* published by an antislavery newspaperman who had had to leave the *Evening Post* because of his views, praised the book.[17] Aside from these reviews, *Archy Moore* was noticed only by the abolitionist press—most importantly by *The Liberator.* Two months after its appearance, Garrison belatedly welcomed the first abolitionist novel by announcing its sale at the Antislavery Office, republishing excerpts, and printing a short notice which, despite its emotional tone, revealed the essence of *Archy Moore:* "It purports to be the story of a slave— but it is rather the harrowing record of the toils, the trials, the woes unutterable of A MAN. . . ." Three weeks later, in the "Communications" column, he printed a letter from the abolitionist writer Lydia Maria Child that began: "Dear Brother Garrison—Have you yourself read Archy Moore? If you have, why don't you bestow upon it hearty, fervent, overwhelming praise? Why, my dear friend, it is a *wonderful* book!" Commending the "intellectual vigor and dramatic talent exhibited in the power of language, the choice of circumstances, the combination of events, and the shadings of character," Mrs. Child asserts that the work displays "intimate knowledge" of the South. She warns that abolitionist readers must not be dismayed by Archy's lack of perfection: It shows the consequences of "the degrading influence of slavery" on "a man of powerful character"; and she reminds her readers that "It would be unnatural to suppose elevated purity of sentiment, or unimpaired moral strength, either in slaves or their masters"—though she does wish that the author had shown just one regenerate planter who, "wrought upon by the precepts of Christ," had emancipated his chattel. Mrs. Child ends with a writer's highest praise: "If I were a man, I should rather be the author of . . . [*Archy Moore*] . . . than of anything ever published in America." [18]

In the same issue, *The Liberator* began republishing reviews from other antislavery papers. Two weeks later, it reprinted a letter praising the handling of point of view in *Archy Moore:* "It purports to have been written by a slave, and it is no more difficult to imagine this to be the case, than to imagine who could write it, if a slave did not." A subsequent issue republished a review which pointed out that, through fiction, abolitionists might reach an audience who otherwise never read antislavery literature. Another excerpt from the novel was republished six weeks later. As a result of this steady publicity, the Antislavery Office did a brisk trade, and the first edition sold well, although the book remained unknown outside the abolitionist community, and even some antislavery men—suspicious of all fiction, and shocked by *Archy Moore's* inclusion of immorality and profanity —disapproved of it.[19] In 1839 *Archy Moore* was brought out by "a respectable Boston house" and reviewed in the Boston *Christian Examiner* which, questioning its handling of point of view, complained that "We read, in what professes to be the language of a slave, that which we feel a slave could not have written," but the book did not move fast enough to satisfy its commercial publishers, and sale reverted to the Boston Anti-Slavery Society. In 1846, welcoming a sixth edition, Garrison commented that while *Archy Moore's* continued reappearance indicated its perennial appeal, the novel was still unknown to "the great reading public." A dozen years after publication, *Archy Moore* had become something of an underground classic.[20]

In 1840, the prestigious London *Spectator* which, as Hildreth later pointed out, was "not less known . . . for its opposition . . .

to the whole abolition movement, than distinguished for the learning, sagacity, and taste displayed in its critical notices of books," gave a lengthy review to a new English edition combining *Archy Moore* with its companion volume *Despotism in America,* the treatise Hildreth had written concurrently with his novel, but which had only recently been published.[21] The reviewer points out the organic relationship between the books:

> In *Despotism in America,* the author discusses the principles of slavery and the general results they produce; after which he proceeds to unfold their alleged effects, both upon the privileged and unprivileged classes. In *The Slave, or Memoirs of Archy Moore,* he creates a character, and conducts him through the various stages of misery and misfortune, which the passions, the caprice, the avarice, the carelessness, or the insolvency of the owner inflict upon his slaves. By this double means, the author exhibits his subject in two phases, and uses the two distinct kinds of materials which his observations and reflections have provided him with. In *Despotism in America,* he confines himself to the broad and general features of Southern slavery, as it affects the social, economical, political, and moral character of masses of men, and the strength and prosperity of the state. In *Archy Moore* he paints individuals; exhibits the arcana of plantation life and practice amongst masters, overseers, and slaves; and animates, by the aid of fiction, those trifling but characteristic details which would have been out of place in the general treatise.

He praises the anonymous author for the Defoe-like quality of his novel: the narrative is "matter-of-fact," and "strong, real, but literal"; and, favorably comparing his polemic with its evident model, Tocqueville's recent *Democracy in America,* states that the treatise exhibits "the results of observation and reflection, set off by a methodical arrangement and powerful style."

Hildreth begins *Despotism in America* by broadening Tocqueville's view to encompass a double image Americans were to hold of themselves for the next generation: In addition to being an experiment in democracy, America is an experiment in despotism. Citing the dramatic disparity between Jefferson's role as slavemaster and as revolutionary—like Banneker and Walker, most antislavery men were struck by this duality—Hildreth proposes that American democrats examine the despotism to which they are tied. His analysis of the nature of the servile relation lies at the heart of both his polemic and his novel:

> The relation of master and slave, like most other kinds of despotism, has its origin in war. By the confession of its warmest defenders, slavery is at best, but a substitute for homicide. . . . Slavery then is a continuation of the state of war. It is true that one of the combatants is subdued and bound; but the war is not terminated. If I do not put the captive to death, this apparent clemency does not arise from any good-will towards him, or any extinction on my part of hostile feelings and intentions. I spare his life merely because I expect to be able to put him to a use more advantageous to myself. And if the captive, on the other hand, feigns submission, still he is only watching for an opportunity to escape my grasp, and if possible to inflict upon me evils as great as those to which I have subjected him. . . . The relation of master and slave . . . is a relation purely of force and terror. Its only sanction is the power of the master; its best security, the fears of the slave. It bears no resemblance to any thing like a social compact. Mutual interest, faith, truth, honesty, duty, affection, good will are not included, in any form whatever, under this relation. (35, 36, 38)

Hildreth proceeds to discuss the means by which the master enforces his will for his economic gain. In his treatise he describes the varying methods of plantation management which he dramatizes in *Archy Moore: force* (as was applied at Spring Meadow and Loosahachee); *fear* (exemplified on the Thornton plantation by the constant threat of sale); and *fraud* (as demonstrated by Carleton's perversion of Christianity into a device for servile control). He asserts that most slave-owners applied all of these methods at one time or another (as does Mrs. Montgomery) and that in consequence, plantation life is a constant struggle. Then he discusses servile resistance to this despotism, and argues that although overt rebellion (such as Thomas') is rare, it is inevitable, and that covert rebellion (like Archy's) is all but universal. This passive resistance, Hildreth says, takes the form of deception, falsehood, theft, and evasion. Always the countenance shown the master is a mask. Thus, like all forced laborers, the slave

yields his time from day-light, until dark; or rather he seems to yield it; for if he be not constantly watched, he contrives to regain hours and moments, which as he can apply them to no better use, he spends in idleness or sleep. His capacity is a thing more in his own power. It is in general, only certain simple acts of manual labor that can be exacted by force. The mind is free. A master cannot force his slave to reason, to remember, or except in certain cases, to hear, or see. If he is sent with a message, he forgets it. He never considers that if the fence is broken, the cattle will get among the corn; and if they do, he neither sees nor hears them. The master would go hunting, and he sends his slave to bring his powder-flask. The slave sees there is no powder in it;—but what is that to him?—he does as he was bid, and carries the flask. When the gun is to be loaded, it appears then there is no ammunition. "Go home," says the master, "in the closet on the upper shelf there is a canister of powder; fill the flask, and bring it to me." As it happens, there are two canisters, one good, the other damaged. The slave takes down the damaged canister first, and without further examination fills the flask with powder that cannot be used, and carries it to his master. He is set to planting corn. The seed, it

chances, is worm-eaten and decayed. What is that to him?
He goes on planting. It is just so in every thing else. He
neglects to exercise his reasoning faculties at all. He becomes apparently as stupid and thoughtless as the mule he
drives. Whatever capacity or understanding he may have,
he sinks it, hides it, annihilates it, rather than its fruits
should be filched from him by his owner. (50, 51)

Hildreth examines the living standard of slaves and concludes that "considered as animals" they live on a lower level than
the inmates of Northern prisons; when they are "considered as
men" their plight is even worse. His characterization of the psychological violence done the slave, which he calls "the murder
of the soul," reflects a perception of the destructiveness of racism
that is modern. Disagreeing with Jefferson, he sees American
slavery as more oppressive than classical slavery because it is "an
artful, deliberate, and well-digested scheme to wreck . . . [the
slaves'] . . . spirit; to deprive them of courage and of manhood;
to destroy their natural desire for an equal participation in the
benefits of society; to keep them ignorant, and therefore weak; to
reduce them if possible to a state of idiocy; to crowd them down
to a level with the brutes" (63). Worse, when the slaves' degradation is complete, its cause is assumed to be not condition but
race, and the repugnance felt by the master class is now seen as
the "innate promptings of nature." Hence members of the privileged group become hardened to the plight of the slave, and
"cease to consider the servile class as belonging to the same scale
of being with themselves" (70). Even the kindest members of the
master class attempt only to provide for the animal needs of their
black slaves; "to entertain the idea that they are men—is considered an absurd, a misplaced and a fanatical tenderness, certain,
if persevered in, to uproot the foundations of society, and to end
in results indeterminate, but terrible." Terrible, explains Hildreth, who thus exposes one of the central metaphors of late
nineteenth-century fiction, because the blacks are seen not merely
as animals, but as wild beasts; as "tigers, trained to draw the
plough, whom nothing but fear, the whip, and constant watch-

fulness, keep at all in subjection; who would take advantage of the slightest relaxation of the discipline that restrains them, to break away from their unwilling labors; and who if left to themselves, would quickly recover their savage nature, and find no employment except to riot in blood" (71). This first section of *Despotism* enunciates the idea shaping *Archy Moore:* Slavery is an evil that is not susceptible to partial solution. "The only cure for slavery, is freedom!" (78)

Following his central statement, Hildreth discusses the political consequences of slavery. He asserts that if we deny civil liberties to an abhorred minority—here, the abolitionists—we inevitably destroy the political liberties of all. He then analyzes the disastrous economic consequences of a slave labor system, dramatized in *Archy Moore* in sketches of poor whites and impoverished land; and the detrimental effects of slavery on the personalities of masters and slaves, another theme of the novel. The treatise argues that the system produces immorality among both oppressor and oppressed: "Ferocity of temper, idleness, improvidence, drunkenness, gambling—these are vices for which the masters are distinguished, and these same vices are conspicuous traits in the character and condition of slaves" (157).

Hildreth concludes that slavery must end, either by forceful or peaceful means. Arguing against colonization as a solution—he sees it as unfeasible and rejects its racist assumptions—he advocates immediate abolition. His final remarks rebut Tocqueville's conclusion, which was dramatized in Beaumont's novel, "that there is such a natural repugnance and antipathy between the two races that it is impossible for them to live together upon any terms of equality. That either one race or the other must rule, or one race or the other must be exterminated. Let us reply, that . . . this narrow and cruel theory [is] the greatest libel upon human nature ever yet propounded" (184).

In the five years since his return to Boston, Hildreth had acted on his abolitionist beliefs. In articles in the *Atlas* he disclosed the schemes of proslavery expansionists to annex Texas and attempted to rally opposition to them.[22] In a witty polemic against Catharine E. Beecher, Lyman Beecher's elder daughter, he argued in support of Garrisonian tactics, including the use of invective and the involvement of women in the movement.[23] But, though he was an antislavery man, Hildreth did not support Birney's Liberty party in 1840; instead he wrote a campaign biography for Harrison, the successful Whig candidate.[24] After the election, in which he was intensely involved, Hildreth was near exhaustion. This time he chose to recuperate not in the American South, but in British Guiana, which had recently abolished slavery (1833). While there, he edited two abolitionist newspapers and became involved in a controversy with the colonial legislature over his criticisms of army repression of slave insurrectionists.

When he returned to Boston he married Caroline Neagus, an accomplished artist, and resumed his active role in the New England Anti-Slavery Society. In 1844 Garrison denounced the Constitution as a proslavery document, "a covenant with death and an agreement with hell" and advanced the slogan, "NO UNION WITH SLAVEHOLDERS!" Hildreth, disagreeing with Garrison's revolutionary notion that antislavery citizens should peacefully withdraw from the Union because to cooperate with the federal government was to "compromise with tyranny," argued instead for political action to end slavery.[25] But this dispute over tactics did not lead him to desert the cause. In addition to his antislavery writing and his aid to the legal defense of those seized under proslavery laws, Hildreth joined a Vigilance Committee of Forty to prevent the kidnapping of fugitive slaves from Massachusetts.[26]

While maintaining this level of intense involvement in the antislavery movement, Hildreth participated in a number of other controversies, and was often engaged in pamphlet warfare. His far-ranging interests and unflagging study are indicated by his publication of a history of banking and a translation of Jeremy Bentham's *Theory of Legislation;* and of *The Theory of Morals* and *The Theory of Politics,* the first two volumes of a projected series in which he hoped to develop an inductive Science of Man.[27] The work for which he is remembered, however, is not polemical or speculative, but factual. Hildreth's *History of the United States* was written during the seven years following his return to Boston.[28] Though a standard work for a generation, his *History* was later neglected, and has only recently been rediscovered by revisionist historians interested in its abolitionist critique of the Constitution.[29]

In 1852, at the prompting of a Boston firm which had once refused to publish his abolitionist novel but now hoped to capitalize on the success of *Uncle Tom's Cabin,* Hildreth got out an expanded version of *Archy Moore*.[30] In the new edition Hildreth includes the earlier text and goes on to depict how Archy fulfills the vow he had made at the end of the 1836 version to return to the United States in search of his son and his wife and friend.

Twenty years after his escape, Archy travels to America as Captain Arthur Moore, Englishman. The lapse in time and the change in name signal the subtle difference in tone between the fugitive slave narrator of the earlier section and the British commentator we now hear. The narrative is now more distant and has something of the qualiy of a traveler's account, reminiscent perhaps of Miss Martineau, or of Captain Hall. Hildreth also has shifted his focus. In the new material he does not emphasize the life of the black slaves, but that of white America. These changes do not destroy the integrity of the work—it is held together by character, plot, locale—but they do account for the difference in tone between the first thirty-six chapters, which had comprised the 1836 text, and the balance of the 1852 edition.

In the original version of *Archy Moore* Hildreth had dramatized the nature of slavery, which he had analyzed in *Despotism in America*. In his sequel he dramatizes the disastrous political and economic consequences of the slave system in the South and of the complicity with this system in the North, another major theme of his treatise. The landscape through which Archy searches is the America of 1835 and 1836. Perhaps influenced by Beaumont, who in *Marie* had fictionalized the violence against the black community during the New York race riots of 1834, Hildreth makes his protagonist an observer of the anti-abolitionist violence that took place in 1836, while he was convalescing and writing his novel and treatise. Thus Archy sees an abolitionist mobbed in Massachusetts—as was Garrison; a Northern official expelled from South Carolina—as was Samuel Hoar; and a citizen under siege in Mississippi—as was Patrick Sharkey.[31] The attacks against antislavery men and women that he witnesses in the North only hint at the terror and the economic and political decay he encounters below the Mason-Dixon line. Archy travels through the Old South—Virginia, North Carolina, and South Carolina—revisiting the scenes of his youth. Everywhere the land is worked out and desolate; everywhere the bankrupt aristocracy—the Moores, the Carletons—have moved west, leaving behind the worn-out land and the poor whites who, like Jemmy Gordon, are too broken to emigrate. Civil government has broken down. Mobs plunder the mail, burn antislavery papers in the streets, and run suspicious strangers out of town. Mob law prevails.

The scene in which Archy is hauled before a vigilante group is a brilliant parody of the operations of a thought control committee and, although written in 1852, speaks directly to American experience a century later.[32] Archy produces his letters of introduction to establish his identity. But upon reading "Tappan, Wentworth, & Co." the chairman becomes excited; only later does he understand that the signature does not refer to the American abolitionists Arthur and Lewis Tappan, but to a British bank. After this is cleared up, things get worse. Archy's possessions, which have been searched, include a copy of Sterne's *Sentimental Journey* with the frontispiece of a chained prisoner and the motto "Disguise thyself as thou wilt, still, Slavery, still thou art a bitter draught, and though thousands have been made to drink thee, none the less bitter on that account!" The passage produces "a profound sensation" when it is read before the committee. Archy is saved from punishment for possessing illegal abolitionist propaganda only because some of the committee members have heard of Sterne. The case against him finally is reduced to the testimony of seven witnesses who swear that they heard him disrespectfully joke about Virginia's fear of antislavery picture books. In a gesture aimed at upholding the tradition of Southern hospitality to the stranger, the committee dismisses him with the warning that he had better leave town.

A craven Yankee merchant, interrogated at the same time,

narrowly escapes a more serious fate. When his house was searched, some illustrated children's books were found and seized.

> At the very sight of the picture books, the committee grew very solemn, and the chairman cast another look over the top of his spectacles, half of pity and half of reproach, at the Yankee merchant, whose teeth began to chatter worse than ever, and who rolled up the whites of his great eyes in as perfect an agony as if he had just been caught in the very act of horse-stealing or forgery. But after a solemn and serious inspection, during which the whole assembled multitude held their breath, clinched their fists, set their teeth, and looked daggers at the suspected offender, nothing worse appeared than Jack the Giant-Killer, and Little Red Riding-Hood. One very fierce-looking old gentleman on the committee, with puffing cheeks and blood-shot eyes, apparently not very familiar with juvenile literature, and a little the worse for liquor, thought there was something rather murderous in these representations, especially as the pictures were pretty highly-coloured. But his colleagues assured him that these were very ancient books, which had been long in circulation, and though, perhaps, considered in themselves, like the Declaration of Independence, the History of Moses and the Deliverance of the Israelites, as recorded in the Bible, or the Virginia Bill of Rights, they might seem to have rather a malign aspect, yet they could not be set down as belonging to that class of incendiary or abolitionist publications, the having which in one's possession would be proof of conspiracy. (193)

Archy encounters a violent consequence of the repression near Loosahachee. Traveling along the road, he comes upon a slave-catching party returning with its prey Wild Tom, the fugitive slave who has harassed the surrounding countryside for twenty years. Archy recognizes the prisoner as his old friend Thomas, and accompanies the posse, which is bringing back the body of an overseer killed in the slave hunt. They are met by a crowd of idlers and slaves and, the jail being full, Thomas is chained to its window grating while the men argue about what to do with him. Archy is able only to give him some water and to identify himself surreptitiously before Thomas is dragged forward for interrogation by the drunken angry mob. Asked who his master is, Thomas asserts that he is a free man, belonging only " 'to the God who made us all!' " They find him guilty of killing the overseer, and ask him whether he has anything to say before they kill him. His response is defiant:

> "Go on, . . . hang me, kill me, do your will. I was held a slave for the best years of my life. My wife was flogged to death before my eyes. As a free man, you have hunted me with bloodhounds, and shot at me with rifles, and placed a price upon my head. Long have I fooled you, and paid you back in your own coin. That white man to-day was not the first who has found me too much for him. One by one, two by two, three by three, I defy and would whip the whole of you, but the whole dozen, mounted and armed, with dogs to boot, were too much for one poor black man, with nothing but his feet, his hands, and his knife. They have not always been too much; but I am getting old. Better die now, while I have strength and courage to defy your worst, than fall into your hands a broken-down old man." (229)

Infuriated, they burn him alive.

Violence characterizes the life Archy encounters during his search through the New South—Georgia and Mississippi. His experiences with lynch mobs at Vicksburg and with trigger-happy committees of vigilance in Hinds and Madison Counties convince him that, in contrast to the Old South where traditional social and legal patterns at least somewhat restrained slavery, in the New South it operates openly, displaying its violent nature. He finds that the ruined landscape—"gullied fields, especially on the hillsides, from which the soil had been completely washed away; over which still stood erect the blackened trunks of the tenants of the original forest, killed by the process of girdling" is symbolic of "the natural effects of the plundering system upon which the whole organization of the slave-holding state is based, and which extends even to the land itself, rifled of its virgin strength by a shiftless system of ignorant haste to be rich—and then abandoned to hopeless sterility" (259-60). He describes the varied population of the Southern frontier: bankrupt aristocrats from Virginia— like Paulding's Dangerfield; slave gangs clearing new lands; poor white squatters from Georgia and the Carolinas—Simms had sketched them, then placed them in the past; Yankees, preachers, slave traders, horsethieves, land speculators, "all, except the preachers, and not all of them, with but one idea in their heads, the growing rich suddenly; and with but two words in their mouths, namely, 'niggers' and 'cotton' " (260).

In his original story, Hildreth had demonstrated the problem of slavery and the impossibility of reform. In his sequel, he presents a debate over the desirability of colonization or abolition, the two proposed solutions. The proponent of colonization, who like Tocqueville quotes Jefferson to support the theory that black and white cannot live together as equals, admits that his scheme caters to "the inveterate prejudice" of white Americans. Hildreth makes Mason, a slave holder who plans to emancipate and settle his slaves in the North, the proponent of abolition (and thus fulfills Lydia Marie Child's earlier request for "just one regenerate planter"). Mason argues that it is impractical to expel the entire labor force of the South and, although at times he is ambiguous in assigning the cause of the degradation of the blacks, voices the central thought of the sequel: The immediate abolition of chattel slavery is necessary not alone to improve the welfare of "our coloured inhabitants," but to make possible the continued existence of democracy in America.

As the dead trees standing above abandoned fields symbolize the abuse of the land under slavery, so the dough-faced Northern merchant and the Southern gambler show the impact of slavery on the American character. The finest product of Southern decadence, John Colter, a bankrupt younger son who turned slave trader and then became a gambler, conjugates for Archy the morality of a capitalist system based on slave labor:

"Suppose we do plunder the planters—don't they live by plundering the negroes? What right have they to complain? Isn't sauce for the goose sauce for the gander? I tell you our whole system here is a system of plunder from beginning to end. 'Tis only the slaves, and some of the poor whites who own no slaves, who can be said to earn an honest living. The planters live on the plunder of the slaves, whom they force to labour for them. The slaves steal all they can from the planters, and a good many of the poor whites connive at and help them in it. A parcel of bloodsucking Yankee pedlars and New York agents overrun our country, and carry off their share of the spoils; and we who have cool heads and dexterous hands enough to overreach the whole set, planters, Yankees, and New Yorkers—we stand, for ought I see, upon just as sound a moral basis as the rest of them. Everything belongs to the strong, the wise, and the cunning; that is the foundation stone of our southern system of society." (256)

Although he renounces all morality by asserting that " 'The living upon the plunder of others is one of the organic sins of this community; and . . . for the organic sins of a community, nobody is individually responsible,' " Colter becomes Archy's aide in his search for Cassy and their son, Montgomery, which is carried out in the final five chapters, laid in New Orleans (256). By chance Archy finds Cassy in a slave market there and rescues her. She tells him of the last twenty years of her life: She was sold to the New England wife of a Southerner after Mrs. Montgomery's bankruptcy and, when this woman died, was bought in New Orleans by a Boston gentleman who intended her for his mistress. Miraculously, she was able to remain true to Archy; but although freed before her master's death, she was seized and had been taken to be sold when Archy found her. Her great concern

—and Archy's, when he learns of it—is the fate of their son and of Eliza his betrothed. Montgomery has been educated in the North by his Boston master, but is on his way to New Orleans and is in danger of being kidnapped. Cassy also fears for Eliza, who is being held prisoner. Thus, with his first generation of white slaves finally free and reunited, Hildreth doubles the cast and proceeds to entangle, then extricate the second generation. The action is melodramatic, its denoument nice and tidy, and, mercifully, over quickly. All sail for England.

While Hildreth bases the intricacies of his plot in the institution of slavery, he raises the issue of rescuing slaves who have already been emancipated in the last section of the book. At first glance, the melodrama involved in the kidnapping and escape of freed mulatto lovers seems tangential to a serious dramatization of American slavery, a system which exacted forced labor from millions of black people for the enrichment of their white masters. But closer analysis reveals that the final section of Hildreth's novel dramatizes the antislavery argument that as long as slavery persisted in the South, black people were not safe from enslavement anywhere in the nation.[33] The abolitionism in *Archy Moore* is firmly rooted. The original story, which makes up the greater part of the expanded version, portrays the destructive nature of the servile relation to the slave and his master; the new material dramatizes—with an added force because of its reference to actual events—the destructive effects of slavery on free America.

This shift in focus, when coupled with the introduction of Montgomery and Eliza, both of whom have been passing for white, raises the possibility that Hildreth has written a racist sequel to his abolitionist novel. But Hildreth rejects racism in the expanded edition and redevelops the doctrine of racial equality. In addition, he provides an important new insight. His brief revelation of the link, in the mind of Cassy's New England mistress, associating sin as slavery, the blackness of sin, and the blackness of the slave, is a profound comment on the psychology of white supremacy.[34] More immediately significant, in his expanded work (which appeared only months after the publication of Harriet Stowe's best-seller) Hildreth developed his

earlier sketch of the slave who asserted his freedom, into the portrait of a black man who lived and died a rebel. Wild Tom
stands defiant, a towering contrast to his kneeling namesake, the
saintly Christian victim Uncle Tom.

In *Archy Moore* Hildreth created something new out of
materials the Southern novelists and the French writer already
had handled. *Archy Moore* exemplifies militant abolitionism in
its moral indignation, urgent tone, and conscious attempt to
identify with the black slave.[35] The antislavery writers that followed fragmented Hildreth's synthesis. The melodrama incidental to American slavery which Beaumont had shown and
Hildreth included but kept submerged—the enslavement of the
son by his father, the abandonment of the mulatto by her lover,
the seizure of free men and women, often heirs, by their grasping
relatives—all became common themes in sentimental abolitionist
fiction. His "powerful . . . realism," praised a generation later by
William Dean Howells, was to characterize the slave narratives
that soon began to appear in numbers.[36] But few white novelists
would attempt what Hildreth had. It is a rare thing, in white
America, to try to think black.

NOTES—CHAPTER VI

1. David Walker, *David Walker's Appeal, in Four Articles; Together with a Preamble, to the Coloured Citizens of the World, but in particular, and very expressly, to those of The United States of America*, ed. Charles M. Wiltse (New York, 1965), pp. 65-66.
2. William Lloyd Garrison's statement of purpose, published in *The Liberator*, January 1, 1831, as quoted in *Documents of Upheaval*, ed. Truman Nelson (New York, 1966), pp. xiii-xiv.
3. [Richard Hildreth], *The Slave, or Memoirs of Archy Moore*, 2 vols. (Boston, 1836). Parenthetical page citations in my text refer to the following edition, which has been more accessible to me: *The White Slave: or, Memoirs of a Fugitive. A Story of Slave Life in Virginia, etc.*, ed. R. Hildreth (London, 1852).
4. Hildreth's biographer, Donald E. Emerson, *Richard Hildreth*, The Johns Hopkins University Studies in Historical and Political Science,

Series LXIV, No. 2 (Baltimore, 1946), concerned primarily with Hildreth's work as an historian, seems unaware of the significance of *Archy Moore* and treats Hildreth's abolitionism as incidental. Biographical information in this chapter is drawn from Emerson, and from W. S. Thayer, "Richard Hildreth," *The Cyclopedia of American Literature,* ed. Evert A. Duyckinck and G. L. Duyckinck (Philadelphia, 1854, photo-reproduced Detroit, 1965), II, 298-301; "Death of Richard Hildeth," *New-York Daily Tribune,* August 2, 1865, p. 6; K. B. Murdock, "Richard Hildreth," *Dictionary of American Biography,* ed. Dumas Malone (New York, 1932), IX, 19-20.

For the disparity between Hildreth's historical works and his journalism and fiction, see Arthur M. Schlesinger, Jr., "The Problem of Richard Hildreth," *New England Quarterly,* XIII (June 1940), 223-45.

5. Articles by Hildreth in N. P. Willis' *American Monthly Magazine* include: "The Republic of Letters," I (1829), 16-24; "Homer," I (1829), 164-73; "Shakespeare," I (1829), 264-74; "National Literature," I (1829); 379-85; "Review of Captain Hall's Travels," I (1829), 532-40; in the *New England Magazine,* "Reminiscences of a Retired Militia Officer," II (1832), 403-05, 479-83; "Romance and Reality," III (1833), 392-97.

6. While in Florida, Hildreth translated from the French of Etienne Dumont a work which he published as *Bentham's Theory of Legislation,* 2 vols. (Boston, 1840).

7. In 1835, both Tocqueville's book and *Marie, ou l'Esclavage aux Etats-Unis, Tableau de Moeurs Américaines* were published in France. The first American edition of Tocqueville is dated 1838. Although *The National Anti-Slavery Standard* serialized an English version of the first sixteen and a half chapters, from July 17, 1845, to April 16, 1846, inexplicably breaking off without completing the last chapter and a half, *Marie* has been so little known in this country that Alvin A. Tinnen, in his introduction to an edition translated by Barbara Chapman (Stanford, California, 1958), erroneously claims that the novel had never before been translated into English. Parenthetical page citations in my text refer to this edition. Helpful discussions of the novel can be found in Tinnen's introduction and in the standard reference, George Wilson Pierson, *Tocqueville and Beaumont in America* (New York, 1938).

8. Richard Hildreth, "Introduction," *Archy Moore, The White Slave: or, Memoirs of a Fugitive* . . . (New York, 1857), p. viii. Hereafter cited as "Introduction."

9. *Despotism in America or, an Inquiry into the Nature and Results of the Slave-Holding System in the United States.* . . . (Boston, 1840).

10. See, for example, Vernon Loggins, *The Negro Author: His Development in America to 1900* (Port Washington, N.Y., 1964), p. 98; or Charles Harold Nichols, Jr., "A Study of the Slave Narrative," unpubl. diss. (Brown, 1948), p. 6.

11. Thus Hildreth imaginatively deals with a problem scholars are debating today: See, for example, Stanley M. Elkins, *Slavery: A Problem in*

American Institutional and Intellectual Life (Chicago, 1959); *The De-bate Over Slavery: Stanley Elkins and His Critics,* ed. Ann Lane (Urbana, 1971).

12. Pp. 4-5. It is inaccurate to quote this uncharacteristic passage as if it were representative, as does Cowie, *The Rise of the American Novel* (New York, 1948), p. 293; or in order to link Hildreth's attitude toward race with that of Harriet Beecher Stowe, as does Charles Nichols in his otherwise excellent article, "The Origins of *Uncle Tom's Cabin,*" *Phylon,* XIX (1958), 331.

13. See Emerson, p. 76; and Cowie, pp. 297-98.

14. Richard Hildreth, "Introduction," p. xx. Douglass, who escaped from slavery in 1838, first spoke before an astonished antislavery convention in 1841. His veracity was questioned, and he published his *Narrative* in 1845 to establish his identity as a fugitive slave. See Chapter Eight, below.

15. Unlike mulatto heroines to follow, Hildreth's Cassy is fortunate in the constancy of her lover; and the tragedy of Beaumont's Marie rests in her rejection by society, not in her betrayal by the white man she adores. Neither is the stock figure of the worshipping "tragic mulatto" abandoned by her white lover.

    Penelope Bullock, "The Mulatto in American Fiction," *Phylon,* VI (1945), 78-82, points out that the stereotype of the tragic mulatto plays on "the race pride and sentiments of the Caucasian group" (79). Jules Zanger, "The 'Tragic Octoroon' in Pre-Civil War Fiction," *American Quarterly,* XVIII (Spring 1966), 63-70, develops the idea that "the octoroon became the visible sign of an incremental sin," that her very existence supported Wendell Phillips' charge that the South was "one great brothel, where half a million women are flogged to prostitution . . ." (66, 67). For an early, important discussion of the mulatto in fiction, see Sterling Brown, "Negro Character as Seen by White Authors," *Journal of Negro Education,* II (April 1933), 179-203.

16. Richard Hildreth, "Introduction," p. ix. For a discussion of the obstacles faced by antislavery writers, see Donald E. Leidel, "The Antislavery Novel, 1836-1861," unpubl. diss. (Michigan, 1961), Chapter I; and Clement Eaton, *The Freedom-of-Thought Struggle in the Old South,* rev. ed. (New York, 1964).

17. Excerpts of these reviews appear in Richard Hildreth, "Introduction," pp. ix-xii, xiv-xv.

18. *The Liberator,* February 25, 1837; March 18, 1837.

19. *The Liberator,* March 31, 1837. In New York, the American and Foreign Anti-Slavery Society refused to stock *Archy Moore.* See Hildreth, "Introduction," p. xx.

20. The *Christian Exemainer* is cited in Hildreth, "Introduction," p. xvii. Garrison's comment is in *The Liberator,* June 12, 1846. Lyle H. Wright, "A Statistical Survey of American Fiction, 1774-1850," *Huntington Library Quarterly,* II (April 1939), 309-18, includes *Archy Moore* in a list of best-sellers prior to 1850; he notes a 7th edition in 1848.

21. "Spectator's Library," *The Spectator: A Weekly Journal of News,*

Politics, Literature, and Science, July 4, 1840, 638-40. Hildreth's comment appears in "Introduction," p. xvii. I have been unable to examine the first edition of *Despotism,* published anonymously in Boston in 1840. Parenthetical page numbers in my text refer to a second edition (Boston: Massachusetts Anti-Slavery Society; New York: American Anti-Slavery Society, 1840).

22. Thayer, *Cyclopedia,* II, 299.
23. Miss Beecher had attacked abolitionist methods and criticized female meddling in public affairs, in *An Essay on Slavery and Abolitionism, with Reference to the Duty of American Females* (Philadelphia and Boston, 1837), addressing her book to Angelina E. Grimké, a South Carolina aristocrat who, with her sister, Sarah Grimké, had joined the Quakers, renounced slavery, and published an *Appeal to the Christian Women of the South* (New York, 1836) urging abolition. Miss Grimké rejoined, setting forth the basic premises of abolitionism, in a series of letters published first in *The Liberator,* and then in pamphlet form as *Letters to Catharine E. Beecher, in Reply to An Essay on Slavery and Abolitionism, Addressed to A. E. Grimké* (Boston, 1838). Hildreth's pamphlet, *Brief Remarks on Miss C. E. Beecher* (Boston, 1837), signed only "by the author of Archy Moore," endorses Miss Grimké's position.
24. *The People's Presidential Candidate, or The Life of William Henry Harrison of Ohio* (Boston, 1840).
25. The phrase is from Garrison's "Address" of May 20, 1844. For the full text and for Hildreth's statement, in which he was joined by William A. White and David H. Barlow, see *Documents of Upheaval,* ed. Nelson, pp. 202ff. Hildreth later developed his position into an antislavery interpretation of the Constitution. See "Has Slavery in the United States a Legal Basis?" *Massachusetts Quarterly Review,* I (1848), 145-67, 273-93; and "The Legality of American Slavery," *ibid.,* II (1849), 32-39. Hildreth appended these articles to a new edition of *Despotism in America* (Boston and Cleveland, 1854). Also see his pamphlet, *What Can I Do for the Abolition of Slavery?* (Boston, 1844).
26. For example, he helped in the trial of Daniel Drayton, who was convicted of attempting to carry slaves to freedom on the schooner *Pearl;* and then edited *Personal Memoir of Daniel Drayton, for Four Years and Four Months a Prisoner (for Charity's Sake) in a Washington Jail* . . . (Boston and New York, 1853). He was also involved in the Shadrach affair, and in the attempted rescue of Anthony Burns. See Emerson, pp. 150-51.
27. He enjoyed controversy. When Andrews Norton attacked Ralph Waldo Emerson's *Divinity School Address,* Hildreth—though no Transcendentalist—joined the war of words against orthodoxy in a *Letter to Andrews Norton on Miracles as a Foundation of Religious Faith* (Boston, 1840). Works referred to are: *The History of Banks* (Boston, 1837); Jeremy Bentham, *Theory of Legislation,* trans. Richard Hildreth, 2 vols. (Boston, 1840); *The Theory of Morals* (Boston, 1844); *The Theory of Politics* (New York, 1853).
28. *The History of the United States of America from the Discovery of the*

Continent to the Organization of Government under the Federal Constitution, 1497-1798, 3 vols. (New York, 1849). *The History of the United States of America from the Adoption of the Federal Constitution to the End of the Sixteenth Congress, 1788-1821,* 3 vols. (New York, 1851-1852).

29. See, for example, Staughton Lynd, "The Abolitionist Critique of the United States Constitution," in *The Antislavery Vanguard,* ed. Martin Duberman (Princeton, N.J., 1965), pp. 209-39.

30. [Richard Hildreth], *The White Slave; or, Memoirs of A Fugitive* (Boston and Milwaukee, 1852). Emerson, p. 113, suggests that Hildreth wrote the sequel while in British Guiana a dozen years earlier, but references to the Fugitive Slave Law place composition after 1850, and other internal evidence suggests that it was written after the appearance of *Uncle Tom's Cabin.*

31. See Beaumont, "A Note on the New York Riots of 1834," Appendix L. For a study of the mobs, see Leonard L. Richards, *"Gentleman of Property and Standing": Anti-Abolition Mobs in Jacksonian America* (New York, 1970). I have been able to document a number of the incidents Hildreth fictionalized. For example, the violence against Garrison is discussed in *Documents of Upheaval,* pp. 79-80; the expulsion of Hoar is described in Eaton, p. 115; Sharkey's defense of his home against a mob is noted in Eaton, pp. 98-99.

32. For provocative discussions of antislavery and proslavery notions of conspiracy, see *The Fear of Conspiracy: Images of Un-American Subversion from the Revolution to the Present,* ed. David Brion Davis (Ithaca, 1971), Chapter 5; and David Brion Davis, *The Slave Power Conspiracy and the Paranoid Style* (Baton Rouge, 1969).

33. See Stanley W. Campbell, *The Slave-Catchers: Enforcement of the Fugitive Slave Law, 1850-1860* (Chapel Hill, 1970), Chapter 8, for a discussion of kidnapping and the Personal Liberty Laws.

34. This suggests an added dimension to the study of the symbolism of the major white nineteenth-century writers who used black-white schemes to signify good and evil.

35. Wendell Phillips linked the fortunes of Hildreth's novel to the vicissitudes of the movement in "The Abolition Movement," *Speeches, Lectures, and Letters* (Boston and New York, 1884), pp. 131-32. Among Hildreth's later antislavery writings are *The "Ruin" of Jamaica,* Anti-Slavery Tracts, No. 6 (New York, 1855); and *Atrocious Judges. Lives of Judges Infamous as Tools of Tyrants and Instruments of Oppression . . . With an Appendix Containing the Case of Passmore Williamson. —Edited with Introduction and Notes by R. Hildreth* (New York and Auburn, 1856). Hildreth continued to publish antislavery works. His writing for the New York *Tribune* from 1855 to 1861 was instrumental in giving the paper its antislavery tone. In 1861 Lincoln appointed him U.S. Consul at Trieste. Hildreth died at Florence, Italy in 1865.

36. William Dean Howells, *Literary Friends and Acquaintances . . .* (New York and London, 1901), p. 97.

CHAPTER VII

HARRIET BEECHER STOWE

All of the resources of the United States government—marshals, courts, and the army—were placed at the disposal of slave catchers when in September, 1850, Congress passed a new Fugitive Slave Law. Five months later a deputy from Virginia snatched the fugitive Shadrach while he waited on tables in a Boston restaurant and dragged him still in his apron before the U.S. Commissioner, but other blacks rescued him. In April, Thomas Sims, a fugitive from Georgia, was seized and, despite the efforts of his would-be rescuers, he was sent back to Savannah under armed guard while Edward Beecher, alone among Boston ministers, preached the shame of Massachusetts. In September black men defending William Parker of Christiana, Pennsylvania, from seizure as a fugitive, shot a U.S. Marshal and killed a Maryland slaveholder.[1]

For pacifist abolitionists, the blood spilled at Christiana sharply raised the moral question of whether violence was ever justified, even when used in self-defense. Harriet Beecher Stowe's *Uncle Tom's Cabin* embodies one set of answers to this problem.[2] Her ideas were instantly challenged by William Lloyd Garrison, who asked in *The Liberator,* "When it is the whites who are trodden in the dust, does Christ justify them in taking up arms to vindicate their rights? And when it is the blacks who are thus treated, does Christ require them to be patient, harmless, long-suffering, and forgiving? And are there two Christs?" [3] Black people today, equally concerned with violent and nonviolent resistance, have so utterly rejected the Christian resignation practiced by Mrs. Stowe's hero that his name is a epithet.

Harriet Beecher Stowe's antislavery novels dramatize the tension between a loving Jesus and the angry God of her father Lyman Beecher and of her husband Calvin Stowe. Born in 1811, the seventh child of one of the most eminent clergymen in America, Harriet's girlhood was spent in his crowded, rollicking farmhouse outside Litchfield, Connecticut. [4] Lyman Beecher's children read the Bible for pleasure; and Harriet immersed herself in Mather's *Magnalia,* Baxter's *Saint's Rest,* Bunyan's *Pilgrim's Progress,* the *Arabian Nights, Ivanhoe,* and a smuggled volume of Byron as well. In adolescence she announced to her father, "I have given myself to Jesus, and He has taken me," and Lyman Beecher wept tears of joy at her conversion. But the minister's sharp probing revealed that his daughter's blessed state had been achieved with too little agony. Because of his doubt, she struggled for years for certain knowledge of salvation. Beecher was called to Hanover Church in Boston, but Harriet spent her youth at Hartford, where she was sent to study and teach at the Female Seminary presided over by her older sister Catharine. When Harriet was twenty-one, she followed Lyman Beecher, his sister, his second wife, and eight of his children west to Ohio where he assumed the leadership of Lane Theological Seminary. She lived for eighteen years in uncongenial Cincinnati.

Beecher had encountered abolitionists in Boston, when Garrison, a member of his congregation, had come to him with a wild idea for a newspaper, claiming that Beecher's insistence on immediate repentance had revealed to him the necessity of immediate emancipation. The minister had scoffed at the young man's zeal and counselled moderation, gradualism, and colonization.

Now at Lane Seminary, he pledged himself to wrest the Ohio Valley from the devil's grip, but though he knew that Satan's shape is various, he could not have anticipated that his scholars would be seduced to antislavery by a fellow student. Theodore

Weld, a newly converted abolitionist, organized the other young men of Lane to work in the black ghetto in Cincinnati and began to agitate the slavery question. He modeled his debates on the "protracted meetings" of the Great Revival, and after days of discussion the students unanimously voted to condemn colonization and to constitute themselves an abolition society. The Seminary trustees promptly prohibited all further meetings, ordered the students' society disbanded, and threatened to expel those who did not comply. In a remarkable demonstration of student power, all but three or four of the hundred students withdrew from the school and, led by Weld, established themselves at Oberlin. Lane Seminary never recovered. The antislavery press published full accounts of the Lane debates, and they became an important instrument of conversion to abolition.[5]

Harriet Beecher Stowe later commented that during her years in the West she viewed the subject of slavery as "so dark and painful . . . so involved in difficulty and obscurity, so utterly beyond human hope or help, that it was of no use to read, or think, or distress one's self about it." Indeed, she reports that it was said "nobody could begin to read and think upon it without becoming practically insane. . . ." [6] But the issue of slavery was almost impossible to ignore in Cincinnati. Located on the river separating North from South, the city sheltered both fugitives and slave catchers. Three years before Lyman Beecher had led his band across the Alleghenies, the State of Ohio, in an attempt to conciliate her Southern sisters, enforced the Black Laws. As a result, white mobs terrorized the ghetto, and half the black inhabitants sought refuge in Canada. The precarious settlement of one or two thousand black people who remained did not escape the racist antiabolitionist violence—described by Hildreth—which erupted throughout the nation in 1835 and 1836.

When James G. Birney, who had been driven out of Kentucky, attempted to establish his antislavery newspaper, the *Philanthropist*, in Cincinnati, the press and civic leaders twice whipped up mobs to destroy his presses and pillage the black community. Birney left Cincinnati after the riots, but his associate Galamiel Bailey continued to publish the newspaper there until 1847, when he went on to Washington to edit the *National Era* and serialize

Uncle Tom's Cabin. The first mob outbreak prompted Harriet Beecher to write in her journal, "already my sympathies are strongly enlisted for Mr. Birney, and I hope he will stand his ground and assert his rights. The office is fire-proof and inclosed by high walls. I wish he would man it with armed men and see what can be done. If I were a man, I would go, for one, and take good care of at least one window." After the second attack, when the mayor finally called for volunteers to control the violence, she found her brother Henry Ward in the kitchen "making bullets," as he said, "to kill men with." [7]

Another brother, Edward Beecher, also bore arms to defend abolitionists from violence. In 1836, when a St. Louis mob broke into jail, seized a black prisoner, and burned him alive, Elijah Lovejoy reported the lynching in his newspaper, and a mob destroyed his press. Undaunted, he criticized the leniency of the judge's charge to the Grand Jury investigating the outrage, and then moved his print shop to Alton, on the free side of the river. In Illinois, although his press was twice broken, he made his *Observer* as important an antislavery organ as the Cincinnati *Philanthropist*. After the loss of his third press, Lovejoy and his friends determined to install and defend new equipment. Among those who set up the fourth press on November 16, 1837 was Lovejoy's closest friend, Harriet's brother Edward. With everything in place, Beecher left Alton the next afternoon. That night, Lovejoy was killed by the mob. There were reports that Beecher had died with him, and it was several days before the family in Cincinnati learned that he was safe. [8]

Since the move West, Harriet Beecher had been busy teaching and writing. In 1836 she married Calvin Stowe, a distinguished Biblical scholar who had followed her father into the wilderness. She bore six of her seven children in Cincinnati, and buried one there. As the years passed, she came to feel overburdened by the heavy responsibilities of caring for her home and family in the border river town. She later wrote that their house on the seminary grounds more than once served as a haven for black refugees from the Cincinnati mob, which renewed its periodic attacks against the black community in 1841. In 1843 Mrs. Stowe described sleeping with guns and ammunition at hand, and "a large bell ready

to call the young men of the adjoining Institution, in case the
mob should come up to search the house." She believed that only
the two miles of steep muddy road that separated the seminary
from the city saved her family from violence.[9]

But neither the mud nor her own absorption in domestic life
could keep the issue of slavery out of her home. Its victims were
constantly before her: a servant who appeared suddenly begging
for help, saying she was a fugitive and that her master was in Cincinnati hunting for her; a lonely little quadroon, her children's
playmate, who moped for his mother, still in slavery; her mulatto
cook who revealed that her Kentucky master had fathered all her
children, explaining, "You know, Mrs. Stowe, slave women cannot help themselves," while the horrified minister's wife remembered her aunt Mary Hubbard, who had gone off a planter's
bride and had met his black wife and mulatto children.

Harriet Beecher Stowe's attitude toward black people was
also shaped by her domestic life in Cincinnati. She commented
in her journal:

> If anybody wishes to have a black face look handsome, let
> them be left, as I have been, in feeble health in oppressive
> hot weather, with a sick baby in arms, and two or three
> other little ones in the nursery, and not a servant in the
> whole house to do a single turn. Then, if they could see
> my good Aunt Frankie coming with her honest, bluff, black
> face, her long, strong arms, her chest as big and stout as a
> barrel, and her hilarious, hearty laugh, perfectly delighted
> to take one's washing and do it at a fair price, they would
> appreciate the beauty of black people.[10]

After eighteen years of hard work, frustration, invalidism,
and debt, the Stowes returned to the East in 1850, the year the
Fugitive Slave Law was enacted. While in Cincinnati, Harriet
Beecher Stowe had helped pay the bills by composing and selling
a series of pious domestic stories and sketches. Now she received a
letter from her sister-in-law urging her to compose something

"that will make the whole nation feel what an accursed thing slavery is." And Mrs. Stowe, always more certain of eternity than of time, vowed to her children, "I will write something. I will if I live." [11]

After the New Year, she visited the staunchly abolitionist Edward Beechers in Boston, and probably met Josiah Henson, who had published his *Life* the previous year.[12] His autobiography is an example of the slave narrative, the uniquely American literary genre which appeared in 1760 and has re-emerged in each succeeding generation, reaching the height of its popularity during the abolitionist agitation before emancipation.[13] The narratives are a literary protest against chattel slavery and doctrines of racial inferiority. Their central theme, classic in our national letters, is the struggle for self-realization. Their protagonists oppose duly constituted authority in order to achieve, quite literally, manhood. They are by definition vernacular heroes, underclass and practiced in deceptions which they use to reach an illegal goal. Although successful in realizing their own liberty, the narrators are ultimately dissatisfied; their personal triumphs are not fulfilling because they perceive themselves not only as individuals, but as members of a group which is still opposed and despised. Hence they chronicle their achievements out of a sense of responsibility to their fellows.

In structure, the narratives generally follow a standard pattern. They begin with a portrayal of life under slavery which usually includes facts about food, clothing, shelter, relationships between master and slave, and information about slavery as an economic system—working conditions, the organization of agriculture under the plantation system, methods of servile control, and the slave trade. Through a series of incidents, they build to a climactic escape. They end with a portrayal of life in freedom, frequently commenting on racial discrimination and discussing the narrator's work in the antislavery movement.

The narrator characteristically reveals his inner life: his alienation resulting from his first encounter with brutality, and inevitably, his separation from his mother (often the only functional family for the slave child); his crucial decision to attempt escape; his devising a plan and concealing it from those around him; his fears during his escape; his triumph at his success; and his reponses to his new life in freedom. What emerges most strongly from each of these works is a sense of the character of the narrator—his energy, resourcefulness, and courage. In style and tone as individual as the personalities of their authors, taken together the slave narratives constitute an heroic literature.

Josiah Henson wrote his book in a simple straightforward style, though he became more mannered and long-winded in later editions. His mild tone is unique among the narratives. The author emerges a benign old man looking back over rich years, although his earliest recollections are of brutality and horror. He remembers seeing his father's back lacerated and his head bloody after he had been whipped and one of his ears had been cropped for attempting to defend his wife from rape by an overseer, but Henson's memories of his later childhood on the farm of his mother's master are pleasant. Josiah grew up a capable field hand, and in young manhood he was converted to Christianity.

He identified his interests with those of his master, working so hard and so well that he was made superintendent of the farm. Although he was maimed for life because his mistress gave him inadequate medical care after he was beaten by a neighboring overseer, Henson expresses no rancor. Instead, he proudly reports that he was able to learn to perform his tasks efficiently without full use of his arms. When his master went bankrupt and asked Henson to keep the slaves out of the sheriff's hands by spiriting them away to his brother's farm in Kentucky, Henson promised to save his master's property. As the group traveled down the Ohio River, crowds at Cincinnati shouted that if they came ashore they would be free, but Henson, believing that a slave should attain his liberty only through purchase, carried the people back into bondage, proud of his master's trust. He was a willing slave. Not until he was cheated of his freedom after he had attempted to buy his liberty—he earned the money preaching—did Henson learn that the interests of the oppressed are not those of his oppressor. Though he continued to play the role of faithful servant, he was one no longer. Now he searched for a way to escape to freedom.

Henson's Christianity was tested when his master suddenly decided to send him South to be sold. His dreams of running away were shattered, and only his religion prevented him from killing the whites on board the river boat in a desperate attempt to gain his liberty. His Christianity not only enabled him to conquer the temptation to murder his master, but prompted him to care for the young man, who fell seriously ill in New Orleans. Instead of leaving him to die, Henson nursed his young master, then took him back to his family in Kentucky. Upon their return, however, it became clear that instead of being rewarded, Henson would again be sent South to be sold. The Christian slave awaited his chance, and one evening, after bidding his master goodnight, he ran away with his wife and four children.

He recounts the hardships of the escape: It took two weeks of steady walking to reach Cincinnati; Henson had to carry the two younger children in a large sling on his back, while his exhausted, frightened wife led the others by the hand. In late October of 1830 the family reached Canada, aided by Quakers, free blacks and Indians. In time, Henson became acquainted with the immigrants at Wilberforce who had fled Cincinnati when the Black Laws were enforced, but dissatisfied with the subsistence life among the refugees, he later attempted to establish a colony at Dawn.

Four years earlier a slave autobiography had appeared whose tone contrasts dramatically with Henson's book. After passionately recounting the brutalities he suffered, Lewis Clarke barely managed to conclude his *Narrative* with the conventional plea for the salvation of those who enslave their fellow men.[14] The realities of Clarke's life are similar to Hildreth's fictional portrayal of the patriarchal relations on Colonel Moore's plantation. Clarke was born on his grandfather Campbell's Kentucky estate, the son of an immigrant Scottish weaver who had fought in the Battle of Bunker Hill, and Letitia, Campbell's mulatto daughter by one of his slave women. Clarke, his mother, and his eight brothers and sisters had believed they would be freed by his grandfather's will, but after the old man's death, they were seized as slaves by their white relatives. At the age of seven, Lewis Clarke was given to his aunt

Betsey Banton. He suffered ten years of her sadistic abuse. His aunt hated the sight of the child's light skin, and forced him to stay in the sun until he was burnt. She punished him by pulling his hair so frequently that, as an adult, he felt no pain when it was yanked. Clarke was at first relieved when he was mortgaged to the owner of a tobacco plantation and put to work as a field hand. Life on the farm, however, turned out to be a constant struggle between the overseer, who drove the slaves to work harder and punished them by withholding their food and by whipping them, and the slaves, who retaliated by shirking, stealing food, and by running away from beatings. For a time he was hired out for wages, which, of course, were taken by his master. Finally he decided to try to obtain his freedom. On his second attempt Clarke succeeded in reaching Ohio by passing for white. After continuing north to Canada, he returned to Oberlin—the new home of the Lane rebels and an antislavery stronghold—where he was reunited with his brother Milton, who had escaped the previous year.

In an expanded edition of the memoirs published in 1846, Milton Clarke adds a sketch of his early life and describes his experiences as an agent of the underground railroad in Ohio, where abolitionists systematically used deception as a weapon in their war against slavery. He gives the details of one fantastic adventure, in which he and a number of other blacks masqueraded as a group of fugitives and permitted themselves to be seized. When captured, the black men played the familiar roles according to the old script. Their spokesman alighted from his carriage, drawling, " 'Well, 'den, 'dis nigger must get out.' " Milton Clarke was taken before a Justice of the Peace and waited until he had been positively identified as a slave girl sought by her master before he dropped his woman's disguise. While he and his friends acted as decoys to divert the slave catchers, the real fugitives had escaped. As a consequence of this audacity, Milton Clarke later was kidnapped, but the Ohio abolitionists rescued him. Of his energetic work with the underground railroad, Milton Clarke writes, "The masters accused me of *stealing* several of . . . [their slaves]. This is a great lie. I never stole one in my life. I have assisted several to get into possession of the true owner, but I never assisted any man to steal another away from himself" (LMC 84).

Both brothers relate reminiscences of their light-skinned sister Delia, who, as punishment for rejecting the sexual demands of her master (who was also her uncle), was dressed in finery and auctioned off in New Orleans as "a fancy article." Delia was fortunate. She was bought by a Frenchman who emancipated and married her. At his death, she inherited his money and used it trying to find and free the members of her family. After she had successfully located some of them, Delia died suddenly. The estate, which she had willed to a freed brother, was confiscated.

The Clarke narratives, with their mood of "restrained outrage" and their tale of suffering and militant struggle against the slave owners, differ greatly from Henson's mellow recital of his early identification with his master.[15] In his crisis, the Christian Henson had transformed hatred for his oppressor into love, but at the conclusion of Lewis Clarke's narrative, he manages to choke out that he would "take the worst slaveholder by the hand, even Mrs. Banton, and freely forgive her, if I thought she had repented of her sins." He ends with a threat: On Judgment Day "the testimony of the slave will be heard" (LC 63). Nonetheless even Henson, the most Christian of slaves, finally deceived his master as did the militant Clarkes, masking his defiance under a passive exterior until he could assert his identity as a man. Ultimately, all of the slave narratives chronicle overt and covert rebellion.

One of the many stories explaining Harriet Beecher Stowe's inspiration for *Uncle Tom's Cabin* is that while attending communion service at Brunswick a few weeks after meeting Henson, she saw a vision of a tortured black man, heard Christ's words, "Inasmuch as ye have done it unto one of the least of these my brethren, ye have done it unto me," and that afternoon wrote "The Death of Uncle Tom." [16]

Uncle Tom's Cabin begins with the central situation of the plantation novel: the threatened loss of the estate and the resultant sale of the slaves. Mrs. Stowe first depicts the pleasant ways of the Shelby's Kentucky plantation. But after she has established this view of harmony, instead of dramatizing subsequent vicissitudes in the lives of the masters, as is done in *The Valley of Shen-andoah, Westward Ho! Swallow Barn,* and *Woodcraft,* she focuses on "life among the lowly," and follows the fortunes of the slaves who are sold. The little mulatto Harry escapes North in the arms of his mother Eliza, and black Uncle Tom is sold South. Thus the action, which in the slave narratives and in *Archy Moore* moves sequentially, first south through the slave trade and then north through the underground railroad, here moves in opposite directions simultaneously, creating a double stream which adds to the energy of the novel.

Harriet Stowe next depicts Tom's servitude at the Louisiana homes of Augustine St. Clare. This episode utilizes the plantation convention of the Northern visitor debating slavery with his host, but here the conclusions are reversed: The New Englander converts her Southern cousin. In this central section the author, adopting an attitude that will become standard in fiction after the Civil War, romanticizes the Southern aristocracy. Her emphasis is not on the slave, but on the master. The Byronic St. Clare, trapped by a bad marriage and racked by the approaching death of his daughter, manages to achieve self-realization and salvation through the agencies of his angel child Eva, his upright New England cousin Ophelia, and his faithful slave Tom (not to mention the memories of his sainted mother), before he dies.

If the homely quality of life on the Shelby place reminds one of the ladies' stories Mrs. Stowe had written, and the exoticism of the passage on St. Clare is reminiscent of her childhood favorite the *Arabian Nights,* the final section, located on Simon Legree's plantation, evokes the hellish terrors of Jonathan Edwards' "Sinners in the Hands of an Angry God," a favorite sermon of her father's. Here she finally establishes Uncle Tom at the center of the action. In this section Harriet Beecher Stowe dramatizes his martyrdom and, counterpointing his role, narrates the escape of a second pair of mulatto fugitives, Cassy and Emmeline. She ends her novel in Kentucky where she began it, with young Masr George freeing the slaves on the Shelby place.

Unlike *Archy Moore* and the slave narratives, which are concerned with the efforts of the black man to win his freedom, at the heart of *Uncle Tom's Cabin* is the dilemma faced by the white American who must choose his role in regard to the Fugitive Slave Law and chattel slavery. Colonel Shelby's reluctant decision to sell Uncle Tom and Eliza's Harry is the mistake which precipitates the events of the novel. Eliza's instant response, depicted as an automatic maternal reaction, is to run off with her child; her husband George Harris has already determined to escape before he first appears on the scene. Thus we do not agonize with the fugitives over their decisions to run away. But we are involved in the moral problems of the people they encounter in their flight, some of whom, quite unexpectedly, must decide whether to respond to their feelings of charity and break the law to aid them. The situation is posed repeatedly: when Eliza is helped by Mr. Symmes and Senator Bird, George Harris by his former employer Mr. Wilson, and both by the Quakers.

Tom does not deliberately choose to acquiesce to his slavery any more than Eliza deliberately chooses to escape with little Harry. Both react by reflex, automatically and instantly. The moral conflict on which Harriet Beecher Stowe focusses in the episodes involving Tom, like that in the sections concerning the fugitives, is not the problem faced by the slaves, but the dilemma which the whites must resolve. Shelby chooses wrongly; St. Clare suffers from paralysis of will; when offered repentance at the last minute, Legree deliberately hardens his heart; young George Shelby finally attempts to rectify his father's mistake and rescue Tom. Although he arrives too late, young Masr George is so moved by Tom's death that he deliberately breaks the law to aid in Cassy's and Emmeline's escape, and he manumits his slaves.

George Shelby thus serves as a model both for the Northern reader who is meant to identify with Mr. Symmes, the Birds, the Hallidays, and Mr. Wilson in their resistance to the Fugitive Slave Law, and for the Southern reader who, instructed in the evils that can be perpetrated under slavery, is taught to renounce his mastery. In her preface to the book, Mrs. Stowe wrote that she hoped "to awaken sympathy and feeling" for the black slave (I. xcii). *Uncle Tom's Cabin* dramatizes the successful struggle of white Americans to achieve this "sympathy and feeling." It concludes with white charity triumphantly ending black slavery. Once free, black people, whose peculiar racial character and experience uniquely fit them for the task, will fulfill the aims of Providence by returning to Africa and spreading the Gospel among the heathen.[17]

Although, as omniscient author, Harriet Beecher Stowe intensely and repeatedly asserts that the evil of slavery lies not in its abuses but in its usage, it is perhaps difficult to analyze what she really finds wrong with the system. At Lane Seminary years before, she had listened to the slavery debates, and now in the section devoted to St. Clare she includes and rebuts all of the proslavery arguments: the historical argument that all peoples must pass through slavery; the patriotic argument that the English are responsible; the anticapitalist argument that Southern slaves are better off than Northern (or British) wage-slaves; the moral argument that the civilized white man must accept the painful responsibility of raising the savage black; the racist argument that black people are incapable of freedom; the Biblical argument that black men bear the curse of Canaan; the hedonist argument that slaves are happier than their masters. But none of her answers to these really strikes to the heart of the problem.

Mrs. Stowe does not share Jefferson's fears that slavery may prevent the development of a democratic personality and a democratic society in America. In *Uncle Tom's Cabin* she does not present mastery as affecting personality adversely. (An exception to this is the single scene depicting Eva's cousin Henrique.) She specifically counters the contention that slave-holding causes the master to become aristocratic by showing the New England Sinclair to be as autocratic as his Southern brother. She refutes the argument that mastery breeds callousness and tyranny in her portrayal of Mrs. Shelby and her son, of St. Clare and his heavenly daughter, and even in her characterization of Legree, who was so brutalized that he struck his mother before he owned a single slave. (St. Clare's wife Marie, we are told, would be selfish anywhere.) Jefferson's fear that slavery would corrupt political democracy, while alluded to by St. Clare, does not figure in *Uncle Tom's Cabin* at all.

Richard Hildreth had dramatized Jefferson's perception, an

insight corroborated by the slave narratives, that hatred is at the center of the servile relation. But although Mrs. Stowe at one point has St. Clare assert that the fundamental fact of slavery is brute power, she dramatizes the opposite. As Eva points out to her Papa, she prefers the Southern way of life to that of New England because "it makes so many more round you to love, you know." The assumption that love is the basis of the servile relation is what makes Mr. Shelby's sale of Harry and Tom so terrible. He destroys love, for money. Similarly, Marie St. Clare's lack of feeling for her slaves is an exact indicator of her inability to care about anyone at all. It is precisely this which makes Legree diabolical. His hatred is a perversion, not a sign of the norm.

What, then, is the problem? If mastery produces excellent men and women, if the political structure is healthy, if the normal social relationship is rooted in love, why is slavery evil? Mrs. Stowe's brilliant exposure of the falsity of the use of familial metaphor in describing a system which breaks up families might suggest that her major concern is the destruction of the family under slavery.[18] She does indeed show this as a major abuse of slavery, and makes it her central theme in the episodes involving Eliza, George Harris, and Harry, as well as in a number of fragmentary incidents in the book. But this criticism does not strike at the heart of the servile institution, for by 1850 proslavery apologists like Kennedy had conceded the need for legal reforms to guarantee the integrity of the slave family; and it is not the main thrust of Mrs. Stowe's condemnation of slavery. Tom, not Eliza, is the protagonist of *Uncle Tom's Cabin*.

Tom's refusal to submit to spiritual tyranny as he had earlier submitted to separation from his family dramatizes the major theme of the novel. His assertion that he belongs body and soul not to Masr, but to Jesus, constitutes his rebellion. He will not disobey God to obey his earthly master. Thus Tom becomes a Christian martyr, tortured on earth and triumphant in heaven. Richard Hildreth recognized this immediately: "It is to its character as a religious novel, it is to Uncle Tom exclusively, to whom all the other characters serve, but as foils to help him shine, and to Uncle Tom not as a slave, but as a Christian hero that Mrs. Stowe's book owes its singular popularity." [19]

The sin of slavery—and it is a sin—rests in one of God's creatures having such complete power over another that he can control not only his physical life here on earth, but his spiritual life here and hereafter. In his strongest condemnation of slavery, St. Clare builds up to this crucial climax:

> This cursed business, accursed of God and man, what is it? Strip it of all its ornament, run it down to the root and nucleus of the whole, and what is it? Why, because my brother Quashy is ignorant and weak, and I am intelligent and strong,—because I know how, and can do it,—therefore, I may steal all he has, keep it, and give him only such and so much as suits my fancy. Whatever is too hard, too dirty, too disagreeable, for me, I may set Quashy to doing. Because I don't like work, Quashy shall work. Because the sun burns me, Quashy shall stay in the sun. Quashy shall earn the money, and I will spend it. Quashy shall lie down in every puddle, that I may walk over dry shod. Quashy shall do my will, and not his, all the days of his mortal life, and have such chance of getting to heaven, at last, as I find convenient. This I take to be about what slavery *is* (I. 292-93).

The slave may be purified by his suffering; at worst he is absolved of spiritual responsibility as a result of his enforced submission to the will of another. He never sins as utterly as does his master. What is really wrong with the institution of chattel slavery in *Uncle Tom's Cabin* is that it entrusts the souls of black slaves to whoever can afford to buy their bodies, thus endangering their salvation and almost certainly condemning white America to everlasting hellfire.

Hence the urgency, the intensity, the note of hysteria, in the novel. Not political and economic manumission but the salvation of the immortal soul is at stake. The slave becomes the occasion and the test. In her novel, Lyman Beecher's daughter has dramatized the perception of "good, motherly Cotton Mather," who a

century and a half earlier had warned his people that the importa-
tion of black slaves into America was Providential:

> God, whom you must remember to be "your Master in
> heaven," has brought them, and put them into your hands,
> who can tell what good he has brought them for? How if
> they should be the elect of God, fetched from Africa, or
> the Indies, and brought into your families, on purpose, that
> by the means of their being there, they may be brought
> home unto the Shepherd of souls! [20]

The white man's sin is made even worse by the nature of the
black man. In contrast to the "hard and dominant Anglo-Saxon
race," Mrs. Stowe tells us that the African is soft and helpless (I.
[xci]). Because of "their gentleness, their lowly docility of heart,
their aptitude to repose on a superior mind and rest on a higher
power, their childlike simplicity of affection, and felicity of for-
giveness," black people lack aptitude for earthly success (I. 236).
Their heritage is one of "ages of oppression, submission, ignorance, toil and vice (I. 324)." But what the world sees as the curse
of racial inferiority and cultural deprivation, Mrs. Stowe views as
the blessing of racial spirituality and earthly trial.

This Christian transvaluation enables Mrs. Stowe to include
the racist stereotypes of plantation fiction in her antislavery
novel.[21] Her color scheme is rigid. Black people are inevitably sub-
servient; mulattoes, who do not exist in plantation fiction, com-
bine the sensitivity of their black mothers with the strengh of
their white fathers. Unlike the characters met with in the slave
narratives and in *Archy Moore,* the black people in *Uncle Tom's
Cabin* always show their true faces to their masters. The black
figures we meet on the Shelby place include comic minstrel types
Sam and Andy (who trick the slave trader to win Missis' approval),
and Mammy Chloe and the giggling pickaninnies; at the St. Clare
mansion the devoted Mammy, comic cook Dinah, victimized and
debauched Old Prue, and minstrel showgirl Topsy; on the Legree
plantation the subhuman brutes Sambo and Quimbo. The mu-

latto slaves in the New Orleans section are stock spoilt servants, but they are attractive and intelligent; the mulatto figures on the Legree plantation include the distraught Cassy and innocent Emmeline, both of who run to freedom. Against this throng, we watch mulatto Eliza escape heroically with little Harry, and her mulatto husband George Harris defend his family with arms; in contrast to black Tom—the type of pious steady slave familiar in plantation fiction—who transcends his traditional acquiescent role and suffers martyrdom.

Tom's refusal to obey his master in obedience to a higher law was a truly revolutionary position in the midcentury America of Thoreau and John Brown, as it had been in Jefferson's time, and is in our own. (This caused the nineteenth-century worldwide democratic movement to embrace the novel.) [22] But the way in which Tom acts out his refusal has in recent years turned his name into a curse. While the mulatto fugitives and their white abolitionist allies portrayed in the novel practice resistance, both passive and active, black Uncle Tom practices Christian resignation.

The merits of the tactics of resistance and nonresistance to the new Fugitive Slave Law, crucial since the events at Christiana, were discussed in articles on *Uncle Tom's Cabin* published in the abolitionist press during the first six months after the book appeared. Garrison examined the alternatives in a review in *The Liberator*:

We are curious to know whether Mrs. Stowe is a believer in the duty of non-resistance for the white man, under all possible outrage and peril, as well as for the black man; whether she is for self-defence on her own part, or that of her husband or friends or country, in case of malignant assault, or whether she impartially disarms all mankind in the name of Christ, be the danger or suffering what it may. . . . That all the slaves at the South ought, 'if smitten on the one cheek, to turn the other also'—to repudiate all carnal weapons, shed no blood, 'be obedient to their masters,' wait for a peaceful deliverance, and abstain from all insurrectionary movements—is everywhere taken for granted, because the VICTIMS ARE BLACK. . . . Nothing can be plainer than that such conduct is obligatory upon them; and, when, through the operation of divine grace, they are enabled to manifest a spirit like this, it is acknowledged to be worthy of great commendation, as in the case of 'Uncle Tom.' But, for those whose skin is of a different complexion, the case is materially altered. When they are spit upon and buffeted, outraged and oppressed, talk not then of a non-resisting Savior—it is fanaticism! Talk not of overcoming evil with good—it is madness! Talk not of peacefully submitting to chains and stripes—it is base servility! Talk not of servants being obedient to their masters —let the blood of the tyrants flow! How is this to be explained or reconciled? Is there one law of submission and non-resistance for the black man, and another law of rebellion and conflict for the white man? [23]

The discussion was continued by Henry C. Wright, a noted reformer and abolitionist, in a Letter to the Editor:

God, in the heart of a slave, is but a call to freedom; and an instigation to exert his own will and energies to obtain it. But so thinks not the author of Uncle Tom's Cabin. In her view, God, in the slave's heart, is but a call to submit the question of his liberty to the will and pleasure of his master, and, in the meantime, to endure all the cruelties and horrors he shall see fit to inflict on him, uncomplaining and submissive, till it shall seem good to the despot to settle that question.[24]

The faithful were advised to be more expedient in a letter published in September. This writer agreed that " 'Uncle Tom' is not the highest type of Christian perfection, by any means. . . .

[N]o person can be a Christian and consent to remain a slave, but as soon as God's spirit takes up his abode in the slave's heart, he will be induced to seek to obtain his freedom." Nonetheless, he complained that abolitionists should recognize the aid *Uncle Tom's Cabin* had given the antislavery cause: "It seems almost like justifying benevolence, or defending virtue, to attempt to plead in favor of such a work." [25]

But black militants were already voicing a more modern judgment of the character of Uncle Tom. In the December 10 issue of *The Liberator,* William C. Nell clearly distinguishes his position from Uncle Tom's and in the columns of *Frederick Douglass' Paper,* William G. Allen concurs in phrases as timely as Watts, Detroit, and Washington:

> Uncle Tom was a good old soul, thoroughly and perfectly pious. Indeed, if any man had too much piety, Uncle Tom was that man. I confess to more of "total depravity." . . . I believe, as you do, that it is not light the slaveholder wants, but fire, and he ought to have it. I do not advocate revenge, but simply resistance to tyrants, if it need be, to the death.[26]

While committed abolitionists were debating the racism in *Uncle Tom's Cabin,* it became a runaway best-seller in the North, but it was excoriated and suppressed in the South.[27] The editor of the leading Southern journal *Southern Literary Messenger* ordered his critic to produce a notice "as hot as hell-fire, blasting and soaring the reputation of the vile wretch in petticoats who could write such a volume." Unsatisfied by the reviewer's denunciation, he added his own, which he concludes by shouting:

> every holier purpose of our nature is misguided, every charitable sympathy betrayed, every loftier sentiment polluted, every moral purpose wrenched to wrong, and every patriotic feeling outraged, by its criminal prostitution of the

high functions of the imagination to the pernicious intrigues of sectional animosity, and to the petty calumnies
of wilful slander.[28]

William Gilmore Simms, at this time editor of the Charleston
Southern Quarterly Review, disdained to notice the book himself.
Preferring "the seemingly poetic justice of having the Northern
woman answered by a Southern woman," he published Mrs.
Louisa McCord's wild attack which, syntax flying, denounces
Uncle Tom's Cabin as a wicked lie:

> To disprove slanders thus impudently uttered and obsti-
> nately persevered in is impossible unless those who are to
> judge the question had some little insight into the facts of
> the case, and could know something of our habits and our
> laws, thus being enabled to judge of the respective worth
> of the testimony brought before them. . . . To such as are
> willing to hear both sides we have endeavoured to invali-
> date Mrs. Stowe's testimony by proving that so far from
> being well acquainted with our habits and manners she
> has probably never set foot in our country, and is ignorant
> alike of our manners, feelings, and even habits of
> language.[29]

In response to the attack by Southerners on the factual accuracy
of *Uncle Tom's Cabin*—as if this were the point—Mrs. Stowe
bgan gathering information about slavery upon which to base a
reply. One of her sources was a work entitled *American Slavery
As It Is,* published by the American Antislavery Society in 1839.[30]
It is a powerful indictment compiled by Theodore Weld, his wife
Angelina Grimké Weld, and her sister Sarah Grimké. After leading Lyman Beecher's students away from Lane, Weld had spread
antislavery gospel throughout the West and helped train The

Seventy, antislavery agents who preached slavery as sin and immediate abolition as repentance. When Congress invoked gag rule
in 1836 and refused to entertain abolitionist petitions, Weld was
involved in the campaign for signatures, and in response to appeals by antislavery volunteers for help in convincing prospective
signers, he conceived of a fact book exposing slavery through the
words of white Southerners. With his Charleston-born wife and her
sister, Weld gathered the materials for *American Slavery As It Is*
by excerpting published criticism (he includes Jefferson, Tucker,
and Paulding); by asking ex-Southerners and Northerners who
had traveled in the South for personal "testimony"; and by comb-
ing twenty thousand copies of Southern newspapers published between 1837 and 1839, searching for ads, speeches, legal decisions,
news stories, and facts about slavery.[31]

The introduction to the thick pamphlet addresses the reader
as juror, and invites him to examine a Southern indictment of
chattel slavery. Specific charges are listed in three sections. The
first concerns servile living conditions: food, clothing, shelter,
labor, and treatment of the sick. The second discusses punishment:
slave-driving, cruelty, and torture. The third deals with the general condition of the slaves. Preceding and following these are
longer testimonies, each signed and attested, describing conditions
under slavery.

The inevitable verdict is that slavery rests on force; labor is
performed out of fear; the men under whom slaves work are of
necessity brutal; the interests of the master are in opposition to
those of his slave; and the master lives by robbing the slave of the
fruits of his labor. Those conclusions are followed by a section
enumerating and rebutting the standard proslavery arguments,
and by an excellent index designed to help an antislavery worker
come up with a quick answer to convince a prospective signer to
add his name to the antislavery petitions. A unique combination
of public and private commentary on chattel slavery in the nineteenth century, *American Slavery As It Is* is an exciting and impressive book today, and was a best-seller in its own time. Harriet
Beecher Stowe later said she had kept it "in her work basket by
day, and slept with it under her pillow by night, till its facts
crystallized into Uncle Tom." [32]

Under attack from Southern critics, she used Weld's book—along with the slave narratives of Frederick Douglass, Josiah Henson and the Clarke brothers—as a major source for her *Key to Uncle Tom's Cabin*. Douglass hailed her efforts. In contrast to the "soft impeachment" of chattel slavery he found in her novel, he judged that "since the publication of . . . *'The Testimony of a Thousand Witnesses'*—there has not been an exposure of slavery so terrible as the *Key to 'Uncle Tom's Cabin.'* " [33]

It has been thoroughly established, despite Mrs. Stowe's claims, that most of the materials she mentions in the *Key* were not sources for *Uncle Tom's Cabin*. Actually she compiled them after the veracity of the novel was attacked, and they were corroborative in nature.[34] What is of interest, then, is not the transformation of this mass of data into fiction, but the shift in emphasis and tone from the documents—the slave narratives and *American Slavery As It Is*—to the *Key*. In each case, Mrs. Stowe transforms her straightforward, often angry sources into an amalgam of sentimentality, sensationalism, and piety.[35]

In the introduction to the *Key*, Mrs. Stowe makes her aim explicit: "The great object of the author in writing has been to bring this subject of slavery, as a moral and religious question, before the minds of all those who profess to be followers of Christ, in this country" (iii-iv). In the first section of the *Key* Mrs. Stowe cites origins of various characters and incidents in *Uncle Tom's Cabin*. It is worth noting that although she links a number of them to actual people and events, she does not connect the martyrdom of Uncle Tom with a description of a Christian slave whipped to death because of his refusal to renounce his religion signed by Sarah Grimké in *American Slavery As It Is* (p. 24). But because Mrs. Stowe is here concerned with the factual, and not the fictional, sources of the novel, it is not surprising that she does not mention *Archy Moore,* although her reference to *The White Slave* shows that she knew Hildreth's novel at least by the time she wrote the *Key,* if not earlier (156).[36]

She opens the second section with an extensive quotation from a criticism of *Uncle Tom's Cabin* which rejected as inaccurate its portrayal of black codes and slave laws. She then presents a full-blown discussion of servile law, complete with comparisons of

American with classical and biblical slave codes. The third section is a miscellany dealing with slavery and public opinion and with the social consequences of tolerating the slave trade, the separation of families, prostitution, and kidnapping. It includes a composite picture of the slave as seen by his master, and a sociological discussion of the consequences of slavery on the poor white Southerner. All of this is preparatory to her discussion of the American churches and chattel slavery. Her final chapter recommends that "the whole American church, of all denominations, should unitedly come up, not in form, but in fact, to the noble purpose avowed by the Presbyterian Assembly of 1818, to seek the entire abolition of slavery throughout America and throughout Christendom" (250). The *Key* concludes with a statement of the unresolved religious dichotomies embraced by Lyman Beecher's daughter. Urging Christians to show their love by espousing the cause of the suffering Jesus, she invokes the terror of sinners before the Triumphant Christ at the Last Judgment.

The diverse demands made by the God of Righteousness and the God of Love on slaves and their masters are again portrayed in *Dred,* Mrs. Stowe's "other slave novel." [37] In the initial situation, reminiscent of *Swallow Barn,* the author portrays the Southern belle, Nina Gordon, returning to her decaying plantation home and beginning a series of romantic exploits with various beaux. Largely as a result of counsel by Milly, her aunt's black slave woman who has substituted Christian love for her hatred of the grasping mistress who sold away her children, and of Bible reading undertaken at the behest of black Uncle Tiff, a neighboring slave devoted to his déclassé young mistress and masr, coquette Miss Gordon is transformed into a responsible Christian young woman. She engages herself to Edward Clayton, an idealistic Southern gentleman who wants somehow to renew Southern life. A dangerous undercurrent involves the antagonism between Nina's exemplary mulatto half-brother Harry, and her depraved white brother Tom. Despite Harry's devotion to Nina's interests, Tom's despotism threatens to incite him to rebellion, and his insurgency is encouraged by the exotic black rebel Dred. Identified as the son of the slave insurrectionist Denmark Vesey, Dred wan-

ders the swamps bordering the plantation, muttering apocrypha
and prophecying divine retribution against slaveholders. Harry is
divided between his love for sister-Mistress Nina and his hatred
of brother-Masr Tom; between black Milly's counsel of forgive-
ness and Dred's cry for justice. But the slave's conflict is not central in the novel.[38]

The main plot pits Nina's aristocratic fiancé Edward Clayton
against the slavocracy. Believing that the only justification for
black slavery is as "a guardian relation, in which our superior
strength and intelligence are made the protector and educator of
their simplicity and weakness," Clayton initiates legal prosecution
against a white man who assaulted Milly. In court the judge re-
luctantly lays bare the central fact of the slave system: The end of
the servile relation is not the protection of the slave, but the profit
of the master. Awakened to the immorality of slavery, Edward
attempts to convince the Southern church to mount an abolitionist
crusade. Near the end of the first volume, it would appear that
the forces of repression, exemplified by Southern law and Tom
Gordon, can possibly be overcome by the forces of progress, represented by Clayton, Nina, and a purified Southern church, and
that, in consequence, Dred's apocalyptic prophecies will remain
unfulfilled. But suddenly Nina dies, and Tom goads Harry into
running off to Dred's swamp refuge.

The second volume recounts Clayton's failure to reform the
Southern churches, and the triumph of Tom's immorality and
lawlessness. Driven from his plantation by mobs and forced to
leave the State, Clayton finally settles his newly freed slaves in
Canada. This turn of events would seem to dictate that mulatto
Harry must decide either to follow Milly's example and practice
Christian resignation or to respond to Dred's appeals for retribution and insurrection. But Dred is shot, and, instead of resolving
his dilemma, Harry, who evidently agrees with Clayton that the
black man is incapable of successful rebellion and self-government,
escapes North. At the end, both enlightened whites and virtually
all the blacks, including even acquiescent Milly and Uncle Tiff,
abandon the South. The final chapter reproduces the central
scene of plantation fiction—loving black Uncle Tiff caring for

his loving young Massa—incongruously transplanted to Boston, Massachusetts.

Mrs. Stowe's biographers suggest that the caning suffered on the floor of Congress by Massachusetts Senator Charles Sumner at the hands of South Carolina Representative Preston Brooks, which occurred while she was working on the novel, convinced her that the time for reform had passed. For whatever reason, it is clear that the author changes her point of view in the middle of *Dred*. The first volume celebrates the charm of the Southland; the second is in fact what *Uncle Tom's Cabin* was falsely accused of being, anti-Southern.

Although Mrs. Stowe shifts her attitude toward the white South, her vision of black people remains constant. As in *Uncle Tom's Cabin,* because of his race and his condition, the black man is seen as intellectually incompetent in the business of this world, but he has a special spiritual talent. Black characters are all static and straightforward. There is no irony here. With the single exception of the valet Jim, who appears only briefly, they are either the clichés of plantation fiction and the minstrel show—Aunt Katy, Old Hundred, Aunt Rose, Dulcimer, Tomtit; or representatives of the religious impulse—Milly, Uncle Tiff, and Dred.

The mulatto women—Harry's wife, his sister Cora, and the dying Emily—are conventionally beautiful victims, actual or potential, of white lust. By virtue of their "white blood," the mulattos are more complex than their black brothers. The most suggestive moment in the novel occurs when Harry, goaded beyond endurance, walks into the forest and encounters first Dred, then Milly. Here is a portentious meeting: The half-black, half-white man confronts a black man urging Old Testament vengeance and a black woman counseling Christian love. But Harry's dilemma is not pursued. The alternatives black people face are not at the heart of *Dred*. Even Harry is a static figure who vacillates between the choices before him and defaults any significant action.

Mrs. Stowe shows that slavery is consistently bad, and worst of all for the Southern white, whom it makes hypocritical and brutal, and whose society it destroys. (Here she comes to Jeffer-

son's view.) Although black men demonstrate their moral superiority not by striking for their rights but by learning to love their
enemies, in *Dred* even this exemplary morality will not convert
their masters to abolition, as did Uncle Tom's; and good white
men cannot end slavery as did George Shelby. In *Uncle Tom's
Cabin*, chattel slavery is an evil which whites, through sympathy
with their black victims, can be moved to correct, but here black
sufferer and white sympathizer are powerless to do anything but
run away.

Like the models Mrs. Stowe used for her first novel, the
people on whom she has patterned her characters in *Dred* have
power and force. Milly is based on Sojourner Truth and Milly
Edmundson; Dred, on Nat Turner.[39] But in the novel, these figures lose the stature of their originals. Beside the wonderfully
vital *Uncle Tom's Cabin*, *Dred* is a tired book.

The emotional impact *Uncle Tom's Cabin* had on the North
cannot be disputed, and its success ended the prohibition on publishing books on the subject of slavery. Following the appearance
of *Uncle Tom's Cabin*, new novels dealing with slavery appeared
and older ones, including Paulding's *Puritan and His Daughter*,
Kennedy's *Swallow Barn*, Simms' *Woodcraft*, and Hildreth's *The
White Slave*, were published again.[40] But despite the significance
of *Uncle Tom's Cabin*, its portrayal of black people does not
challenge white racism.

Uncle Tom's Cabin and *Dred* are Christianized, sentimental-
ized, sensationalized versions of *Archy Moore* and *The White
Slave*. Character types, incidents, even names repeat from one to
the other. But the Christian slave, who rebels in *Archy Moore*,
patiently endures martyrdom in *Uncle Tom's Cabin*. The defiant
rebel, lynched in *The White Slave*, in *Dred* becomes a mystic who
never leads his insurrection. The relation between master and
slave is shown as being based on hatred in *Archy Moore*, but
Uncle Tom's Cabin shows love betrayed. *The White Slave* dramatizes the violence inherent in the slave system directed first against
the black chattel and then engulfing an entire society, but in *Dred*
the white reformist is the principal victim of brutality. *The White
Slave* ends with a call for immediate abolition; *Uncle Tom's*

Cabin concludes with a plea for colonization. Mrs. Stowe's mixture of antislavery and white supremacy had led her back to Jefferson's *Notes on Virginia.*

Working with the historical precedent of the Nat Turner revolt and with the literary precedents of *Archy Moore* and the slave narratives, Mrs. Stowe produced Uncle Tom. It is not surprising that, a few months after the book's publication, an ardent abolitionist should write, "I wonder not at the unprecedented popularity of *Uncle Tom's Cabin.* The conscience of this nation is lashed to madness by uncompromising antislavery. *Uncle Tom's Cabin* comes as a quietus, to some extent." [41] With Mrs. Stowe's shift in emphasis from this world to the next, all is revealed as part of God's plan. The suffering endured under slavery is seen as morally beneficial to the savage African (who will ultimately Christianize the Dark Continent), and the sin of white America can be absolved merely by an extension of sympathy to the lowly. In the years that followed the publication of her sensational book, Mrs. Stowe warned that if the Southerner, unlike his black victim, would not heed Jesus' love, he must suffer His wrath at the hands of His chosen instrument: not black militants, but the Grand Army of the Republic. For Lyman Beecher's daughter, there were indeed two Christs.[42]

NOTES—CHAPTER VII

1. The Shadrach case is discussed in Marion Gleason McDougall, *Fugitive Slaves (1619-1865),* Publications of the Society for the Collegiate Instruction of Women, Fay House Monographs, No. 3 (Boston, 1891), pp. 47-50. Also see Frederick Douglass, *Life and Times of Frederick Douglass* (New York, 1962), p. 280. The Sims case is discussed in McDougall, pp. 44-45. For Edward Beecher's position see Forrest Wilson, *Crusader in Crinoline, The Life of Harriet Beecher Stowe* (Philadelphia and New York, 1941), p. 261. The Christiana affair is discussed in McDougall, pp. 50-51; and in Douglass, pp. 280-82.
2. *Uncle Tom's Cabin* appeared as a serial in the *National Era,* June 3, 1851-April 2, 1852. It was published in book form at Boston in 1852. Parenthetical page references to *Uncle Tom's Cabin* in my text refer to vols. I and II, *Writings of Harriet Beecher Stowe,* Riverside ed., 16 vols. (Cambridge, Mass., 1896).

For nonviolence and the antislavery movement, see *Nonviolence in America: A Documentary History*, ed. Staughton Lynd (Indianapolis, New York, Kansas City, 1966), pp. 25-108; and Carleton Maybee, *Black Freedom: The Nonviolent Abolitionists from 1830 Through the Civil War* (London, 1970).

For Garrison's unique mixture of pacifism and abolition, see *Documents of Upheaval: Selections from William Lloyd Garrison's The Liberator, 1831-1865*, ed. Truman Nelson (New York, 1966).

3. [William Lloyd Garrison], "Uncle Tom's Cabin," *The Liberator*, March 26, 1852.

4. Biographical information was obtained from the following sources: Wilson, *Crusader;* John R. Adams, *Harriet Beecher Stowe* (New York, 1963); Constance Rourke, *Trumpets of Jubilee* (New York, 1927, 1963); Edward Wagenknecht, *Harriet Beecher Stowe, the Known and the Unknown* (New York, 1965); Charles Edward Stowe and Lyman Beecher Stowe, *Harriet Beecher Stowe: The Story of Her Life* (Boston and New York, 1913); *Life and Letters of Harriet Beecher Stowe*, ed. Annie Fields (Boston and New York, 1899).

5. Materials on the Lane Debates can be found in Rourke; Gilbert Barnes, *The Antislavery Impulse 1830-1844* (New York, 1933, 1964); "Introduction," *Letters of Theodore Dwight Weld, Angelina Grimké Weld and Sarah Grimké 1822-1844*, ed. Gilbert H. Barnes and Dwight L. Dumond, 2 vols. (New York, 1934). For an account of the confrontations between Garrison and Beecher, see *Documents of Upheaval*, pp. xii, 96-100.

6. "Introduction," 1878 edition of *Uncle Tom's Cabin*, quoted in *Life and Letters*, p. 142.

7. For a discussion of Northern racist violence, see Leon F. Litwack, *North of Slavery: The Negro in the Free States 1790-1860* (Chicago and London, 1961, 1965); Lorman Ratner, *Powder Keg: Northern Opposition to the Antislavery Movement: 1831-1840* (New York, 1968); and Leonard L. Richards, *"Gentlemen of Property and Standing"; Anti-Abolition Mobs in Jacksonian America* (New York, 1970). For Mrs. Stowe's responses, see Forrest Wilson, pp. 186, 188.

8. See Joseph and Owen Lovejoy, *Memoir of the Rev. Elijah P. Lovejoy* (New York, 1838); and Edward Beecher, *Narrative of Riots at Alton* (Alton, 1838, New York, 1965). Lovejoy's use of arms is discussed in Maybee, Chapters 4-11.

9. *Life and Letters*, pp. 133-34. Litwack, p. 100.

10. *Life and Letters*, p. 175.

11. Wilson, p. 252.

12. Wilson, following Charles and Lyman Stowe, assumes this. Marion Wilson Starling, "The Slave Narrative: Its Place in American Literary History," unpubl. diss. (New York University, 1946), believes that Mrs. Stowe's view of Henson as The Christian Slave was influenced by Ephraim Peabody's review, "Narratives of Fugitive Slaves," *The Christian Examiner*, 4th Ser., XLVII (July 1849), 61-92. Charles Harold Nichols, "A Study of the Slave Narratives," unpubl. diss. (Brown,

1948), pointing out several discrepancies, conjectures that Mrs. Stowe and Henson did not meet until 1858.

Josiah Henson, *The Life of Josiah Henson, Formerly a Slave Now an Inhabitant of Canada, as Narrated by Himself* (Boston, 1849). The *Life* was republished in London in 1851. A new edition, with an introduction by Harriet Beecher Stowe, was entitled *Truth Stranger than Fiction: Father Henson's Story of His Own Life* (Boston and Cleveland, 1858). A later version entitled *Truth Is Stranger Than Fiction: An Autobiography of the Rev. Josiah Henson . . .* is dated Boston, 1879. For a critical biographical study see Brion Gysin, *To Master—A Long Goodnight* (New York, 1948).

13. Vernon Loggins, *The Negro Author: His Development in America to 1900* (New York, 1929; Port Washington, N.Y., 1964), p. 95, states that the earliest is dated 1760. The last full-length narrative appeared in 1900. Recently several collections of brief narratives, like the classic *Lay My Burden Down*, ed. B. A. Botkin (Chicago, 1945), based on the Slave Narrative Collection of the Federal Writers' Project, have appeared.

For an excellent introduction to the narratives, see Anna Bontemps, "The Slave Narrative: An American Genre," *Great Slave Narratives* (Boston, 1969). Major studies include Starling, "The Slave Narrative"; Nichols, "A Study of the Slave Narrative"; Margaret Young Jackson, "An Investigation of Biographies and Autobiographies of American Slaves Published Between 1840 and 1860 . . . ," unpubl. diss. (Cornell, 1954). Also see "The Significance of Slave Narratives," *Puttin' On Ole Massa*, ed. Gilbert Osofsky (New York, 1969), pp. [9]-48. For the slave narratives as a criticism of plantation fiction, see Charles H. Nichols, "Slave Narratives and the Plantation Legend," *Phylon*, X (1949), 201-10.

14. *Narrative of the Sufferings of Lewis Clarke, During a Captivity of More than Twenty-Five Years, Among the Algerines of Kentucky, One of the So-Called Christian States of North America, Dictated by Himself* (Boston, 1845). Parenthetical page citations in my text referring to this edition are labelled LC. The following year a new edition, including the reminiscences of Clarke's brother Milton, was published under the title *Narratives of the Sufferings of Lewis and Miton Clarke, Sons of a Soldier of the Revolution, During a Captivity of More than Twenty Years Among the Slaveholders of Kentucky, One of the So-Called Christian States of North America. Dictated by Themselves* (Boston, 1846). Parenthetical page citations in my text referring to this edition are labelled LMC.

15. The quoted phrase is Charles Nichols'. All of the students of the narratives point out the ironic fact that while "Uncle Tom" Henson was acclaimed by white Americans, his fellow fugitives feared he was a self-seeking charlatan. See, for example, the warning letter from William Wells Brown to Frederick Douglass which appeared in *The Liberator*, October 20, 1854, republished in *The Mind of the Negro As Reflected in Letters Written During the Crisis 1800-1860*, ed. Carter G. Woodson (Washington, D.C., 1926), p. 365.

16. This account is included in Stowe and Stowe, pp. 144ff. Mrs. Fields points out discrepancies among the various versions, *Life and Letters,* p. 165.

17. For a similar view—reached through a study of millennialism—see Ernest Lee Tuveson, *Redeemer Nation: The Idea of America's Millennial Role* (Chicago, 1968), Chapter 6. Mrs. Stowe's position on colonization is discussed in Litwack, pp. 254-55. Also see Sterling A. Brown, "The American Race Problem as Reflected in American Literature," *Journal of Negro Education,* VIII (July 1939), 275-90.

18. For discussions of her handling of plantation "familial rhetoric," see Kenneth S. Lynn, "Introduction," to the 1962 Cambridge edition; and especially Severn Duvall, "Uncle Tom's Cabin: The Sinister Side of the Patriarchy," *New England Quarterly,* XXVI (March 1963), 3-22. John William Ward, *"Uncle Tom's Cabin,* As a Matter of Historical Fact," *Columbia University Forum,* IX (Winter 1966), 42-47, suggests that this is Mrs. Stowe's major theme.

19. "Uncle Tom, The White Slave, Ida May and the New York Evening Post," *Boston Evening Telegraph,* November 12, 1854. Most modern critics agree; see Rourke; Lynn, "Introduction"; Vernon L. Parrington, *Main Currents in American Thought,* 3 vols. (New York, 1927, 1930, 1954), II, 364ff; Edmund Wilson, *Patriotic Gore: Studies in the Literature of the American Civil War* (New York, 1962, 1966).

20. The description of Mather is from Harriet Beecher Stowe's *Oldtown Folks,* Chapter 18, and is quoted in Wagenknecht, p. 198. His statement can be found in Thomas F. Gossett, *Race: The History of an Idea in America* (Dallas, 1963; New York, 1965), p. 31. For a similar view, see Cushing Strout, *"Uncle Tom's Cabin* and the Portent of Millennium," *Yale Review,* 57 (1968), 375-85.

21. For a similar interpretation, see George M. Frederickson, *The Black Image In the White Mind* (New York, 1971), Chapter Four. Scholars of Southern literature have long recognized the plantation elements in *Uncle Tom's Cabin.* See Francis A. Shoup, "Uncle Tom's Cabin Fifty Years After," *Sewanee Review,* II (1893), 88-104; Paul H. Buck, *The Road to Reunion, 1865-1900* (Boston, 1937), Chapter 8; Francis Pendleton Gaines, *The Southern Plantation* (New York, 1925), pp. 36ff. Thomas F. Gossett makes the point that while insisting on an end to slavery, *Uncle Tom's Cabin* views the black man as innately inferior (p. 261). Although J. C. Furnas, *Goodbye to Uncle Tom* (New York, 1956), correctly identifies this racism, he wrongly attacks Harriet Beecher Stowe and the abolitionists as its originators.

22. George Sand praised the book extravagantly, as did Tolstoi in *What Is Art?* and Heine in his *Confessions (Gestandnisse).* See Forrest Wilson, pp. 329-30, and *Life and Letters,* pp. 151-57.

23. *The Liberator,* March 26, 1852. An extract is reprinted in *Documents of Upheaval,* pp. 239-40.

24. *The Liberator,* July 9, 1852.

25. *The Liberator,* September 17, 1852.

26. Nell's letter is republished in Woodson, p. 338. At various times asso-

ciated with *The Liberator* and with *Frederick Douglass' Paper,* Nell is most often remembered as a pioneer black historian, author of *The Colored Patriots of the American Revolution* . . . (Boston, 1855).

Allen's letter is quoted from the issue of May 20, 1852. Allen, who had published the *National Watchman* at Troy, New York and taught at an abolitionist college, emigrated to England after he and his white bride faced mob violence in New York. He contributed letters to *The Liberator* after their expatriation.

27. For an account of the fantastic popularity of *Uncle Tom's Cabin,* see Frank Luther Mott, *Golden Multitudes* (New York, 1947), pp. 117-18. For a discussion of Southern suppression, see Forrest Wilson, pp. 297-98.

28. Letter from editor John R. Thompson to reviewer George F. Holmes, September 11, 1852, quoted in Clement Eaton, *The Freedom-of-Thought Struggle in the Old South,* rev. ed. (New York, 1964), pp. 36-37. Holmes' review is in *Southern Literary Messenger,* XVIII (October 1852), 630-38. Thompson's article appears in *Southern Literary Messenger* XVIII (December 1852), 721-31.

29. The comment on Simms' motives is from William P. Trent, *William Gilmour Simms,* American Men of Letters Series (Boston and New York, 1892), 174-75.

Louisa S. Cheves McCord's review appeared in *Southern Quarterly Review,* n.s. VIII (January 1855), 81-120. I have not been able to examine this journal; excerpts in my text are taken from sections quoted in Arthur B. Maurice, "Famous Novels and Their Contemporary Critics, I: *Uncle Tom's Cabin,*" *Bookman,* XVII (1903), 23-30.

Simms commented on *Uncle Tom's Cabin* in the late versions of a proslavery polemic which he revised and republished over a twenty-year period. (See Chapter V, above.) Simms' most complete statement on the novel is included in his review of Harriet Beecher Stowe's *A Key to Uncle Tom's Cabin,* Southern Quarterly Review, n.s. VII (July 1853), 214-54. Claiming that the appearance of *Key* has necessitated a reexamination of *Uncle Tom's Cabin,* this time not as fact but as fiction, he argues against the use of the romance as a vehicle for social protest.

30. American Anti-Slavery Society, *American Slavery As It Is: Testimony of a Thousand Witnesses* (New York, 1839).

31. Both Barnes and Dwight Lowell Dumond, *Antislavery: The Crusade for Freedom in America* (Ann Arbor, 1961; New York, 1966), include discussions of the agency system and of the compilation of *American Slavery As It Is.* Additional information on Weld is available in the introduction to the Weld-Grimké *Letters,* which they edited jointly. These materials all stress the divergences between Weld and Garrison. But see Weld's eulogy of Garrison, republished in *The Abolitionists,* ed. Louis Ruchames (New York, 1964), pp. 250-55.

32. Unpublished manuscript by Sarah Weld of reminiscences of her mother Angelina Grimké Weld, quoted in Barnes, p. 231.

33. Harriet Beecher Stowe, *A Key to Uncle Tom's Cabin, Presenting the Original Facts and Documents Upon Which the Story is Founded* . . .

(Boston, Cleveland, and London, 1853). *Key* is included in Vol. II of *Writings*, but because this edition is much abbreviated, page references in my text refer to the first edition. I am grateful to Professor Philip Foner for calling to my attention Douglass' comment, which appeared in *Frederick Douglass' Paper*, April 29, 1853; it is reprinted in *Life and Writings of Frederick Douglass*, ed. Philip S. Foner, 4 vols. (New York, 1950), II, 242.

34. Forrest Wilson, pp. 332ff.
35. The peculiar tone of Mrs. Stowe's writings has been remarked upon by her modern critics. See Kenneth S. Lynn, "Mrs. Stowe and the American Imagination," *New Republic*, June 29, 1963, 20-21; James Baldwin, "Everybody's Protest Novel," *Notes of a Native Son* (Boston, 1949, 1955), pp. 13-24; and Edmund Wilson, pp. 47-48.
36. It is remarkable that in the quest for the literary sources of *Uncle Tom's Cabin*—although Alexander Cowie, *The Rise of the American Novel* (New York and Cincinnati, 1948), quoting Quinn, hints at them —with the exception of Charles Nichols, "The Origins of Uncle Tom's Cabin," *Phylon*, XIX (1958), 328-34, critics have overlooked its obvious similarities to *Archy Moore* which Hildreth had pointed out in 1854 in "Uncle Tom, The White Slave, Ida May, and the New York Evening Post." See, for example, the discussion of sources in Charles H. Foster, *The Rungless Ladder* (Durham, N.C., 1954), pp. 13-17.
37. Harriet Beecher Stowe, *Dred: A Tale of the Great Dismal Swamp*, 2 vols. (Boston, 1856). The standard edition is Vols. III and IV of *Writings;* a number of Mrs. Stowe's shorter antislavery writings are collected in Vol. IV.
38. For another view, see Alice Crozier, *The Novels of Harriet Beecher Stowe* (New York, 1969).
39. Mrs. Stowe has deliberately linked her characters to their sources. The Cambridge edition of *Dred* includes Nat Turner's *Confessions* as an appendix; and among the "anti-slavery tales and papers" which fill out the volume is an essay on Sojourner Truth. Milly Edmundson's story is included in *Key*, pp. 155-67. In discussing sources for the novel, it should be noted that Mrs. Stowe provided an introductory note to C. G. Parsons, *Inside View of Slavery: or, A Tour Among the Planters* (Boston and Cleveland, 1855). The book includes an anecdote about a rebellious slave named Dread, pp. 224-31.
40. Proslavery "answers" to *Uncle Tom's Cabin* are discussed in Jeanette Tandy, "Pro-Slavery Propaganda in American Fiction in the Fifties," *South Atlantic Quarterly*, XXI, 41-50, 170-78. "Tommania" is handled in Charles Briggs, "Uncle Tomitudes," *Putnam's Monthly Magazine*, I (January 1853), 97-102. For Uncle Tom on the stage, see F. S. Arnett, "Fifty Years of Uncle Tom," *Munsey's*, XXVII (September 1902), 897-903. See also Chester E. Jorgenson, *Uncle Tom's Cabin as Book and Legend* (Detroit, 1952); and Herbert Ross Brown, "Uncle Tom's and Other Cabins," *The Sentimental Novel in America, 1789-1860* (Durham, 1940). The publishing revolution is discussed in Donald E. Liedel, "The Antislavery Novel, 1836-1861," unpubl. diss. (Michigan, 1961).

41. Henry C. Wright in *The Liberator,* July 9, 1852.
42. Mrs. Stowe's militant Unionist position is recounted in *Life and Letters,* Chapter 9, and elsewhere. Her increasingly simplistic stereotyping of black people is made clear in *Life in Florida After the War,* "Our Florida Plantation," *Palmetto Leaves,* and in her letters. See, for example, *Life and Letters,* pp. 304, 381. She died in 1896.

CHAPTER VIII

WILLIAM WELLS BROWN

Black militant Henry Highland Garnet delivered an impassioned speech urging the slaves to strike for freedom at a National Convention of Colored Citizens held in Buffalo, New York, in 1843.

> Brethren, arise, arise! Strike for your lives and liberties. Now is the day and the hour. Let every slave throughout the land do this, and the days of slavery are numbered. You cannot be more oppressed than you have been—you cannot suffer greater cruelties than you have already. *Rather die freemen than live to be slaves*. Remember that you are FOUR MILLIONS!

Criticized in *The Liberator* for the aggressiveness of his position, Garnet answered with a letter to the editor articulating the tensions between black and white abolitionists:

> [T]he address to the slaves you seem to doom to the most fiery trials . . . you say that I "have received bad counsel."

You are not the only person who has told your humble
servant that his humble productions have been produced
by the 'counsel' of some anglo-saxon. I have expected no
more from ignorant slaveholders and their apologists, but
I really looked for better things from Mrs. Maria W. Chapman, an anti-slavery poetess, and editor *pro tem.* of the
Boston Liberator. I can think on the subject of human
rights without 'counsel' either from the men of the West,
or the women of the East.[1]

Among the black antislavery men who heard Garnet's words
was William Wells Brown, a fugitive slave serving as delegate from
Buffalo, his adopted home. Brown's first published writing is a
letter to the *National Anti-Slavery Standard* correcting Garnet's
report of the proceedings of this convention. Ten years later, a
celebrated refugee in England, he would publish a novel. His book
Clotel, like Garnet's speech written to advance the antislavery
cause, is the first major attempt of an Afro-American to reshape
his experiences into fiction.[2]

William Wells Brown was born near Lexington, Kentucky
about 1814—he never was certain because no records of slave
births were kept—one of seven children of Elizabeth, a field hand
on Dr. John Young's farm. Each of his mother's children was
fathered by a different man—William by his master's white half-
brother. His status is symbolized by his names. He was originally
named William, but, to avoid confusion in the Big House after a
young nephew of his master, similarly named, came there to live,
was called Sanford. When the slave boy refused to answer to this,
he was beaten. This arbitrary denial of his name signified to him
his lack of identity and his status as chattel. For him, the assertion
of manhood involved the assumption of a name. Scorning to call
himself after his natural father or his master, he gratefully assumed
the name of the Quaker Wells Brown, who sheltered him in his
flight. For the young fugitive, freedom transformed the thing
called Sanford into the man William Wells Brown.

When he escaped North at the age of twenty or twenty-one,

William Wells Brown had traveled widely and experienced many diverse forms of slavery. He had lived on farms in Kentucky and Missouri, on the river traveling the Mississippi between St. Louis and New Orleans, and in the city of St. Louis. He had worked at dozens of jobs for his owners, and for masters to whom he had been hired. From earliest childhood the young man had dreamed of freedom and had made one disastrous effort to reach Canada before he successfully escaped from slavery in the midwinter of 1834. Familiar with shipping as a result of his work on the Mississippi, Brown found employment on the Great Lakes. For nine years, he worked on Lake Erie, making his home first in Cleveland, then in Buffalo.

Brown had gotten a little learning while in slavery. In later reminiscences he wrote that with some of the first wages earned as a free man, he bought a spelling book and some candy to bribe the two small sons of his employer to teach him his letters. He then practiced writing his new name on fences and noted the corrections made by children who watched. As soon as he had achieved minimal literacy, Brown, who like many later immigrants used newspapers as textbooks, subscribed to the *Genius of Universal Emancipation* and *The Liberator*. When he had been hired out to a tavernkeeper as a slave boy, Brown had been repelled by drunkenness; as a free man, he attended meetings of the local temperance society, and became accustomed to public speaking through discussions condemning John Barleycorn.

Like many other black sailors, Brown helped smuggle fugitives to freedom in Canada—Henson was aided by such a man—and by the 1840s he had made his home a haven for runaways and a hostel for traveling abolitionist lectures. Nine years after his escape from slavery, he joined their ranks.

As a black abolitionist, Welliam Wells Brown was a potential target for violence. In 1844, at a church in Aurora, New York, he faced an angry mob after being pelted with rotten eggs, and came down from the pulpit to taunt them as cowardly, saying that if they had been enslaved, as he had, not one would have had nerve enough to escape. Startled by his audacity the crowd quieted, and he spoke for more than an hour, telling the story of his life, and ending with an appeal for black freedom. One of his listeners, impressed by his performance, let slip that the exit had been rigged so that, on signal, Brown, who was to have been run out of the church, would be doused with flour. When the most respectable members of the mob passed underneath, Brown himself hollered, "Let it slide!"—and relished his revenge. Trained in this rough school, he became a skillful speaker, and after four years of lecturing in western New York, he accepted an appointment from the New England Anti-Slavery Society. He moved his wife and children to Boston, the center of the movement, where except for the five years he would spend in exile, Brown would live for the rest of his long life.

In late 1847, with the help of Edmund Quincy, Brown quickly composed his memoirs, shaping his book as he shaped his speeches, into a weapon against racism and chattel slavery.[3] He dedicated his *Narrative* to Wells Brown:

> Thirteen years ago, I came to your door, a weary fugitive from chains and stripes. I was a stranger, and you took me in. I was hungry, and you fed me. Naked was I, and you clothed me. Even a name by which to be known among men, slavery denied me. You bestowed upon me your own. Base, indeed, should I be, if ever I forget what I owe to you, or do anything to disgrace that honored name! ([iii])

In contrast to the self-justification of Henson and the self-pity of Clarke, the special note of Brown's autobiography is his use of humor, his revelation of the witty combat waged by the slave in his struggle against his master.[4] He had seen much in his twenty years of bondage, as he worked in the field, the Big House, the office, the stable; in taverns, steamboats, restaurants, print shops, barbershops, slave coffles. Brown crammed his book with incident, detail, and anecdote, in addition to snatches of polemic and sentimental poetry.

In the main Brown tells his tale simply and directly, with enough detachment to write with humor. He is passionate, however, in his outraged recital of his childhood initiation into the brutalities of slavery, when he had heard his mother's cries as she was whipped. He recalls the "breaking" of the defiant slave Randall; the whipping of the pretty slave girl Patsy by her jealous master (reminiscent of *Archy Moore*); himself being hunted and treed by dogs, then jailed, whipped, and "smoked" as punishment for running off to the woods to escape a violent master; being caned by a white man for defending himself against the man's son.

Early determined to attempt escape, he was deterred by his sister, who begged him not to leave her and their mother behind in slavery. His desire for freedom was intensified by his experiences serving Walker, the slave trader. "Heart-sick at seeing my fellow creatures bought and sold," after his first trip to the Southern market, William begged his owner not to make him complete his services with the slave trader, but he was forced to make two more trips with the coffle. There, among other jobs, it was William's task to prepare the slaves for sale. Accordingly, he shaved their gray beards, plucked out or blackened their white hairs, schooled them to answer queries about former masters, and assigned them younger ages. He describes how they were displayed in the New Orleans slave pens:

> Before the slaves were exhibited for sale, they were dressed and driven out into the yard. Some were set to dancing, some to jumping, some to singing, and some to playing cards. This was done to make them appear cheerful and happy. My business was to see that they were placed in those situations before the arrival of the purchasers, and I have often set them to dancing when their cheeks were wet with tears. (46)

He returned to St. Louis to learn that his sister had been sold South and that his owner, short of cash, planned to sell him to a new master. William fled North with his mother. Although they got across to the Illinois shore and followed the star, after walking ten nights they were captured and taken back to St. Louis. As punishment, William's mother was sold South. The final scene between mother and son, in which she absolves him of responsibility for her plight and urges him to continue to try to escape to freedom, is extremely sentimental; but Brown's description of his subsequent adventures is more straightforward.

His uncle-owner, who had promised William's father not to sell him South, now sold him to a St. Louis man, and despite the kindness of his purchaser, the young slave brooded. Sold again, he accompanied his new master on a trip to Cincinnati, and escaped on New Year's Day, 1834. In his second attempt to reach Canada, he was extremely wary:

> I had long since made up my mind that I would not trust myself in the hands of any man, white or colored. The slave is brought up to look upon every white man as an enemy to him and his race; and twenty-one years in slavery had taught me that there were traitors, even among colored people. (95-96)

He matter of factly describes how he suffered from hunger; worse, from cold. After traveling several days, in desperation he hailed a man in a broad-brimmed hat and long coat. It was Brown, the Quaker, who sheltered and nursed the fugitive for a fortnight, then directed him north. In another week the newly named William Wells Brown reached Cleveland and got a job in a hotel, intending to wait for the ice to break up so that he could get to Canada. Instead, he moved on to Buffalo, where he studied, worked, and involved himself in the abolitionist movement. The *Narrative* is a conglomeration of sensational violence, sentimentalism, long discussions of servile marriage and religion, and diatribes against the hypocrisy of American democracy and Christianity. Its over-all style is anecdotal.

Brown tells a story well. Most interesting is his reversal of the plantation convention: Here the white master is the butt of the black slave's humor. Thus Brown includes sketches illustrating the battle of wits between master and slave, in which the clever black man triumphs, often by playing dumb; he sometimes even outsmarts himself. He tells how, as house servant, he took care to sit near the julep pitcher when his newly converted master combined the routine of morning devotions with his time-honored practice of julep drinking—then wryly comments that "by the time prayer was over, I was about as happy as any of them" (37). In Vicksburg, sent to the jail by the slave trader Walker with a note ordering his whipping, Brown paid a man fifty cents to deliver the letter; he then wet his eyes and returned home while the other received his punishment. (This hoax bothered Brown because it involved not only outsmarting his master, but exploiting another black man; after recounting it, he comments that it demonstrates the meanness slaves resort to under a brutal system. He dropped the episode from later editions of his *Narrative*.) Only by means of deception was he able to make the trip which culminated in his escape. When questioned by his apprehensive new master, who feared he might run away if taken North, Brown lied, saying that he had traveled to Ohio before, but "never liked a free State" (90). In these anecdotes, Brown develops a black figure of central importance in the oral tradition of Afro-Americans, but omitted in plantation fiction, the Henson and Clarke narratives, and the Hildreth and Stowe novels: the trickster who outsmarts The Man by "hitting a straight lick with a crooked stick." [5]

By 1847, when his book appeared, Brown was becoming well known as an antislavery lecturer, and reviewers who had begun to notice slave autobiographies found his lively narrative "interesting," even "thrilling." It sold well—8000 copies in less than eighteen months—and Brown brought out an expanded edition two years later, which is strengthened because he omitted much of the sentimental poetry and added an exciting chapter describing a battle in which he and other black residents of Buffalo defeated an attempted kidnapping by slave catchers.[6]

Like all the other slave narratives, however, Brown's book suffers in comparison with a slim volume that appeared in 1845. Most slave autobiographies chart the writer's adventures as a slave, fugitive, and freeman, but this powerful book traces the author's unfolding consciousness from unquestioning chattel to ungovernable rebel. Frederick Douglass' *Narrative* is a classic American autobiography.[7]

The book begins with the small boy's enforced separation from his mother, and recounts his initiation into the evil of slavery when, hiding in a closet, he watched a jealous master whip his pretty Aunt Hester. The distance between naive protagonist and self-conscious narrator is established in a short passage on the music of the slaves:

> I did not, when a slave, understand the deep meaning of those rude and apparently incoherent songs. I was myself within the circle; so that I neither saw nor heard as those without might see and hear. They told a tale of woe which was then altogether beyond my feeble comprehension; they were tones loud, long, and deep; they breathed the prayer and complaint of souls boiling over with the bitterest anguish. Every tone was a testimony against slavery, and a prayer to God for deliverance from chains. The hearing of these wild notes always depressed my spirit, and filled me with ineffable sadness. . . . To those songs I trace my first glimmering conception of the dehumanizing character of slavery.[8] (37)

The controlled intensity which is the hallmark of Douglass' *Narrative* results from this detachment. Despite his inclusion of villainous characters and sensational incidents, Douglass indicts a system rather than individuals. His restraint and objectivity give his book force.

The young slave early learned the necessity of masking his thoughts before his master. After describing childhood in the quarter, he tells of his providential reprieve from the farm and his service in Baltimore under a different branch of the family. At first, he was enchanted by his new kind mistress who taught him his letters; but his studies were soon stopped. Douglass learned an important lesson about the opposing interests of master and slave, and about the means he could use to achieve his goals, when he heard his master admonish his mistress for her dangerous foolishness in teaching a slave to read:

> What he most dreaded, that I most desired. What he most loved, that I most hated. That which to him was a great evil, to be carefully shunned, was to me a great good, to be diligently sought. . . . In learning to read, I owe almost as much to the bitter opposition of my master, as to the kindly aid of my mistress. I acknowledge the benefit of both. (59)

The young slave's awareness was fed by his stolen contact with white boys with whom he discussed the future, and by his covert study of nineteenth-century schoolbooks which featured the standard orations on liberty. He began to notice newspaper references to "abolitionists," and one day a sympathetic Irishman, whom he had helped on the docks, advised him to run away. His consciousness of his condition was intensified when, on the death of his owner, he was ordered back to the farm to be inventoried with the rest of the property. There he was witness to the abandonment of his old grandmother, whose offspring peopled the plantation and comprised its wealth, by the callous heirs. Douglass was luckily sent back to Baltimore, but a few years later, in consequence of a quarrel in his master's family, he was returned to the farm to serve as field hand. The young slave's contempt for his new master's hypocritical religiosity must have been obvious, for after a few months he was sent to Covey, a poor white neighbor who had a local reputation as a slave-breaker.

As the narrator describes his degradation under Covey's brutal regime, the story moves toward its climax. After six months of mistreatment, exhausted and ill, Frederick was attacked by Covey, who intended to tie and whip him as a punishment. The young man unexpectedly fought back. After two hours the slave was still unsubdued. Although he remained in bondage for four more years, Frederick had asserted his freedom:

> I felt as I never felt before. It was a glorious resurrection, from the tomb of slavery, to the heaven of freedom. My long-crushed spirit rose, cowardice departed, bold defiance took its place; and I now resolved that, however long I might remain a slave in form, the day had passed forever when I could be a slave in fact. I did not hesitate to let it be known of me, that the white man who expected to succeed in whipping, must also succeed in killing me. (105)

He was never beaten again.

After this climactic assertion of his independence, the narrator quickly recites his subsequent adventures. In consequence of plotting an escape with friends, he is betrayed, seized, and imprisoned. Miraculously sent back to Baltimore, he learns a trade, fights racist apprentices, is permitted to hire his own time, and plans another escape. The contrast between the psychological bias of this narrative and the externality of those which climax in an exciting escape is heightened by Douglass' suppression of the story of his run for freedom. He briefly discusses his fear and loneliness as a fugitive in the North, then tells of his acquaintance with abolitionists and of their aid. A description of his life in freedom—his naming, his work, and his encounters with Northern race prejudice—provides a quiet ending to the *Narrative,* which closes with a short discussion of his early efforts on behalf of his enslaved brothers.

Douglass' *Narrative* is somehow less an American success story than a hero tale. This is due not only to the distancing between protagonist and narrator and to the handling of concrete character and incident as suggestive of a larger pattern, but also to the sparseness and the symbolic richness of the detail. Thus the chapter devoted to the lavish wealth of the master, which follows a discussion of the impoverishment of the slaves, begins with a description of Colonel Lloyd's walled garden. Rich with fruits and flowers, it is a forbidden Eden which tantalizes the boy Frederick and the other slaves. The symbol is natural, unstrained, and significant. Similarly, Douglass' first whipping by

Covey results from his awkwardness in handling a half-wild team
of oxen, a Herculean labor, surely. Douglass' *Narrative* is not a
flawless work of art, but it expresses more than the boundless incident and passion of the other slave autobiographies and of contemporary plantation and abolitionist fiction. Its symbolism, restraint, and intelligence give it a classic quality.

In 1855 Douglass published a new autobiography entitled
My Bondage and My Freedom.[9] The book differs greatly from
his earlier work. The *Narrative* is terse, dramatic, urgent; it is
the effort of a young man only seven years out of bondage to
establish the truth of his indictment of slavery, even at the risk of
endangering his precarious freedom by identifying himself publicly. (When Wendell Phillips first read the manuscript, he advised Douglass to burn it and avoid the chance of recapture.)
My Bondage and My Freedom, while powerful, is less intense, as
befits the autobiography of a free Afro-American abolitionist
orator and journalist who, despite his "somewhat positive repugnance to . . . personal notoriety," has published his memoirs both
to advance the cause of emancipation "by letting in the light of
truth upon a system," and to combat the racist assertion that
enslaved black people are "so low in the scale of humanity, and
so utterly stupid, that they are unconscious of their wrongs, and
do not apprehend their rights" (vii).[10]
    Douglass had become a lion on the platform in 1855, address-
ing audiences not only in the North, but throughout the British
Isles, where he had sought refuge after publication of the *Narrative.* On his return to America he had assumed an independent
role within the antislavery movement by establishing his own
newspaper, *The North Star.*[11] He had subsequently broken with
Garrison over his interpretation of the Constitution and had
become a leading advocate of political abolitionism. Douglass
indicates these changes in *My Bondage and My Freedom* when
he substitutes a tribute to Gerrit Smith for the earlier dedication
to Garrison, includes an introduction by black abolitionist James
McCune Smith in place of those by Garrison and Phillips, and
appends excerpts of his writings and orations instead of the de-

fense of his indictment of religion which had followed the *Narrative*.

Douglass expresses his two main purposes in the two sections into which he divides his book. The first twenty-one chapters deal with his life as a slave and his efforts to achieve his liberty, and the last three with his life in freedom and his work to end slavery in the South and prejudice in the North. The book is written in the easy manner of a skilled editor and orator, confident of both his audience and himself.

In *My Bondage and My Freedom* Douglass gives a much fuller account of his life, both subjectively and objectively, than he did in the *Narrative*. He expands the description of his early childhood into five full chapters, in which he presents a detailed discussion of his boyhood on a great Maryland plantation in the early 1820s. (They provide a fascinating contrast to *Swallow Barn*.) Douglass writes of his first glimmerings of his condition and—bitter fruits of his growing self-awareness—of his hatred for his master and despair for his future. Perhaps to answer the critics who had accused him of atheism, he adds a chapter dealing with his religious conversion at adolescence and develops the incident which he had barely mentioned in the 1845 edition, of his church-going master leading a white mob to smash a Sabbath school for slaves Douglass was organizing. He expands the climactic center of the first section, his victimization by Covey and his ultimate assertion of his manhood, from one into three chapters, and he fills four more chapters with accounts of his subsequent adventures in slavery.

In the second section, inevitably less spectacular, he handles his early experiences in freedom, and brings his story up to date by adding a discussion of the abolitionist work he had undertaken in America and in England in the decade since the appearance of the *Narrative*. In the first of two new chapters, he describes the circumstances surrounding the writing of the book and tells of his experiences as a refugee in England, where for the first time he felt free not only from slavery but also from prejudice. In the last, Douglass stresses his battle against Northern racism and comments on prejudice within the antislavery movement. Discussing his break with Garrison, he argues the value of political action as a weapon against slavery, and ends with the vow to work for "the universal and unconditional emancipation of my entire race."

In *My Bondage and My Freedom* the mature Douglass produced an autobiography which ranks with the memoirs of his greatest countrymen, and critics have judged it his most finished work.[12] But by reason of its very completeness and of the ease with which it moves from detailed description to comment and argument, the book lacks the dramatic impact of the *Narrative*. That stark volume stands on its own, a complement to the fuller autobiography.

In 1882 Douglass, now everywhere recognized as the spokesman of his people, published his *Life and Times*.[13] Like *My Bondage and My Freedom,* the book is divided into two sections. Although he worked the text into a more succinct form, in the first part Douglass follows the plan of his earlier autobiography. In the second he gives an inside view of the political history of the preceding half-century. Building on the materials included in the latter section of *My Bondage and My Freedom,* Douglass tells the story of his escape North—slavery long abolished, it is now safe to do so—and adds countless reminiscences of his abolitionist days, including memories of Harriet Stowe and John Brown. He describes the long struggle waged during the Civil War to achieve Emancipation. Discussing Reconstruction, he tells of the fight for the Fourteenth and Fifteenth Amendments, and chronicles his public career in the recent past. A massive new edition of the book appeared in 1892 with a third section, concerning Douglass' later life, added to the 1882 text.[14] The value of both versions of Douglass' third autobiography is expressed in his concluding remarks to the 1882 edition, formulated in his finished style:

> I have written out my experience here, not in order to exhibit my wounds and bruises and to awaken and attract sympathy to myself personally, but as a part of the history of a profoundly interesting period in American life and

progress. I have meant it to be a small contribution to the
sum of knowledge of this special period, to be handed
down to after-coming generations which may want to know
what things were allowed and what prohibited—what
moral, social, and political relations subsisted between the
different varieties of the American people down to the
last quarter of the nineteenth century and by what means
they were modified and changed. The time is at hand when
the last American slave and the last American slaveholder
will disappear behind the curtain which separates the living from the dead and when neither master nor slave will
be left to tell the story of their respective relations or what
happened to either in those relations. My part has been
to tell the story of the slave. The story of the master never
wanted for narrators. (478-79)

In 1848, while Douglass was lecturing in England and
Brown was speaking in New England, the daring escape of a young
slave couple who traveled from Georgia to Pennsylvania masquerading as master and servant, made a sensation in abolitionist
circles. Like Douglass and Brown, most fugitive slaves escaped
furtively, but a few had reached freedom by passing for white.
Black William Craft and his light-skinned wife Ellen adopted
the conventional social roles of devoted slave and invalid master
as a means of escaping the system they mimicked. Their use of
this deception appealed to the imagination (and perhaps stuck in
Melville's mind when a few years later he dramatized another
masquerade in "Benito Cereno"). The Crafts told their incredi-
ble story on antislavery lecture circuits on both sides of the
Atlantic and published an account of their escape in 1860. While
it shares the abolitionist purpose of the other narratives, *Running a Thousand Miles for Freedom,* a recital of the adventures
of a devoted husband and wife risking all for the chance to raise
a family in freedom, suggests not only the success story but the
domestic romance.[15]
    The Crafts, like Douglass, divided their book into two sec-

tions. They begin with brief sketches of their lives, and after numerous digressions, many illustrating the plight of the white slave girl, settle down to a recital of their exciting escape. After years of trying to think of a feasible plan, William hit on the idea of traveling as servant to Ellen, who would pass as white and masquerade as a man. (The male guise was essential because a young lady would not travel with a manservant.) He convinced his frightened wife to agree, and within a few days they had made preparations. William bought Ellen a suit of clothes and dark glasses, cut her hair, and bandaged her to hide her beardless chin and to give the appearance of an invalid perhaps too sick to socialize. Finally, knowing that in her role as traveling slaveholder the illiterate Ellen would be expected to sign hotel registers, he bandaged her right arm. Then they parted, and William went to the "Negro car" while Ellen bought train tickets North for herself and her slave.

Each stage of their flight was accompanied by narrow escapes. Ellen barely missed being detected when a friend of her master who had known her since childhood took a seat near her and began a conversation. Later, passengers who thought the invalid's actions strange questioned her slave William, but were satisfied by his answers. At Charleston, she was required to sign the register for passage north despite her bandages, but was saved when a drunken fellow passenger vouched for her. En route through North Carolina, two young ladies flirted with her while their accommodating father offered medical advice and invited the handsome invalid to his Virginia home for a visit. In Richmond a woman claimed William as her runaway slave—they all look so alike—and at Baltimore, required to produce proof of ownership before crossing to a free state, Ellen played the affronted South Carolina gentleman and stalled until the intimidated officer decided against delaying her. She almost panicked when she lost sight of William at Havre de Grace, but they finally arrived safely in Philadelphia.

In the second section, dealing with their life after fleeing the South, the Crafts recount a second escape from the North. They received aid from Philadelphia abolitionists (whom Ellen assumed were mulatto because she believed whites incapable of such kindness) and settled down in Boston. Here William resumed his trade as carpenter and Ellen found work as a seamstress. But their escape had been widely publicized, and they were much too prominent to remain safe after the Fugitive Slave Law of 1850 was passed. When federal writs were served against them, William bought a gun and secured his wife in hiding; but when word came that militia had been sent to Boston with Presidential orders for their arrest, the Vigilance Committee convinced him to leave the country.

Just as the flirtatious Southern belles provided some comic relief in the account of their first escape, anecdotes lampooning the color prejudice of Canadians add a humorous note to the second: Happy to accommodate a white lady, hotelkeepers were appalled when she shared her room with the black man they assumed was her servant. The Crafts end their account with a description of their voyage to Liverpool and a tribute to British democracy.

At the center of the book is the figure of Ellen, the white slave. Like Hildreth's fictional heroine, she was the daughter of her master by one of his slave women. Although like Lewis Clarke, she was given as a gift to a near relation, Ellen had a relatively easy life serving her sibling-mistress as lady's maid. She was permitted to marry the skilled slave William, whom she had long loved. But the story the Crafts tell about Ellen's mulatto aunt is a pathetic contrast to the Clarkes' romantic tale of their sister Delia, heiress of the Frenchman who bought, freed, and married her. Although Ellen's aunt was married by her master, at his death she and her children, legally slaves, were sold by the man claiming to be heir. The aunt died; and, while two of Ellen's cousins escaped, a third, bought to serve as concubine, committed suicide. The stress on the special pathos of the lives of these light-skinned slave women and the sensational revelation of William and Ellen Crafts' escapes made their story a smashing success on the lecture platform and between bookcovers, despite its lack of stylistic merit.

A year before the Crafts made their second escape, William Wells Brown, now a celebrated black abolitionist, was sent to Britain to rally antislavery support for the movement, as Douglass had done. He represented the American Peace Society at an International Peace Congress held in Paris, where he linked American militarism with racism, condemning the "war spirit of America which holds in bondage three million." [16] Then to avoid returning home and risking seizure under the newly passed Fugitive Slave Law, he settled in London and attempted to make his living as a man of letters. Brown wrote, read enormously, and lectured widely—on at least one tour, sharing the platform with the Crafts —in his five years abroad. His articles appeared regularly in the London press, and as foreign correspondence in *Frederick Douglass' Paper, The Liberator,* and other American abolitionist journals. In 1852 Brown compiled some of his letters in a volume entitled *Three Years in Europe; or, Places I Have Seen and People I Have Met.*[17] The book is an important contribution to nineteenth-century American travel literature not because of its easy style or the freshness of some of its matter, but because of its special point of view toward the United States, perhaps most clearly expressed in an open letter written by Brown to his last owner, Enoch Price:

> I will not yield to you in affection for America, but I hate her institution of Slavery. I love her, because I am identified with her enslaved millions by every tie that should bind man to his fellow man. The United States has disfranchized me, and declared that I am not a citizen, but a chattel: her Constitution dooms me to be your slave. But while I feel grieved that I am alienated and driven from my own country, I rejoice that, in this Land, I am regarded as a man. I am in England what I can never be in America while Slavery exists there.[18]

At a time when our classic white writers examined the Old World and returned home with visions of a native literature, our first black author, more akin to their expatriate descendants, saw Europe as a refuge from American tyranny.[19]

Many of Brown's writings, both before and after he met Ellen

Craft, included the figure of the beautiful white slave girl. In both versions of the *Narrative* he had commented on the mysterious light-skinned woman whom Walker, the slave trader, took on board at Hannibal, Missouri, and on the sad life of Walker's quadroon woman Cynthia. In *The Antislavery Harp,* an anthology of abolitionist songs he had edited before leaving America, he widened the circulation of a popular rumor by printing a poem lamenting the fate of the lovely white slave daughter of Thomas Jefferson.[20] He included a pathetic story, similar to that told by the Crafts about Ellen's beautiful cousins, in the catalog he wrote to accompany the Original Panoramic Views of the Scenes in the Life of an American Slave, which he exhibited in England in 1850.[21] Brown published a white-slave story with a happier ending, in which the rejected mulatto daughter of a proud Virginian is finally reunited with her penitent father, in *The Anti-Slavery Advocate.*[22]

In one chapter of *Three Years,* Brown worked up the white-slave theme involving the beautiful girl and her mulatto lover into a fully developed romance. Here the heroic George (slave son of a Congressman), under sentence of death for his participation in the Nat Turner insurrection, escapes from prison by disguising himself as Mary, his white slave paramour who impersonates him and remains in his cell. After a series of exciting adventures much like those Brown had told in his *Narrative,* the fugitive reaches Canada, where he works to earn money for Mary's freedom. Learning that she has disappeared after being sold to New Orleans as punishment for helping him escape, George emigrates to England, where he passes as white and tries to forget his lost love in hard work. Ten years later, after he has become a successful businessman, George vacations in France and encounters the still-lovely Mary, who had been rescued from slavery by a traveling Frenchman and taken home with him as his wife. Mary's husband having conveniently died, the melodramatic tale concludes with the happy wedding of the reunited lovers.

In 1853, a year after the astounding success of *Uncle Tom's Cabin* made it possible to publish abolitionist fiction, William Wells Brown gathered all these white-slave plots into a full-length novel. Guaranteeing its sensationalism by making use of the Jefferson scandal, he entitled his book *Clotel, or, the President's Daughter*.[23] The various melodramatic storylines are set in motion by the sale of the mulatto woman Currer, long-discarded consort of Jefferson, and her two daughters. She is separated from her children when she is bought by a hypocritical slave-holding parson, and dies midway through the novel. A minor plot line follows her lovely younger daughter, whose adventures are patterned after those of Ellen Craft's aunt. Although bought, educated, and wed by a white New England physician, at his death she and her daughters are sold into slavery. All are soon dead: the mother of shock, one girl of suicide, the other of a broken heart.

The main narrative, much of which clearly derives from Lydia Maria Child's sentimental antislavery tale "The Quadroons," concerns the fate of Currer's older daughter Clotel.[24] In Brown's novel, as in Mrs. Child's tale, the beautiful girl is a white slave victimized by the institution of slavery and its ideology of racism, which make her the property of her white aristocratic sweetheart but do not permit her to marry him, though she bears his child. But Brown changes Mrs. Child's pathetic story. When Clotel is cast off by her weak lover and sold by his jealous wife, instead of dying of a broken heart like Mrs. Child's rejected heroine, she disguises herself as Ellen Craft had, and escapes North with another slave masquerading as her black servant. She returns to Virginia in an attempt to find her daughter Mary, but because Nat Turner's insurrection has broken out, strangers are closely watched. Clotel is seized as a fugitive and taken to the slave pens in Washington. When she attempts to escape, slave-catchers trap her on the Long Bridge and, within sight of the nation's capitol, the President's daughter jumps to her death to avoid capture.

Brown's final white-slave plot, like Mrs. Child's, concerns his heroine's daughter. But instead of the pathetic chronicle of betrayal, rape, and suicide described in "The Quadroons," Brown retells the romance of Mary and George, complete with happy ending, which he had included in his travel book.

In addition to following the adventures of three generations of beautiful white slaves, *Clotel* includes as a minor plot a love story of white characters which is suggestive of Harriet Beecher Stowe's *Dred*, published three years later. This involves a Southern belle, an excellent girl who, expounding both abolitionism and Christianity, refutes her proslavery father and converts her antislavery lover. Ultimately she and her new husband free their slaves and settle them in Ohio.

What makes *Clotel* unique among the many antislavery novels published after *Uncle Tom's Cabin* is that in addition to interspersing the standard snatches of poetry and polemic among his melodramatic plots, its fugitive slave author inserts powerful realistic scenes of slave life. Brown, who had had a religious master, had seen the slave trade while serving a trader and as a slave on the block, had run away, been tracked by dogs, captured, and whipped, only to run off again and again, describes the life he has known. His parodies of slave sermons, his scenes of slave life in coffles, pens, and warehouses, his sketches of rebellious slaves, his anecdotes of ruses used by runaways, his examples of Jim Crow in the North—these give his novel value.

Perhaps the most jarring of these harsh digressions is his description, buttressed by newspaper clippings, of a slave hunt through the Mississippi swamps. The runaways are tracked by dogs and found, but, when one resists capture, his hunters judge him guilty of striking a white man. After assembling the slaves from surrounding plantations to teach them a lesson in obedience, the mob burns him at the stake.

Not all the interjections are grim. The humorous anecdotes which added to the vigor of Brown's slave narrative also give freshness to his sentimental novel. Thus the obviously transparent answer of the slave who was instructed to lie about his age says less about the simplicity of the black man than about the unscrupulousness of the white. Similarly, the sketch of the religious interrogation of a slave, who responds to questions about his creator with " 'De overseer told us last night who made us, but indeed I forgot the gentmun's name,' " while apparently attributing clownishness to the slave, actually exposes the hypocrisy of his master, who claimed he had given his people religious instruction (134).

Brown uses this ironic humor not only as a weapon against the white master, but also against black acceptance of the doctrine of white supremacy. Black Sam is comical when he judges mulattoes handsomer than blacks and lies about the color of his mother's skin. Brown lampoons his practice of greasing his hair with butter in precisely the same way, and for the same reason, that in our time Malcolm X ridiculed the conk—because it represents an effort to look white. In contrast to the plantation novels, which find comedy in the crudeness of the slaves' imitations of their masters, what is here seen as ludicrous is the black man's acceptance of white standards, his rejection of his blackness.

The vitality of *Clotel* lies in these passages, but their tone grates harshly against the conventional plots and genteel characters. The sentimental novel was not an adequate vehicle to express black experience, and Brown did not republish his book in this form when, his freedom bought by British abolitionists, he returned to America in 1854 to continue his work as writer and reformer.

The next version is a marked improvement. Retitled *Miralda, or the Beautiful Quadroon,* the novel appeared in an extensively revised form as a serial in the *Weekly Anglo-African* during the winter of 1860.[25] Brown reduces the number of white-slave plots and makes them more cohesive. Although he retains the initial situation, the sale of a mulatto mother and her fair daughters, now they are only incidentally linked to Jefferson. He de-emphasizes the secondary storyline dealing with the younger daughter and omits that concerning the white lovers. The plot concerning the older daughter Clotel, here renamed Isabelle, which dramatizes the victimization of a white slave by her lover-master, is made secondary. His central narrative now follows her daughter, here called Miralda, whose adventures he expands from three chapters to sixteen.

Brown's heroine remains the same genteel figure we saw in the travel book sketch and in the first version of the novel, and the large outlines of her adventures are not varied. But Brown has changed the Mary-Miralda story radically because the man she loves is no longer the rebellious mulatto George, but the black slave rebel, Jerome. In this version, George-Jerome is an heroic African who scorns to submit to a whipping, knocks down his tyrannical master, and escapes. Here it is George-Jerome, not an anonymous slave, who is hunted by dogs and caught. When imprisoned and condemned, he defies his oppressors, asserting that " 'the day will come when the Negro will learn that he can get his freedom by fighting for it,' " and telling them, " 'if I had my life to live over again, I would use all the energies which God has given me to get up an insurrection' " (Jan. 26, 1861). Brown describes his flight North, after Mary-Miralda takes his place in prison, in much greater detail than before, and now sketches a number of incidents included in the *Narrative*. He develops George-Jerome's British adventures at length, and after he has re-united his happy lovers, expands the story to include another white-slave plot. Traveling in Europe, the hero and heroine encounter Mary-Miralda's father who has gone mad with guilt. When his daughter's forgiving love has cured the Virginian, he accepts the black man as a son and liberates the slaves on the old plantation.

In addition to giving a greater coherence to the story line, Brown also improves *Miralda* by deleting much of the distracting poetry and polemic he had included in *Clotel*. The shifts from conventional sentimental romance to stark reportage are less abrupt than in the earlier version because Brown incorporates some of the incidents into his narrative and omits or softens others. For example, the descriptions of the lynching and of the slaves' religious instruction do not reappear, and the sketch of the slave pens is abbreviated. The result is a more unified tone. But though individual passages are not as forceful, the realism which gave substance to the first edition is not completely lacking in *Miralda*. The revised novel has a stronger impact as a result of Brown's deletions and revisions and, most important, in consequence of his characterization of a militant black hero.

In 1864, Brown again republished his novel, this time as *Clotelle*,[26] but this revision was not so fortunate. The various titles of the novel become confusing. In *Clotelle* the structure and characters are essentially those of *Miralda*, but the white slave heroine of the central plot, who takes her lover's place in prison and is reunited with him in France, called first Mary and then Miralda, is here renamed Clotelle. Her pathetic mother is no longer Jefferson's daughter, but the child of an anonymous Senator. In this revision the realistic passages have been weakened still more. The tone is now smooth. The rough humor, stark brutality, and pointed debate which gave the novel vitality are trimmed, toned down, almost obliterated. If the skin of its hero were not colored black, the book would be a conventional sentimental antislavery novel.

After the Civil War, Brown brought the edition up to date and republished it as *Clotelle; or, the Colored Heroine.* Brown, who is perhaps best known as an historian, was then writing a history of Afro-American troops in the Civil War, and he added four new chapters to his novel, in which he recounts how Mary-Miralda-Clotelle and George-Jerome return to America to aid the Union.[27] Jerome joins the gallant black First Louisiana Regiment but is killed in an attempt to recover the body of his white commander. The book ends as Clotelle, who has served as a nurse at Andersonville and aided in the escape of Union prisoners and black slaves, returns to Mississippi to dedicate her life to the education of the freedmen.

An examination of the different versions of William Wells Brown's novel reveals changing views of chattel slavery and of black people. Throughout all the revisions, slavery is seen as evil; but in *Clotel,* although the plots dramatize its wrongs in terms of the sexual victimization of beautiful white slave women and the repression of heroic sons of white Revolutionary fathers, the digressions counterpoint this sensational view by dramatizing a violent struggle waged by masters and darker-skinned slaves. The author shows less of this warfare in *Miralda,* and almost completely ignores it in *Clotelle.* The result is that slavery, while consistently castigated, is attacked in an increasingly sentimental manner. The intense hortatory passages of *Clotel* become the stock platitudes of *Miralda* and *Clotelle.*

The author also shifts his vision of black people. The personalities of his genteel female white slaves are essentially the same, though their tastes and fortunes vary. All the versions of the book include a beautiful mulatto victimized by a white man's betrayal, but in *Clotel* Brown focusses on this figure, while in *Miralda* and *Clotelle* he shifts his emphasis to the mulatto woman who finds happiness with a black rebel. Although in the later versions Mary-

Miralda-Clotelle's lover remains essentially the same figure portrayed earlier, his blackness is now insisted upon, his role is em-
phasized, and he speaks the militant words Garnet had used a generation before. Jerome represents a new character in American
fiction: a militant black man as romantic hero.

   Recognizing that black letters in America has been "a literature of necessity," critics have seen as prophetic William Wells
Brown's use of the novel to achieve social and political ends; but
they have criticized him for focussing on a white-skinned, aristocratic figure, at no time representative of black America.[28] Although his heroine does not die when discarded by her white
lover, like Mrs. Child's quadroon on whom she was modeled,
and although her daughter's lover is a black rebel who is presented as a romantic hero—all of these are essentially conventional sentimental figures. More important for the future of
Afro-American literature is Brown's Black Sam. Early in *Clotel*
he seems a humorous figure; his acceptance of white standards
makes him an object of ridicule and his anecdotes are used for
comic relief. But we later see another Black Sam, whose secret
celebration of a hated master's death while he outwardly expresses conventional sorrow, and whose assumption of responsibility for managing the estate and helping his fellow slaves
prepare for freedom hint at a figure with some of the force and
complexity of the slave narrators. Sketched briefly in *Clotel* and
almost ignored in later versions, in this ironic, tough black man,
Brown suggests the character who will reappear as the vernacular
hero of black fiction. Although in succeeding editions William
Wells Brown sacrificed the vitality which informed his novel to
the demands of the sentimental romance, *Clotel* was not a false
beginning.

NOTES—CHAPTER VIII

   1. For a brief discussion of the Convention Movement before the Civil
   War, see John Hope Franklin, *From Slavery to Freedom*, 2nd ed. (New
   York, 1967), pp. 233-34. The standard work on the Convention Move-

ment is Howard H. Bell, "A Survey of the Negro Convention Movement, 1830-1861," unpubl. diss. (Northwestern, 1953).

According to Vernon Loggins, *The Negro Author: His Development in America to 1900* (New York, 1931; Port Washington, N.Y.,
1964), p. 432, Garnet included his speech, under the title "An Address
—to the Slaves of the United States. Rejected by the National Convention, 1843" in an edition of Walker's *Appeal* which he edited in 1843.
Loggins, p. 192, repeats the tradition that Garnet got out this volume
at John Brown's "instigation and expense."

Antislavery responses to the possibility of servile insurrection are
discussed in Robert H. Abzug, "The Influence of Garrisonian Abolitionists' Fears of Slave Violence on the Antislavery Argument, 1829-
1840," *Journal of Negro History*, LV (January, 1970), 15-28.

Garnet's letter, which appeared in *The Liberator*, December 3,
1843, is reproduced in *The Mind of the Negro as Reflected in Letters
Written During the Crisis 1800-1860*, ed. Carter G. Woodson (Washington, D.C., 1926), pp. 194-95.

2. Information on Brown's life was obtained from the following sources:
William Edward Farrison, *William Wells Brown, Author and Reformer*
(Chicago, 1969); Edward M. Coleman, "William Wells Brown as an
Historian," *Journal of Negro History*, XXXI (January 1946), 47-59;
[Carter G. Woodson], "William Wells Brown," *Dictionary of American
Biography*, ed. Allen Johnson and Dumas Malone (New York, 1929,
1958), II, 161; [Josephine Brown], *Biography of an American Bondman.
By His Daughter* (Boston, 1856); J. C. Hathaway, "Preface," *William
Wells Brown, Narrative of William W. Brown, a Fugitive Slave* (Bos-
ton, 1847); Alonzo D. Moore, "Memoir of the Author," William Wells
Brown, *The Rising Son; or, The Antecedents and Advancement of the
Colored Race* (Boston, 1874); William Farmer, "Memoir of William
Wells Brown," William Wells Brown, *Three Years in Europe; Or,
Places I Have Seen and People I Have Met* (London and Edinburgh,
1852).

Many of Brown's works contain autobiographical materials, includ-
ing the following: "Memoir of the Author," in *The Rising Son; or,
The Antecedents and Advancement of the Colored Race* (Boston,
1874); "Narrative of the Life and Escape of William Wells Brown,"
in *Clotel* (London, 1853); *Narrative of William W. Brown, a Fugitive
Slave* (Boston, 1847); *Narrative of William W. Brown, an American
Slave* (London, 1849); "Memoir of the Author," *The Black Man: His
Antecedents, His Genius, and His Achievements* (New York and
Boston, 1863); *Three Years in Europe: Or, Places I have Seen and
People I Have Met* (London and Edinburgh, 1852).

3. *Narrative of William W. Brown, a Fugitive Slave, Written by Himself*
(Boston, 1847). Quincy, whose letter to Brown serves as introduction
to the book, says that he has merely corrected "clerical" errors (vi).
Parenthetical page numbers in my text refer to this edition.

4. Discussions of Brown's *Narrative* can be found in Margaret Young
Jackson, "An Investigation of Biographies and Autobiographies of

American Slaves Published Between 1840 and 1860 . . . ," unpubl. diss. (Cornell, 1954); Charles H. Nichols, "A Study of the Slave Narrative," unpubl. diss. (Brown, 1948); Marion W. Starling, "The Slave Narrative: Its Place in American Literary History," unpubl. diss. (New York University, 1946); J. Saunders Redding, *To Make A Poet Black* (Chapel Hill, N.C., 1939); Vernon Loggins; and Arna Bontemps, "The Negro Contribution to American Letters," *The American Negro Reference Book*, ed. John P. Davis (New Jersey, 1966), pp. 850-79. I am greatly indebted to Prof. Bontemps' essay, which suggests that *Clotel* is the link between the slave narratives and black fiction.

5. See *Lay My Burden Down: A Folk History of Slavery*, ed. B. A. Botkin (Chicago, 1945), p. 2.

6. *Narrative of William W. Brown, an American Slave, Written by Himself* (London, 1849). Reviews quoted are from the Boston *Whig*, the New Bedford *Bulletin*, and the Lawrence *Courier*. They can be found in the 1849 edition, along with the information about sales. This edition also includes a letter, poems, and testimonials. It is these that thicken the volume; the narrative, while slightly longer, is not, as Redding claims, pp. 23-30, "spun out to twice its original length."

7. *Narrative of the Life of Frederick Douglass, an American Slave. Written by Himself* (Boston, 1845). Parenthetical page numbers in my text refer to an edition edited by Benjamin Quarles (Cambridge, Mass., 1960).

I have obtained biographical information about Douglass from this and the three other versions of his autobiography, cited below; and from Benjamin Quarles, *Frederick Douglass* (Washington, D.C., 1948); and Philip S. Foner, *Frederick Douglass* (New York, 1950, 1964).

8. This is one of the earliest serious discussions of this music. Also see Thomas Wentworth Higginson, "Negro Spirituals," *Army Life in a Black Regiment* (Boston, 1869); and W. E. B. DuBois' seminal essay, "Of the Sorrow Songs," *The Souls of Black Folk* (Chicago, 1903).

9. Frederick Douglass, *My Bondage and My Freedom* (New York and Auburn, 1855). Parenthetical page number in my text refers to this edition.

10. The difference in style is evident in the two versions of the following passage:

> 1845: "You have seen how a man was made a slave; you shall see how a slave was made a man. On one of the hottest days of the month of August, 1833 . . ." (97).
> 1855: "You have, dear reader, seen one humbled, degraded, broken down, enslaved, and brutalized, and you understand how it was done; now let us see the converse of all this, and how it was brought about; and this will take us through the year 1834" (222).

11. In 1851 the title was changed to *Frederick Douglass' Paper*. The newspaper was published weekly at Rochester, New York, from December, 1847 to June, 1860; then monthly until August, 1863. *Douglass'*

Monthly first appeared in June, 1858, and was issued concurrently with the weekly for two years.

12. See Loggins, pp. 143-45. For other discussions of Douglass' literary style, see Redding, pp. 31-38; Alain Locke, "Forward," Frederick Douglass, *Life and Times,* Centenary Memorial Subscriber's ed. (New York, 1941), pp. xv-xx; Rayford W. Logan, "Introduction," Frederick Douglass, *Life and Times* (New York, 1962), pp. 16-17; Benjamin Quarles, "Introduction," Frederick Douglass, *Narrative* (Cambridge, 1960), pp. xvi ff.; George L. Ruffin, "Introduction," Frederick Douglass, *Life and Times* (Hartford, Conn., 1882), pp. 17, 21.

13. Frederick Douglass, *Life and Times of Frederick Douglass, Written By Himself* (Hartford, Conn., 1882).

14. Frederick Douglass, *Life and Times of Frederick Douglass, Written By Himself,* rev. ed. (Boston, 1892). This text is readily available in an edition published by Collier Books (New York and London, 1962). The page reference in my text is to this volume.
   Douglass' public career climaxed in his appointment as Minister to Haiti by President Harrison in 1889. He died in 1895.

15. William and Ellen Craft, *Running a Thousand Miles for Freedom or, The Escape of William and Ellen Craft from Slavery* (London, 1860).
   Most commentators believe that the Crafts wrote their book themselves. See, for example, Starling, p. 333. Sterling Brown, however, in "The American Race Problem as Reflected in American Literature," *Journal of Negro Education,* VIII (July 1939), 275-90, lists this among dictated narratives.

16. Brown is quoted in William Farmer, p. xiii.

17. William Wells Brown, *Three Years in Europe: or, Places I Have Seen and People I Have Met . . .* (London and Edinburgh, 1852).

18. The letter, doubtless inspired by Douglass' famous letter to his former master, is dated London, November 23, 1849. It appeared in *The Liberator,* December 14, 1849, and is included in Woodson, pp. 213-16.

19. According to Farrison, the book was well received, and was reviewed in British journals. After his return to Boston, Brown published a revised edition under the title, *The American Fugitive in Europe; Sketches of Places and People Abroad . . .* (Boston, Cleveland, and New York, 1855). Omitted from this version are "A Narrative of American Slavery," now *Clotel;* and some of the abolitionist material. More travel chapters are added, and in a final chapter Brown discusses his reactions on his return to America. More finished than *Three Years,* yet retaining the lively, conversational tone characteristic of the earlier version, *The American Fugitive* is one of Brown's best literary efforts.

20. *The Anti-Slavery Harp,* compiled by William Wells Brown (Boston, 1848).

21. William Wells Brown, *A Description of William Wells Brown's Original Panoramic Views of the Scenes in the Life of an American Slave . . .* (London, n.d.).

22. Farrison, p. 210. I have not read Brown's sketch.

23. William Wells Brown, *Clotel, or, The President's Daughter: A Narra-*

tive of Slave Life in the United States . . . (London, 1853). Parenthetical page numbers in my text refer to this edition.

24. Lydia Maria Child, "The Quadroons," *Fact and Fiction: A Collection of Stories* (New York, 1846). The story first appeared in *The Liberty Bell* for 1842. For other origins of *Clotel,* see Farrison, pp. 175, 210, 227.

25. William Wells Brown, *Miralda; or, the Beautiful Quadroon. A Romance of American Slavery* . . . , *Weekly Anglo-African,* November 30, 1860-March 16, 1861. The parenthetical date in my text refers to the date of the newspaper in which the quoted material appeared.

26. William Wells Brown, *Clotelle: A Tale of the Southern States* (Boston, 1864).

27. William Wells Brown, *Clotelle, or, the Colored Heroine* (Boston, 1867), Brown's history is entitled *The Negro in the American Rebellion: His Heroism and His Fidelity* (Boston, 1867). His other historical works include *The Black Man, His Antecedents, His Genius, and His Achievements* (New York and Boston, 1863); and *The Rising Son; or, the Antecedents and Advancement of the Colored Race* Boston, 1874. Brown's dramas are discussed in Doris M. Abramson, "William Wells Brown: America's First Negro Playwright," *Educational Theatre Journal,* 20 (October 1968), 370-75. In Brown's final book, an extended essay entitled *My Southern Home; or, the South and its People* (Boston, 1880), he reworks into finished form many of the anecdotes and themes he had dealt with for almost forty years in fiction, drama, and history. Brown died at Boston in 1884. For discussions of his work as an historian, see Earl E. Thorpe, *Negro Historians in the United States* (Baton Rouge, 1958), pp. 24-28; and Coleman, noted above.

28. The phrase is Redding's, taken from the "Preface," of *To Make a Poet Black.* The "tragic mulatto" figure is identified in Sterling A. Brown, "Negro Characters as Seen by White Authors," *Journal of Negro Education, VIII* (July, 1939), 275-90. and more recently in his "A Century of Negro Portraiture in American Literature," *Massachusetts Review, VII* (1966), 73-96. Also see Penelope Bullock, "The Mulatto in American Fiction," *Phylon, VI* (1945), 78-82; and Jules Zanger, "The 'Tragic Octoroon' in Pre-Civil War Fiction," *American Quarterly, XVIII* (1966), 63-70. Blyden Jackson, "A Golden Mean for the Negro Novel," *College Language Association Journal, II* (1959), 81-87, asserts that black fiction, traditionally a literature of protest, could hardly have centered on a less effective embodiment of its message.

Nineteenth-century pictures of armed black men are rare. This portrayal of the Nat Turner revolt is a foldout from a pamphlet published while Turner was still at large.

Part Four:

An Insurrectionist Perspective

As for the black—whose brain, not body, had schemed and led the revolt, with the plot—his slight frame, inadequate to that which it held, had at once yielded to the superior muscular strength of his captor, in the boat. Seeing all was over, he uttered no sound, and could not be forced to. His aspect seemed to say, since I cannot do deeds, I will not speak words.

Herman Melville, "Benito Cereno"

In 1831, a half-century after Jefferson had warned obliquely against servile revolt in *Notes on Virginia* and hinted at the possibility that under slavery the truth about the black man was veiled, Nat Turner rose. His *Confessions* lurks behind the black characters drawn by plantation and abolitionist writers and dramatizes their lack of dimension.

The Nat Turner figure, the figure of the black rebel who attempts the violent overthrow of slavery from within, appears repeatedly in literature written between 1830 and 1863, but is almost always muffled. The slave narrators, many of whom were intensely religious and all of whom shared Turner's hatred of slavery, revealed themselves to be essentially unlike the God-bitten Turner. He deliberately returned to bondage after a successful escape because he believed himself destined not to realize his own mundane liberty, but to fulfill a heavenly injunction to lead an uprising against the oppressors of his people. Even the most otherworldly of the fugitives fixed his eyes a bit lower, escaping to freedom and using less bloody means to work for the liberation of his brothers. In the background of their narratives, however, the writers frequently include figures of black men who wage a guerrilla war against slavery from within the South.

Although the figure of the black insurrectionist is suggested in plantation fiction—in *Swallow Barn* in the guise of Abe's outlaw comrades and in the devil Mike Brown encountered in the swamps, and in *The Yemassee* in the glimpse of diaboloical Indians as blacks—the Nat Turner figure is of course seen more often in the antislavery novels. Hildreth's *Archy Moore* presents him as Black Thomas, executioner of a brutal overseer; and its sequel, *The White Slave,* dramatizes his defiance of his captors. Brown hints at him in *Clotel* in the George-Jerome figure, who expresses his determination to lead a slave rebellion, although he later chooses escape to insurgency. Harriet Beecher Stowe's Uncle Tom, like Nat Turner, has visions, but they teach him to accept his suffering on earth, not to lead the Army of the Lord as Turner did. Although Mrs. Stowe patterns the religious experiences of the protagonist of her second novel, *Dred,* directly on Nat Turner's *Confessions,* significantly, unlike Turner, Dred never carries out his plot. Despite its recurrence, the figure of the black rebel is not fully realized in the narratives, or in plantation and anti-slavery fiction. However, in viewing these portrayals of the insurrectionist figure as inadequate to Turner's *Confessions,* it must be remembered that the *Confessions* themselves cannot be accepted uncritically. They are not the words of Nat Turner, but his statements as transcribed and edited by Thomas R. Gray, a Virginia attorney. Even if one could be certain that the *Confessions* were Turner's own, knowing that the slaves used deception and falsehood as weapons in their war against slavery, one could never be sure they were true. Given the text, it is impossible to know to what extent they reflect the captured black rebel who believes he has done God's work, and to what extent they reflect his victorious white enemy who sees him as a fiend.

An outstanding addition to the portrayals of the black insurrectionist has recently been discovered in a long-lost novel written by Martin Delany, a black nationalist leader who may have been involved in John Brown's conspiracy. In *Blake,* Delany conceals both his hero and his revolutionary mission. A dangerous agitator and organizer, his insurrectionist leader moves in secret, viewed with wonder by his followers as an instrument of God's vengeance. Because the text of the novel, originally published in fragments and then for over a century believed lost, is today incomplete, even the outcome of this fictional black conspiracy remains unknown.

But though Nat Turner's form cannot be seen clearly in the narratives or in popular fiction, and his voice is not directly heard in response to the official interrogation, his ominous presence pervades our literature. The diabolical black man in American letters is of course an Old World devil transported to the new Eden; but his vital force bears the weight of our peculiar American experience. There really were dangerous black men in the American forest in the 1830s, '40s and '50s. It is not idle to suggest that their presence shadows the blackness of our greatest fiction.

CHAPTER IX

NAT TURNER
MARTIN ROBISON DELANY

Now that his skeleton (long the property of Dr. Massenberg) and the purses made from his skin have been lost, all that remains of Nat Turner are his sword, his Bible, and *The Confessions*.[1] Just as the insurrectionist's name belonged to his master (under his last owner he was called Nat Travis) so the *Confessions* are the work of the Virginia attorney Thomas Gray, not of the rebel Nat.[2]

Little is known of the slave insurrectionist.[3] Born in 1800 to an African woman called Nancy who reportedly tried to kill him after birth, and a father who escaped from slavery while the boy was small, Nat grew up in the slave quarter on his master Benjamin Turner's farm in eastern Virginia. He somehow learned to read and write—there is speculation that his literacy might be the result of acquaintance with his master's second son John Clark Turner—and showed himself an apt youngster around the quarter. When his master died in 1810, Nat became the property of Turner's oldest son, Samuel, but was one of twenty slaves sold to raise cash for the heirs at the death of his young owner in 1832. He brought $450, the price of an unskilled fieldhand.

Nat's new master was Thomas Moore, owner of a farm three miles northeast of the Turner plantation. Evidently while at

Moore's, Nat was placed under a new overseer and ran away, but after a month in the woods he returned. He did not escape again. Commentators speak of his wife, who evidently belonged to a neighboring slave holder, and mention children, but information about Nat's personal life, like that of most slaves, is almost non-existent,[4] although it is known that in this period he began to gain a reputation as a religious exhorter. While Nat preached among the slaves, baptized a white man, and was said to see visions, his religious activities evidently did not impair his efficiency on the farm, for he seems to have been made head of a work gang. In 1828 his third owner died, and he was willed to the son Putnam Moore, but continued to live on his widowed mistress' farm. In October of the following year, she remarried, and her new husband, Joseph Travis, moved to her place to live.

On August 21 and 22, 1831, Nat led his fellow slaves in the bloodiest servile insurrection in American history. He disappeared the following day, and for more than nine weeks was at large. Then after capture, torture, jail, interrogation, and trial, Nat Turner was executed November 11, 1831. His deceased master's estate was reimbursed by the government in the amount of his value, $375.

Although by the time Nat Turner was caught, the white community had retaliated for the massacre of fifty-five of its members by murdering at least an equal number of blacks and, through its courts, by executing or transporting twenty-nine more, it was unable to grasp the meaning of the insurrection.[5] As Gray points out, most of the doomed blacks had gone to their deaths "without revealing any thing at all satisfactory, as to the motives which governed them, or the means by which they expected to accomplish their object. Every thing connected with this sad affair was wrapt in mystery. . . ." Thus he reports that "public curiosity has been on the stretch to understand the origins and progress of this dreadful conspiracy, and the motives which influence its diabolical actors." When Nat Turner was finally captured, Gray visited the rebel in his cell at Jerusalem (129). Finding the prisoner "willing to make a full and free confession of the origin, progress, and consummation of the insurrectionary movements of the slaves," the lawyer "determined for the gratificaion of public curiosity to commit his statements to writing, and publish them, with little or no variation, from his own words" (129). *The Confessions* are the result of the conversations Gray had with Turner on November 1, 2, and 3, 1831. They were read at the trial on November 5, and copyrighted by Gray on November 10. The next day Nat Turner was dead.

The Confessions are encased in official documents. First comes Gray's introductory note explaining the conditions under which the manuscript was written and drawing appropriate lessons. This is succeeded by a statement from the Clerk of the Court, and another by its members, certifying the authenticity of the manuscript. Only after these do we reach the confessions themselves; they fill a brief fifteen pages. After them, the attorney describes his questioning of the prisoner concerning the extent of the plot. He then makes an effort to characterize him, and closes with some anecdotes concerning survivors of the massacre. More documents follow: a summary of the trial, the text of the Judge's sentence, a list of the whites murdered in the insurrection and another cataloging the blacks tried.

The narrative divides almost evenly between the story of Nat Turner's religious experiences and the events of August 21 and 22, as if the doomed speaker were determined to communicate the first, and the writer wanted an accurate transcript of the second. Turner's recollections reveal his early sense of destiny. At the age of three or four, he astonished his mother by narrating incidents that had occurred before his birth; when this was coupled with "certain marks" on his head and breast, his parents became convinced that he was "intended for some great purpose"; and his grandmother remarked that he had "too much sense" to be raised a slave, and if he were, he "would never be of service to any one" (133-34). His awareness of his special role was fed by the ease with which he learned to read and write, by his successful experiments at manufacturing paper and gunpowder, and by his unusual manners. Sensitive to the response of those around him, the child assumed the role of a solitary, and spent much time in prayer. He reflected especially on the Biblical passage, "Seek ye

the kingdom of Heaven and all things shall be added unto you"
(135). One day at the plough he heard the Spirit utter these words;
they were repeated two years later. The young man now was certain he was meant for some great deed, and, as he mulled over
what had been said of him during his childhood, became convinced that the old prophecies would be fulfilled.

Although, when placed under an overseer, Nat ran away, he
returned after a month because the Spirit had rebuked him for
addressing himself to earthly trials and not to the Kingdom of
Heaven. Soon after, Nat saw a vision in which "white spirits and
black engaged in battle, and the sun was darkened—the thunder
rolled in the Heavens, and blood flowed in streams." He withdrew still more from his fellows to purify himself, and, cleansed,
received promised knowledge of the tides, the planets, and the
elements. When he was shown more visions—in the sky, "the
lights of the Savior's hands," and in the fields, drops of blood on
corn and hieroglyphs in leaves—he knew the Day of Judgment
was near (136-37).

By this time, his reptation for holiness had spread beyond the
confines of the quarter, and he converted a white man. (Excluded
from the church, they baptized each other in the pond.) In May,
1828, the Spirit assured him that "the time was fast approaching
when the first should be the last and the last should be first" but
instructed him to keep his mission secret until he saw signs in
the sky (138). The solar eclipse of February 12, 1831, was his signal
to organize and prepare to kill his enemies. He immediately revealed his intention to four friends, and they set July 4 as the
date of their uprising; but Nat became ill, and they delayed. When
on August 13, the strange "blue sun" appeared, they knew they
could wait no longer. On Saturday, August 20, the men met. The
insurrection began that night.

The recital of the murders is terse and detailed. Nat confesses
that as leader he was to "spill the first blood" and says he tried to
kill his master but missed in the dark, so Travis was slain by
another (139). After decribing the massacre of the family, he reports going to the Francis', the Reese's, and then to Mrs. Turner's.
There he admits attempting to kill Mrs. Newsome and being prevented by the dullness of his sword; she was finally dispatched by

Will's axe. He says that they then proceeded to Whitehead's, where he confesses to killing a girl with a fence rail, then to Porter's, to Edwards', to Barrows', to Harris', to Waller's, to William's, to Vaughn's, and the battle at Parker's field. He describes their regrouping at Ridley's, the confusion in the night, the retreat from Dr. Blount's next morning, and his realization that he had failed; his concealment; and his arrest.

The confession is presented with few interruptions. Gray mentions in a note evidently designed to establish the prisoner's veracity that he questioned Nat about his manufacturing experiments and received convincing answers. But Gray makes the first break in the narrative when he inquires what Turner meant by "the Spirit." Later, when Nat Turner describes the vision directing him to pick up Christ's yoke and fight the Serpent (that is, to lead the insurrection), Gray stops him to ask whether he now realizes that he was mistaken. The certainty of his answer—"Was not Christ crucified?"—evidently ended further interrogation (138). Turner's recital of his spiritual history is not again interrupted.

When the prisoner begins his chronicle of the insurrection itself, Gray questions him about his delay in joining his men, a query that seems to have been posed out of simple curiosity. He later interrogates the prisoner on a more practical level, demanding to be told the truth about the extent of the servile plot, and examining Turner closely about uprisings in neighboring North Carolina. Evidently satisfied by the reply that others might have been led to revolt by the same causes that had moved Nat, the lawyer then restricts himself to cross-examining the prisoner to establish the truth of his statements.

Gray evidently believed the confession to be true. He cites Nat Turner's admission of his role as evidence of his veracity, and, in the fashion of a lawyer, points out that in his cross-examination he checked the prisoner's statements against those he and others had made earlier. According to the trial transcript, when Gray's manuscript was presented as evidence for the prosecution, the defendant accepted it as accurate.[6] Thus historians and commentators have generally credited Gray's book with being in fact what it purports to be: Turner's confession.

But at each point the narrative reveals itself not Turner's work, but Gray's, and the gulf between narrator and author results in a text which is a curious conglomerate. Although Gray uses the first person in his presentation of the confession, he evidently cannot bring himself to state what Turner believed his mission to be. Instead, the speaker is made to refer vaguely to "some great purpose" and "this great object" and "the purpose for which, by this time, I felt assured I was intended." He never says he will lead a servile insurrection. He never even mentions freedom. These peculiarly veiled statements of intent are followed by a flat recital of violence, and both are interrupted by questions and interpolated comments which, like the introductory and concluding sections, clearly reflect the writer's horror of the speaker.

Gray's imagination and sympathy fail him when he makes an effort to grasp the significance of the insurrection and the character of its leader. He finds only that the black man's confession "reads an awful, and it is hoped, a useful lesson, as to the operations of a mind like his, endeavoring to grapple with things beyond its reach" (130). Gray sees the uprising as an aberration; Turner's acts are not the consequence of his slavery, the central fact of his mundane existence, but the result of his spiritual confusion. The white Southerner knows, however, that he can never be certain about the black. Somewhat uneasy with his conclusions, he finally characterizes Turner as a man who "is a complete fanatic, or plays his part most admirably." In either case, the lawyer's solution to the problem is better police protection; he recommends that the Black Laws should be "strictly and rigidly enforced" (147, 131).

Gray's candid description of his responses to the slave rebel, given near the end of the narrative, fully articulates the unbridgeable chasm between writer and speaker and expresses the white man's horror of the diabolical black:

> I shall not attempt to describe the effect of his narrative, as told and commented on by himself, in the condemned hold of the prison. The calm, deliberate composure with

which he spoke of his late deeds and intentions, the expression on his fiend-like face when excited by enthusiasm, still bearing the stains of the blood of helpless innocence about him; clothed with rags and covered with chains; yet daring to raise his manacled hands to heaven, with a spirit soaring above the attributes of man; I looked on him and my blood curdled in my veins. (147-48)

It is appropriate that the most important nineteenth-century novel portraying the Nat Turner figure was written by an Afro-American paricipant of John Brown's convention in Chatham, Canada, and that the full text of his book has never been published between covers.

Although what happened at Chatham is disputed, historians agree that at Brown's request Martin R. Delany arranged for a number of black men to meet with Brown and a dozen of his Kansas followers in a small schoolhouse on May 8, 1858. There he introduced Brown, who, according to minutes kept by one of his men, explained "the general features of the plan of action in the execution of the project. Mr. Delany and others spoke in favor of the project and the plan, and both were agreed to by general consent." [7] After Delany moved that they swear an oath of secrecy, in the name of "citizens of the United States, and the oppressed people," they considered a "Provisional Constitution" which outlined a government appropriate to a group waging guerrilla warfare. Delany and the other members of the Convention adopted and signed the document, elected officers of the provisional government, and made John Brown commander-in-chief. Eight months later, Delany serialized sections of a novel about an antislavery conspiracy entitled *Blake; or the Huts of America* in the black *Anglo-African Magazine*. For over a century the balance of the manuscript was believed lost. Then, in 1970, all but the final chapters were found in the incomplete files of *The Weekly Anglo-African*.[8]

Delany wrote his novel from the special perspective of a free black man at midcentury.[9] He was born in 1812, the grandson of Africans who had been kidnapped to America. When he was ten, his mother, threatened with prosecution under Virginia law for teaching her children to read and write, fled with them to Pennsylvania. After her husband bought his freedom and joined the family, Northern prejudice prevented him from following his trade, and Martin's parents both worked at menial jobs to give their youngest son an education. At nineteen, Martin Delany walked across the Alleghenies to Pittsburgh, where the black community was alive with ferment. A convention recently held at Philadelphia had demonstrated the importance of black organization, and news of Nat Turner's insurrection and of Garrison's *Liberator* suggested alternatives for Afro-Americans to consider.[10] Delany, attempting to gain both a general and a medical education, joined self-help organizations and became involved in the life of the community. By 1836 he had established himself as a "Cupper, Leecher, and Bleeder."

But life was increasingly difficult for free black Americans. In Pittsburgh, as elsewhere in the North, mobs attacked their neighborhoods. In 1838, while in Texas Americans established an independent republic which abolitionists feared would be divided into slave states, in Pennsylvania free black men lost the franchise. Upset by the growing restrictions at home—and perhaps interested in establishing independent black communities in the West, perhaps curious to see slavery in the South—in 1839 Martin Delany braved the dangers faced by a free black man in the slave states to visit Mississippi, Louisiana, Texas, Arkansas, and the Indian Territory.

When he returned to Pittsburgh, Delany established and edited a newspaper and later served as co-editor of Frederick Douglass' *North Star*. He toured the country, speaking to black audiences about racial pride and uplift, to white audiences about slavery and racism. Once mobbed in Ohio, he armed himself with a butcher knife and hatchet and barricaded himself in his hotel, later writing, "we are not slaves, nor will we tamely suffer the treatment of slaves." [11] But his willingness to defend his rights did not guarantee that he could win them. When accepted to study medicine at Harvard, he was driven out by students who protested

"That we have no objection to the education and elevation of blacks but do decidedly remonstrate against their presence in the College with us." [12] When seeking to patent his invention to improve railroad efficiency, he was denied permission because, as a black man, he was not a citizen.

While he attempted to work within the system to assert his rights as an American, Delany did not hesitate to examine radical alternatives. He counselled black rebellion in the event of an American attempt to annex Cuba in *The North Star* during the spring of 1849. Reminding his readers that the Spanish government, claiming an insurrectionist plot, had executed the mulatto poet Placido and terrorized the free black community a few years earlier, he announced that "the day has arrived when the colored race . . . must defend ourselves and the cause of our brethren, regardless of consequences," and asserted that "at the instant of the annexation of Cuba to the United States, it should be the signal for simultaneous rebellion of all the slaves in the Southern States, and throughout that island." [13] Three years later, waiting for the Patent Office to act on his application, Delany suggested another radical alternative to black Americans: emigration.

His preface to his first book, *The Condition, Elevation, Emigration, and Destiny of the Colored People of the United States, Politically Considered,* marks Delany a maverick:

> The colored people are not yet known, even to their most professed friends among the white Americans; for the reason, that politicians, religionists, colonizationists, and abolitionists, have each and all, at different times, presumed to *think* for, dictate to, and *know* better what suited colored people, than they knew for themselves; and consequently, there has been no other knowledge of them obtained, than that which has been obtained through these mediums. . . . A moral and mental, is as obnoxious as a physical servitude, and not to be tolerated; as the one may, eventually, lead to the other. Of these we feel the direful effects. [14]

Delany argues that despite the fact that "we are Americans" and have made significant contributions to American culture, black people in the United States are "a nation within a nation," treated as second-class citizens even within the antislavery movement (48, 12). He points out that under the provisions of the 1850 Fugitive Slave Law "the colored people of the United States are positively degraded beneath the level of the whites," and reasons that in order to achieve dignity, they must emigrate and establish their own nation (154). Delany asserts that "our elevation must be the result of self-efforts, and work of our *own hands*" (45-46). Like all abolitionists rejecting the Liberia of the Colonization Society, he finds Canada unfit because vulnerable to Americanization, and suggests establishing a black republic in Central or South America. Delany ends with a plea for black pride, and proposes an alternative site for emigration in an appendix entitled "A Project for an Expedition of Adventure, to the Eastern Coast of Africa."

The next year, while Douglass was organizing a new convention to realize the rights of black people within the United States, Martin Delany called a National Emigration Convention to investigate establishing a black republic elsewhere. To implement the work of this Convention, he began raising funds from the black community to finance an expedition to Africa. Before the United States Supreme Court, in the Dred Scott decision, stripped black Americans of their citizenship, he had moved his wife and children to the black settlement in Chatham, Canada West. In May, 1858, John Brown found him there.

There is no question that Delany's role in the Chatham convention was crucial, but there is debate as to whether he knew of Brown's plan to attack the United States Arsenal at Harper's Ferry. The entire affair was of course cloaked in secrecy. In a statement later prepared in prison while on trial for his life, one of Brown's men clearly implied that the plans were discussed at Chatham, and another, in testimony before the United States Senate Harper's Ferry Investigation Committee, stated that Brown had said he would use the mountains as a base of operations. But in 1867, while telling his life story to his biographer, Delany, then

a Major in the United States Army, claimed that Brown had proposed at Chatham only to run an underground railway to the
Kansas Territory—a statement which, as one of Delany's recent
biographers points out, is "strangely at variance with all other
firsthand accounts of the gathering." [15] After the convention,
Brown delayed his attack because of betrayal, and Delany returned to his emigration project.

Delany had consistently opposed white domination of the
black movement. Typically, a few years earlier he had attacked
Uncle Tom's Cabin not only because of its colonizationist position, but on the grounds that Mrs. Stowe *"knows nothing about
us,"* and had found the main value of the book to be its use of
slave narrative materials.[16] It is probable that he had then begun
writing a novel about black people in response to the white
woman's version of "Life Among the Lowly." Three chapters of
his book were serialized in January, 1859, and the following
month, deeply engaged in raising funds for his expedition, he
wrote to Garrison asking for an introduction to a publisher.
Delany explained that he was "anxious to get a good publishing
house to take it, as I know I could make a penny by it, and the
chances for a Negro in this department are so small, that unless
some disinterested competent persons would indirectly aid in
such a step, I almost despair of any chance." Writing that "whilst
I have studiously guarded against harshness and offensiveness, I
have given truth its full force in the pictures drawn," Delany
neglects to point out that in contrast to Mrs. Stowe, his message
is black pride and his theme, black insurrection.[17]

Written in two parts, *Blake* depicts the developing struggle
between Afro-Americans and the American slavocracy. Against a
background of linked proslavery conspiracies, a series of intricate
plots dramatizes the organization of a black insurrection. The proslavery forces scheme to deny black Americans their rights; with
Cuban help, to reopen the African slave trade; and to overthrow
Spanish rule and inaugurate American racist practices on the island of Cuba. The black hero, Blake, opposes them by organizing
a slave revolt throughout the American South, by persuading
Africans to overthrow their venial king who participates in the

international slave trade, and by leading a black insurrection in
Cuba.[18] Throughout the novel, Blake works to unite black people.
Despite differences of racial mixture, caste, class and religion, he
organizes them in the struggle to end chattel slavery and elevate
"the African race" (247).

The action of the first book, which takes place in the United
States, focusses on the slaves. After an introductory chapter in
which Americans and Cubans conspire to run a slaveship from
Africa to the New World, Delany begins with an abolitionist version of life on the old plantation. While a Northern judge assures a Southern slave trader that Northern courts will enforce
the Fugitive Slave Law and implement the Dred Scott decision,
the mulatto slave woman Maggie is sold away from her home and
family in Natchez because she refuses to permit her master-father
to use her sexually. When her husband Henry Holland returns
to the plantation and learns that she has been sold to Cuba, he
denounces her master. Though a free man, he is put on the block,
but runs away before his sale is completed. Here Delany changes
the abolitionist pattern. Before leaving, Henry tells friends of his
plan to organize a massive servile insurrection. Then, following a
path similar to that Delany had undertaken in 1839, he travels
throughout the South, meeting with slaves and teaching them
how to organize to fight for their liberty. Henry later returns to
Mississippi to lead his friends and the remaining members of his
family to freedom. Though captured in an incident reminiscent
of Delany's earlier Ohio mobbing, they escape. In Canada, Henry
vows to rescue his wife from slavery, and at the end of the first
book is en route to Cuba.

The second book, which centers in Cuba where the white
conspirators are outfitting their slaveship, focusses on the plight of
free blacks. As in antislavery fiction, Henry conducts a successful
search to find his wife and arranges for her manumission. But then,
explaining that he had been kidnapped to America when a child,
he reveals himself to black Cuban revolutionaries as Henrico
Blacus.[19] He becomes the leader of a well-organized insurrection,
and to ensure their success decides to seize a ship. Aboard the
craft bound for Africa which the Americans and Cubans have

outfitted for the slave trade, Henry and the proslavery plotters confront each other—but the maritime rebellion he plans is aborted, and with the black crew and cargo, Blake bides his time. When he returns to Havana, an American conspiracy to over-throw Spanish rule threatens not only to entrench slavery, but to inaugurate American racist policies on the island. With the Americans committing provocative acts to precipitate a crisis and the blacks under Blake united and organized to fight slavery and racism—the book stops. Although Delany's style is often awkward, his novel is carefully plotted, and it seems reasonable to assume that in the missing chapters he reveals the fate of the planned insurrection and completes his tale. It is tantalizing that the existing text breaks off with the characters anticipating a violent confrontation, and with Gofer Gondolier's menacing threat, " 'Woe be unto those devils of whites, I say!' " (313)

In and around his complex plots, Delany includes genteel set pieces, sentimental poems, authentic black folk tales and songs, and harsh sketches of slave life which reflect both his rich experiences within black America and his wide reading about black people elsewhere. His views of slavery and of the status of free Afro-Americans in the United States and Cuba are particularly interesting.[20] Delany's inclusion of such disparate elements, coupled with his often clumsy style, at times causes his book to lose coherence, but at its best *Blake* is a vigorous montage of black life at midcentury.

On another level the novel is a revolutionary handbook outlining the organization of a guerrilla army of black liberationists. Blake tells his fellow conspirators that they must "take the slaves, not as we wish them to be, but as we really find them to be" (126). Although without his leadership the American slaves are unable to plan an insurrection, even before Blake begins his mission among them they demonstrate their skill in using deception to wage covert war against their masters. The most humorous instance of this is the interrogation of Mammy Judy concerning the disappearance of her grandson, whom she knows Henry has spirited off to Canada:

"Maus Stephen, yeh sen' fah me?" enquired the old woman, puffing and blowing.

"Yes, Judy. Do you know anything about little Joe? I want you to tell me the truth!" sternly enquired Franks.

"Maus Stephen! I cah lie! so long as yeh had me, yu nah missus neveh knows me tell lie. No, bless de Laud! Ah sen' my soul to de ole boy dat way? No maus Stephen, ah uhdn give wat I feels in my soul—"

"Well never mind, Judy, about your soul, but tell us about—"

"Ah! maus Stephen, ah 'spects to shout wen de wul's on fiah! an—"

"Tell us about the boy, Judy, and we'll hear about your religion another time. . . . Come, come, Judy! what are you crying about! let us hear quickly what you've got to say. Don't be frightened!"

"No maus Stephen, I's not feahed; ah could run tru troop a hosses an' face de debil! My soul's happy, my soul's on fiah! Whoo! Blessed Jesus! Ride on, King!" (45)

Judging the old woman crazy, but "an honest old creature . . . religious to a fault," Colonel Stephen Franks and his lady then interrogate their young slave girl. She reports that on the night in question a man in the woods touched her on the shoulder as she left the cabin where the missing boy slept. Pleased at finding a clue, they press her to identify the man, but drop their questioning abruptly when, evidently embarrassed, she finally murmurs to her mistress, " 'Ah tho't t'wah maus Stephen afteh me' " (48).

Blake teaches the slaves how to mount an insurrection. He trains them to rely on organization, to reject the religion of their masters and to forge a new faith of freedom, to resist being co-opted by the enemy, to beware of agents provocateurs and super-militants, to use their masters' money as a "passport through the White Gap," and to fight to the death before surrendering to slavery.

He has different lessons for the free people of color in Cuba. They have begun to organize even before he announces to Placido,

" 'I have come to Cuba to help free my race; and that which I desire here to do, I've done in another place' " (195). When Blake returns after his African voyage, Placido tells him that while he was away, the conspirators " 'have had our gatherings, held our councils, formed our legions, chosen our leaders, and made Henry Blake General-in-Chief of the army of emancipation of the oppressed men and women of Cuba!' " (241). Henry teaches the Cubans to identify their interests with those of their enslaved brothers, to ignore religious disputes, to renounce class differences, to eradicate their own white racism—indeed, to elevate their black consciousness—and to unite to overthrow slavery and end racism.

Delany's message of black unity, pride, and self-reliance, which he had presented in his treatise, is central to his novel. He dramatizes this with both his black hero and his theme, and makes it explicit in an interchange between a Cuban mulatto who questions being characterized as "Ethiopian," and Placido:

> "Colored persons, whatever the complexion, can only obtain an equality with whites by the descendants of Africa of unmixed blood. . . . the whites assert the natural inferiority of the African as a race: upon this they premise their objections, not only to the blacks, but all who have any affinity with them. . . . Let us prove, not only that the African race is now the principal producer of the greatest part of the luxuries of enlightened countries . . . but that in Africa their native land, they are among the most industrious people in the world, highly cultivating the lands, and that ere long they and their country must hold the balance of commercial power by supplying . . . the greatest staple commodities . . . from their own native shores . . . and that race and country will at once rise to the first magnitude of importance in the estimation of the greatest nations on earth. . . . Do you now understand it, Madame Cordora?"
>
> "Indeed I do, Senor Placido; and although I thought I

had no prejudices, I never before felt as proud of my black
as I did of my white blood. I can readily see that the blacks
compose an important element in the commercial and
social relations of the world. . . . How sensibly I feel, that
a people never entertain proper opinions of themselves
until they begin to act for themselves." (260-62)

Delany later raises questions about black superiority and
racial destiny when he has Placido assert that " 'by a comparison
of the races, you may find the Africans in all parts of the world,
readily and willingly mingling among and adopting all the usages
of civilized life, attaining wherever practicable, every position in
society, while those of the others, except the Caucasians, seldom
acquire any but their own native usages' " (262). In another passage, the poet responds to a question about the relative piety of
black and white people by answering, " 'We really are more re-
ligiously inclined than they' " (282). Still later, the entire Cuban
revolutionary assembly proclaims that "The colored races . . .
were by nature adapted to the tropical regions of this part of the
world as to all other similar climates. . . ." (287).

The language used by several characters reflects their racial
thought. Delany counters the epithets of whites, who here as in
plantation fiction refer to black people as animals and devils,
with the epithets of blacks who call the whites devils, "alabasters,"
and "candlefaces."

Delany's cast of black characters is large and varied. His anecdotes about Zack Parker and Eli and Ambrose, in the chapters
describing Blake's tour of the South, suggest the slave narrators.
A number of his other characters, though based on stock abolitionist patterns, deviate from their models. For example, while
Maggie is sexually threatened by her master, here her black husband ultimately frees her. But he is not a romantic hero. Although he too displays attributes reminiscent of the black heroes
of antislavery fiction, Blake does not follow abolitionist patterns.
He explicitly rejects the role of spiritual leader, telling a fellow

conspirator, " 'I am not fit, brother . . . my warfare is not Heavenly, but earthly; I have not to do with angels, but with men; not with righteousness, but wickedness' " (103). The religious slaves Mammy Judy and Daddy Joe, while partially immobilized by Christian doctrines, use their religion against their master. In Africa the tragic mulatto Angeline, who suffers because her white father is a slave trader, convinces him to renounce his nefarious business. On the Middle Passage the exotic primitives Abyssa and Mendi are prepared to revolt against their white captors. In the Cuba section, the large group of genteel upperclass characters use their soirees to plot revolution.

Although Delany includes among his gallery of insurrectionists Placido, whose name and character are based on the historical Cuban poet-rebel; Gascar, a grotesque young sailor who taunts the Americans; and Gofer Gondolier, an impulsive Cuban caterer who hates whites, most of the conspirators are portrayed as unexceptional. They are of all ages, both sexes, all variations of color, speak all dialects, are enslaved and free, rich and poor. They live throughout the South, Cuba, and Africa. The slaves who join Blake's rebellion in America and Cuba are representative: Charles and Andy, the preacher in Natchez; Sampson and his wife in Texas; old Aunt Rachel and Uncle Jerry in Arkansas; Seth and Phebe with their comrades in New Orleans; the conjurers Gamby Gholar and Maudy Ghamus in the Dismal Swamp; old Uncle Talton, whom Blake encounters near Harper's Ferry; and their Cuban counterparts, the African family Oba and Dominico. All are ready to revolt at the signal. The conspiracy is equally widespread among the free blacks in Cuba and the black sailors on the ship. Despite Delany's inclusion of informers and enemy agents, of black men who own slaves and mulattoes who practice white racism, and of passive slaves in the border states of the South, his message is clear. Black insurrectionists are everywhere.

Their leader's name signifies his color. Blake is "a black—a pure Negro—handsome, manly and intelligent. . . . A man of good literary attainments. . . . He was bold, determined and courageous, but always mild, gentle, and courteous, though impulsive when an occasion demanded his opposition" (16-17). From the moment early in his journey when, faltering, he prays for Divine aid in the wilderness, his political mission is viewed in Biblical terms and Blake is characterized as the "Arm of the Lord."

> "From plantation to plantation did he go, sowing the seeds of future devastation and ruin to the master and redemption to the slave, an antecedent more terrible in its anticipation than the warning voice of the destroying Angel in commanding the slaughter of the firstborn of Egypt. Himself careworn, distressed and hungry, who just being supplied with nourishment for the system, Henry went forth a welcome messenger, casting his bread upon the turbid waters of oppression, in hopes of finding it after many days. (83)

The slaves anticipate his appearance and recognize him instantly:

> "How we knows you!" rejoined the old woman. "Wy, chile, yeh got mahk dat so soon as we put eye on yeh, we knows yeh. Huccum yeh tink we gwine tell yah so much wen we don'o who yeh is? Sho, chile, we ain't dat big fool!"
> "Then you know my errand among you, aunty?"
> "Yes, meh son, dat we does, an' we long been waitin' foh some sich like you to come 'mong us. We thang God dis night in ouh soul! We long been lookin' foh ye, chile!" replied Uncle Jerry. (89)

They see in his coming an answer to their prayers:

> "Blessed be God's eternal name!" concluded the man himself. "I've long been praying and looking, but God has answered me at last."

"None could answer it, but a prayer-hearing God!"
replied his wife.

"None would answer it, but a prayer-hearing God!"
responded the husband.

"None did answer it, but a prayer-hearing God!" ex-
claimed the woman. "Glory to God! Glory to God! 'Tis
none but He can deliver." (117)

Blake himself quotes Scripture in accepting his role: " 'You know
my errand among you; you know my sentiments. I am for war—
war upon the whites. "I come to bring deliverance to the captive
and freedom to the bond." Your destiny is my destiny; the end
of one will be the end of all' " (290).

From his first appearance in the novel, when he announces
his mission by saying, " 'My mind is made up, my course is laid
out, and if life last, I'll carry it out,' " Blake is an enigma (16).
It is not remarkable that he uses a series of names (Henry Holland, Gilbert Hopewell, Jacob) to confuse his enemies, or that
when he meets whites he masks himself—although rarely en-
gaging in role-playing, he often remains silent. But Blake is a mystery even to his family and his friends. Early in the book, Maggie's
mother learns with surprise that he is a free man. When he appears in Cuba, his wife does not recognize him. He writes to
friends in Canada that they do not know him. Although he tells
his cousin Placido his life story, he does not explain his nineteen-
year silence, nor does he make clear his reasons for remaining in
slavery so long. (While he claims that he had to "wait and watch
an opportunity for years," the book dramatizes his almost effort-
less arrangements for his son's deliverance and his own escape
[194]). In Cuba, he deliberately conceals his identity from his
father. When he sails for Africa, he hides his destination from his
wife.

In addition, his plan is shrouded in mystery, although Blake
comments that it is " 'so simple that the most stupid among the
slaves will understand it as well as if he had been instructed for
a year' " (39). Similarly, he hides his interim plans from his com-

rades, expecting them to respond blindly to his instructions. Characteristically he speaks indirectly: In the conspiratorial "seclusions" in the South he uses words to conceal his meanings, and in the fully staged Cuban "seclusions" he speaks a ritualistic language perhaps reminiscent of the Chatham proceedings.

Thomas Gray had seen the black insurrectionist as mysteriously diabolical. Martin Delany reverses this vision, and portrays him as a mysterious instrument of the Divine will.

In January, 1859, *The Anglo-African Magazine* published Chapters twenty-nine through thirty-one of *Blake*. In a headnote, the editors assert that

> This work differs essentially from all others heretofore published. It . . . gives in the most familiar manner the formidable understanding among the slaves throughout the United States and Cuba. . . . The work is written in two parts, so as to make two volumes in one, containing some 80 Chapters and about 600 pages. We do not give these Chapters because of their particular interest above the others, but because they were the only ones the author would permit us to copy. The writer of said work . . . is . . . now in this city arranging for an expedition . . . to Central Africa.[21]

The section that follows shows the hero leading fugitive slaves to Canada, a staple situation in antislavery fiction. From February through July, the first twenty-three chapters, in which Delany dramatizes plantation life, his hero's decision to organize an insurrection, and the beginning of his Southern journey, appeared in order. Publication then ceased. It is suggestive that Chapters twenty-four through twenty-eight were not published. In them, Delany's insurrectionist meets with veterans of Denmark Vesey's conspiracy and, in the Dismal Swamp, with a group of Nat Turner's men; then travels through the area John Brown evidently planned to use for guerrilla outposts (manned by escaped slaves who would govern themselves under the document Delany had voted to ratify at Chatham); and goes on to Harper's Ferry.

By October 16, when Harper's Ferry was struck, Martin Delany was in Abbeokuta, trying to establish an African homeland for his people. On his return he published an *Official Report of the Niger Valley Exploring Party,* then updated his novel, incorporating into it some of his African experiences.[22] The first installment was printed in *The Weekly Anglo-African* in November 1861, and the book ran in serial form all winter. It evidently elicited no comment and doubtless no longer seemed current; after the firing on Fort Sumter, the notion of a proslavery conspiracy was not unusual, and war news eclipsed speculation about slave rebellions. The last chapters appeared only months before Lincoln announced that he would issue an emancipation proclamation, and Delany, envisioning a black army of liberation like that in *Blake,* urged that the Union recruit black troops throughout the South. His subsequent career as the first black Major in the United States Army and as political leader so overshadowed his early effort at fiction that in 1868 his biographer omitted all mention of his novel.[23]

Yet *Blake* is a significant portrayal of a black figure other writers suppressed. In the aftermath of Nat Turner's revolt, abolitionist Richard Hildreth had begun his novel with a plea for a new American hero to arise and destroy chattel slavery: "Chosen Instrument of Mercy! Illustrious Deliverer! Come! come quickly! come!—lest, if thy coming be delayed, there come in thy place, he who will be at once, DELIVERER and AVENGER." [24] Delany's guarded portrait outlines the spectre Hildreth had foreseen and dreaded.

Although Nat Turner was literate and might conceivably have written his own story, it is appropriate that his statements have been preserved in a form imposed by his victorious enemy. His silence symbolizes the condition of his people. Under American slavery, a black man's speech did not legally exist. His testimony inadmissible in court, his literacy forbidden by law, quite literally he was made mute.[25] It seems fitting that Delany's enigmatic novel celebrating the Nat Turner figure has been hidden, lost, and broken. The current edition of *Blake* includes the literary equivalent of a "Wanted" poster, advertising for "any information pertaining to" the missing chapters; even fictional black insurrectionists are hard to track.

NOTES—CHAPTER IX

1. Thomas R. Gray, *The Confessions of Nat Turner, The Leader of the Late Insurrection in Southampton, Va. As fully and voluntarily made to Thomas R. Gray, In the prison where he was confined, and acknowledged by him to be such when read before the Court of Southampton; with the certificate, under seal of the Court, convened at Jerusalem, Nov. 5, 1831, for his trial* . . . (Baltimore, 1831). Page references in my text refer to *The Confessions* as reprinted in Herbert Aptheker, *Nat Turner's Slave Rebellion* (New York, 1966). Information on the insurrection is based on materials in F. Roy Johnson, *The Nat Turner Slave Insurrection* (Murfreesboro, N.C., 1966); William S. Drewry, *Slave Insurrections in Virginia 1830-1865* (Washington, 1900); and Aptheker. For relevant materials, see *The Nat Turner Rebellion; The Historical Event and the Modern Controversy*, ed. John Duff and Peter Mitchell (New York, 1971); for a definitive collection, see *The Southampton Slave Revolt of 1831: A Compilation of Source Material*, ed. Henry I. Tragle (Amherst, 1971).
2. According to Drewry, p. 97, W. C. Parker, James R. French and Thomas R. Gray, "the three most prominent and able lawyers available," were assigned to defend the slave insurrectionists. Parker was appointed by the Court to defend Nat Turner. For a similar view of Gray's role, see Seymour Gross and Eileen Bender, "History, Politics and Literature: The Myth of Nat Turner," *American Quarterly*, XXIII (October, 1971), 487-518.
3. Biographical information on Nat Turner is based on information in *The Confessions;* Thomas Wentworth Higginson, "Nat Turner's Slave Insurrection," *Atlantic Monthly*, XVIII (August, 1861), 173-87 (republished in slightly changed form in *Travellers and Outlaws* . . .); William Wells Brown, *The Black Man* (New York, 1865), pp. 59-75; Russel Blaine Nye, *A Baker's Dozen; Thirteen Unusual Americans* (Lansing, 1956); and materials in the historical works mentioned above.
4. Since the appearance of William Styron's prize-winning novel, *The Confessions of Nat Turner* (New York, 1967), the question of Turner's character and life has been hotly debated. For black critics who polemicize against Styron's portrayal, see, for example, Darwin T. Turner, review of Styron, *The Confessions* . . . , *Journal of Negro*

History, LIII (April, 1968), 183-85; and *William Styron's Nat Turner; Ten Black Writers Respond,* ed. John Henrik Clarke (Boston, 1968).

5. The number of blacks convicted comes from Gray. For a discussion of the massacre that followed the uprising, see Johnson, especially Chapters 13 and 17; and Aptheker, pp. 57ff. Drewry, disagreeing, finds "far less of this indiscriminate murder than might have been expected," pp. 86, 87.

6. All the sources I have examined assume that it is legitimate. The only material I have encountered which contradicts Gray's *Confessions* is a piece attributed to Jerusalem postmaster T. Trezvant and published in the Norfolk *Beacon* which Johnson quotes but discounts, p. 145.

    While Turner was still at large, Samuel G. Warner published a sensational pamphlet, *Authentic and Impartial Narrative of the Tragical Scene Which Was Witnessed in Southampton County (Virginia) on Monday the 22d of August last, when fifty-five of its Inhabitants (mostly women and children) were inhumanly MASSACRED BY THE BLACKS!* . . . (New York, 1831). As a contemporary response to the insurrection the pamphlet is fascinating, but it is of no value as a source of information about Turner or the insurrection.

7. For the minutes, see Richard Hinton, *John Brown and His Men* (New York, 1894), pp. 634-35. For a general discussion of the convention, see W. E. B. DuBois, *John Brown* (New York, 1909, 1962).

8. Martin R. Delany, *Blake; or the Huts of America* (Boston, 1970). Page numbers in my text refer to this edition. Between January and July, 1859, Chapters 1-23 and 29-31 appeared in *The Anglo-African Magazine.* From November 26, 1861, until April 26, 1862, Chapters 1-74, this entire edition, appeared in *The Weekly Anglo-African.* Because files of *The Weekly* are incomplete, the end of the novel—which was composed of approximately eighty chapters—is missing.

9. Biographical information on Martin R. Delany was gathered from the following sources: Frank A. Rollin (pseud. of Francis E. Rollin Whipper), *Life and Public Services of Martin R. Delany* (Boston, 1868, 1883); Floyd J. Miller, "Introduction," Martin R. Delany, *Blake; or the Huts of America* (Boston, 1970); Dorothy Sterling, *The Making of an Afro-American: Martin Robison Delany, 1812-1885* (Garden City, New York, 1971); Victor Ullmann, *Martin R. Delany, The Beginnings of Black Nationalism* (Boston, 1971).

10. See n. 1, Chapter VIII above.

11. *The North Star,* July 14, 1848.

12. Sterling, pp. 130-31.

13. *The North Star,* July 20, 1849; April 27, 1849. For brief reference to the aborted slave insurrection, see Herbert S. Klein, *Slavery in the Americas, A Comparative Study of Virginia and Cuba* (Chicago, 1967), pp. 220-21. For annexation intrigues, see Charles E. Chapman, *A History of the Cuban Republic* (New York, 1927, 1969), pp. 35 ff.

14. Martin R. Delany, *The Condition, Emigration, and Destiny of the United States, Politically Considered* (Philadelphia, 1852; New York, 1969). Page numbers in my text refer to this edition.

15. DuBois discusses Brown's secrecy, pp. 162-63. For the statements by Brown's men, see the interview with Kagi, the account by Realf, and Cook's confession in Hinton, pp. 670-706; a section of Delany's account, which is fully presented in Rollin, Chapters 9 and 10, is also included. The modern commentary is made by Sterling, p. 332.
16. *Frederick Douglass' Paper*, April 1, 1853; April 29, 1853; May 6, 1853.
17. Delany's letter is quoted in Sterling, p. 185. It is generally agreed that while the book was probably begun in 1852 or 1853, Delany wrote most of it while at Chatham and revised it after his trip to Africa in 1859 and 1860.
18. For the idea of conspiracy at mid-century, see David Brion Davis, *The Slave Power Conspiracy and the Paranoid Style* (Baton Rouge, 1969); and *The Fear of Conspiracy*, ed. David Brion Davis (Ithaca, 1971), Chapter 5.
19. This, too, was based on Delany's experience. In 1853 he was involved in the rescue of a fourteen-year-old Jamaican boy who had been kidnapped and brought to Pittsburgh. See *The Anti-Slavery Bugle*, June 11, 1853.
20. For modern comparative studies of slavery, see, for example, Frank A. Tannenbaum, *Slave and Citizen, the Negro in the Americas* (New York, 1947); Stanley M. Elkins, *Slavery* (Chicago, 1959); and Klein.
21. Since the present fragmentary text breaks after Chapter seventy-four, it would appear from this description of the manuscript that the editors of the *Anglo-African Magazine* were familiar with the complete text of the novel. The headnote preceding the serialization of *Blake* in *The Weekly Anglo-African* in 1861, assuring its readers that "we have the entire manuscript in our possession," implies that the *Anglo-African Magazine* had stopped publication because of Delany's departure for Africa; and Miller suggests that possibly Delany did not want his book serialized while he was out of the country. But this seems unlikely in light of both the announcement in the 1859 headnote of his preparations to leave and the publication of the last segment in July, two months after he sailed for Africa.

In a note to the current edition, the editor explains that he has corrected the misnumbering of chapters in the original text. Thus in the book, Chapters twenty-nine through thirty-one bear the titles and follow the text of the chapters which were numbered twenty-eight through thirty when they were published in the *Magazine*, January, 1859.
22. M. R. Delany, *Official Report of the Niger Valley Exploring Party* (New York, 1861).
23. Frank A. Rollin (pseud. of Frances Rollin Whipper), wrote the 1868 biography in close collaboration with Delany. Not only does the book ignore *Blake*, it mentions only briefly *The Condition, Emigration, and Destiny of the Colored People of the United States, Politically Considered*, his most important book, and makes little of Delany's extensive efforts for emigration. Delany had been commissioned by the Army in 1865 and sent to South Carolina, where he later served with the Freedman's Bureau. He was politically active throughout Reconstruc-

tion. After 1876 he again looked to Africa, and following the failure
of the Liberian Exodus Joint Stock Steamship Company in 1878, attempted—unsuccessfully—to obtain appointment as minister to Liberia.
In 1879 he published *Principia of Ethnology*. He died in 1885.

24. [Richard Hildreth], *The Slave, or Memoirs of Archy Moore*, 2 vols.
(Boston, 1836). The quotation cited here can be found in the edition
entitled *The White Slave; or, Memoirs of a Fugitive. A Story of Slave
Life in Virginia, etc.*, ed. R. Hildreth (London, 1852), p. 6.

25. See the discussion of black laws in Kenneth Stampp, *The Peculiar
Institution: Slavery in the Ante-Bellum South* (New York, 1956),
Chapter 5.

Part Five:
The Problem Restated

> *At last, puzzled to comprehend the meaning of such a knot, Captain Delano addressed the knotter:—*
>
> *"What are you knotting there, my man?"*
>
> *"The knot," was the brief reply, without looking up.*
>
> *"So it seems; but what is it for?"*
>
> *"For someone else to undo. . . ."*
>
> Herman Melville, "Benito Cereno"

CHAPTER X

MELVILLE'S "BENITO CERENO"

"Benito Cereno," Herman Melville's tale of a slave revolt, was one of the most profound literary responses to the juxtaposition of the races in America published before the Emancipation Proclamation.[1] The story appeared in 1855, at a time when the slavery crisis had become acute, and many Americans had come to share Jefferson's concern about the black man voiced almost three-quarters of a century earlier.

In the first of the Boston fugitive slave trials, Melville's father-in-law, Justice Lemuel Shaw, despite his personal opposition to slavery, had denied *habeas corpus* to George Latimer, whose freedom was later obtained by purchase. After passage of the 1850 Fugitive Slave Law Justice Shaw, obliged to enter his courtroom by crawling under chains put up to prevent angry antislavery citizens from storming the jails, sent the fugitive Thomas Sims back into slavery. The year before Melville sent "Benito Cereno" to *Putnam's Monthly*, federal troops were used in Boston to return Anthony Burns to slavery in Virginia. In response, William Lloyd Garrison had burned the Constitution at a July 4 picnic, and Henry Thoreau, who shared the platform with him, had announced:

I have lived for the past month . . . with the sense of having
suffered a vast and infinite loss. I did not know at first
what ailed me. At last it occurred to me that what I had
lost was a country. . . . The law will never make men free;
it is men who have got to make the law free. They are
lovers of law and order who observe the law when the
government breaks it. . . . Show me a free state, and a court
truly of justice, and I will fight for them, if need be; but
show me Massachusetts, and I refuse her my allegiance,
and express contempt for her courts.[2]

Melville submitted his story to *Putnam's* in the spring of
1855, when Frederick Law Olmsted, the free-soil journalist who
had recently returned from a tour of the South, assumed editor-
ship of the journal. Under Olmsted, *Putnam's* became the first
important national magazine to take a stand against slavery.[3] In
addition to Melville's tale, the last three numbers for 1855 included articles on the threat of slavery in Kansas, a review of
Frederick Douglass' autobiography, and an announcement of
Putnam's new radicalism, which concludes: "The nigger is no
joke, and no baboon; he is simply a blackman, and I say: Give him
fair play and let us see what he will come to" (612).

New York readers of "Benito Cereno" recognized as their
own the curiosity Melville's American sea captain felt upon encountering an unidentified ship. They had shared his response
fourteen years earlier when, as one prominent citizen noted in
his diary, there was "great interest excited . . . about a mysterious
low, black-looking schooner which was seen and spoken to several
times off Long Island, filled with pirates, as was said." The ship
attracting his attention was a Spanish slaver named, ironically,
Amistad, scene of an insurrection on the high seas. Her captain,
although ordered by the slaves to return to Africa, had surreptitiously shifted course and sailed toward Long Island until ap-
prehended by the U.S. Coast Survey. The insurgent blacks were
arrested and tried for murder at Hartford, while the Spanish
throne demanded their return. When in 1841 defense attorney

John Quincy Adams won freedom for the rebels in the United States Supreme Court, they sailed for Africa. The following year, in another sensational maritime insurrection, captives on board the slave trader *Creole* arose and successfully sailed the ship to the British port of Nassau, where they were granted asylum and freedom despite American protest.[4]

Melville's study of insurrection is not based on any of the numerous recitals of these much publicized recent uprisings, but on a narrative published more than a generation earlier recounting a slave revolt that had occurred a generation before that. The changes Melville made in adapting his source are suggestive. He pushes the events even further back in time: Although the incident on which he bases his story occurred during the winter of 1804, he places the action of "Benito Cereno" in the summer of 1799. In addition, while he retains the actual names of the sea captains involved, Melville alters the names of their ships despite the fact that their real names would seem appropriate to his story. Although *Tryal* was the Spanish craft on which Don Benito actually underwent his ordeal, and *Perseverance* Delano's American sealer that finally delivered him, Melville rechristens the rescuer *Bachelor's Delight* and the slaveship *San Dominick*. Both the temporal and nominal changes suggest the black insurrection that had occurred at Santo Domingo in the last decade of the eighteenth century.[5] The terror evoked by the Santo Domingo rebellion and the Nat Turner revolt sets the mood of Melville's "Benito Cereno."

The story projects a shifting triad of figures, envisioned in the distant past as American, Spaniard, and African, but more familiarly recognized by *Putnam's* readers as Yankee, Slaveholder, and Negro.[6] Through them, Melville probes the problem of reality and the nature of evil. The particular reality and the specific evil in "Benito Cereno" involve their relationship as blacks and whites, as masters and slaves.[7]

Like the other characters, Amasa Delano of Duxbury, Massachusetts, the captain of the *Bachelor's Delight,* is seen doubly. He is characterized as a Yankee—curiously investigating the strange ship; self-righteously expounding the doctrine of work; officiously planning to manage affairs on the *San Dominick;* resentful of any implied social slight; and in no way averse, after helping the distressed Spaniard, to totting up the sum he expects to be paid for his trouble. He smugly believes himself the peculiarly favored child of Providence. When he is contrasted with the aristocratic European, he is seen as representative of New World Man: democratic, compassionate, generous, capable of decisive action, although blind to evil and unable to learn from his experience. Nowhere is Amasa Delano more typically American than in his views of the black people. He is unable to penetrate to the truth on board the *San Dominick* because what he sees appears to be a sequence of familiar versions of reality, none of which involves a basic challenge to his preconceptions about slavery and race.[8] Presented with a series of masquerades, he shifts his belief from one lie to another.

When he boards the *San Dominick,* the tableau shown the captain of the *Bachelor's Delight* confirms his earlier suspicions: As he had surmised, the vessel is an old Spanish slaver in distress. Delano's first view of the aristocratic Don Benito shadowed by his devoted slave Babo is, except for the nationality of the master, typical of numberless portraits done in the plantation tradition:

> The Spanish captain, a gentlemanly, reserved-looking, and rather young man, dressed with a singular richness, but bearing plain traces of recent sleepless cares and disquietudes, stood passively by, leaning against the mainmast. . . . By his side stood a black of small stature, in whose rude face, as occasionally, like a shepherd's dog, he mutely turned it up into the Spaniard's, sorrow and affection were equally blended. (60)

During his day aboard the slave ship, the Yankee is presented with a series of scenes which strengthen his belief in the beneficence of the relation between aristocratic master and favorite slave. Like the typical Northern travelers portrayed in plantation fiction, Melville's Yankee captain is so impressed by the beauty of the patriarchal bond that he proposes to buy Babo for himself; but of course he is rebuffed by the slave, who assures him that his master would never consent to the sale.

In addition to this savage parody of the plantation view of the black as happy slave, Amasa Delano is shown a burlesque of the somewhat less familiar abolitionist vision of black people as victims. The role of victimized slave is first played for him by the gigantic black prince Atufal, who appears in chains before Don Benito, acting as despotic master. When Delano learns that the prisoner is being punished for proudly refusing to submit to the Spaniard's will, he suggests the African be pardoned. When he again encounters the chained black, he criticizes the use of shackles, saying he fears the Spaniard is "a bitter hard master." Later, when the role of victim is played by Babo, the Yankee is so shocked by the master's apparent violence against his devoted slave that he voices his disapproval not only of the abuses of slavery, but of the institution itself.

But neither his intermittent dismay at the tyranny of slavery nor his recurrent pleasure in the beauty of the patriarchal relation forces Delano to question his estimate of black people. He envisions the women as exotic primitives, "unsophisticated as leopardesses; loving as doves," and views the men as naturally inferior:

There is something in the negro which, in a peculiar way, fits him for avocations about one's person. Most negroes are natural valets and hairdressers; taking to the comb and brush congenially as to the castinets, and flourishing them apparently with almost equal satisfaction. There is, too, a smooth tact about them in this employment. . . . And above all is the great gift of good-humor. Not the mere grin or laugh is here meant. These were unsuitable. But a certain easy cheerfulness, harmonious in every glance and gesture; as though God had set the whole negro to some pleasant tune.

When to this is added the docility arising from the

> unaspiring contentment of a limited mind, and that sus-
> ceptibility of bland attachment sometimes inhering in
> indisputable inferiors, . . . [it is not surprising that] . . .
> [l]ike most men of a good blithe heart, Captain Delano
> took to negroes, not philanthropically, but genially, just as
> other men to Newfoundland dogs. (99-100)

Because he is incapable of imagining black people in any but a
passive role—devoted servant, victimized savage, exotic primitive
—the American cannot perceive the true situation on the *San
Dominick*.

The possibility that the blacks might be in control of the
ship never enters his mind. Delano's recurrent suspicions are
not directed at the slaves, but at their master. After rejecting the
notion that Don Benito might be an imposter, the American sees
the Spaniard alternately as a pitiful lunatic needing his aid, or
as a pirate plotting against him. Aware of the menacing atmosphere of the *San Dominick,* frankly skeptical of Don Benito's tale
of calamity, and apprehensive about the inquiries concerning
the *Bachelor's Delight,* although Delano momentarily conceives
of a plot against his ship, his racism prevents him from consider-
ing this seriously:

> [C]ould then Don Benito be any way in complicity with the
> blacks? But they were too stupid. Besides, who ever heard
> of a white so far a renegade as to apostatize from his very
> species almost, by leaguing in against it with negroes? (90)

Thus, though he repeatedly entertains the apprehension that the
Spaniard is a pirate, Delano must always return to the view that
Don Benito is ill and in need of help.

Even after Don Benito jumps, Delano still does not see. Only
when he glimpses the slave, livid with hate, in the very act of
trying to kill his master, does Delano apprehend the truth:

> [T]he Negroes [were], not in misrule, not in tumult, not
> . . . frantically concerned for Don Benito, but with mask
> torn away, flourishing hatchets and knives, in ferocious
> piratical revolt. (119)

Then, like the whites of Santo Domingo and, later, of Southampton County, Delano sees the black man anew: He is a savage wild
beast—a wolf that must be struck down. The scene figured on
the sternpiece of the slaveship symbolizing the inevitable struggle
between enslaver and enslaved is thus acted out. The emblem
of the "dark satyr in a mask, holding his foot on the prostrate
neck of a writhing figure, likewise masked," which at the onset
of the voyage perhaps signified Spanish mastery over the Africans,
and after the uprising seemed to figure the masked supremacy
of the rebels, now becomes flesh as the American tramples the
black (58).

The Yankee acts quickly to restore order; that is, to re-estab-
lish white mastery and black slavery. He commands his men to
subdue the insurgents, sails both ships into port where the rebels
can be punished, and then dismisses the incident as unique.
Although events force him to include among his versions of the
black the active form of the insurrectionist, this does not require
that he reject his basic view of the black man as inferior. And
although he penetrates to the violent center of the relation
between master and slave, like Thomas Gray, interviewer of Nat
Turner, Delano prefers to disregard the meaning of what he
has seen.

But the Spaniard cannot ignore it. Don Benito, who epito-
mizes the decadent Old World, as an American type suggests the
Cavalier, our closest approximation to European aristocracy. The
Yankee sees him as embodying both the virtues and the vices of
his class: His manners, when he troubles himself to heed them,
are flawless; but he is proud, and lacks both energy and self-
discipline. Over-refinement and unchecked authority evidently
have led him not only to melancholy and intermittent tyranny,

but, in Delano's muddled view, to villainy or madness. Even
when the Yankee finally apprehends the truth, his estimate of the
slaveholder's character does not change dramatically. While Don
Benito was Babo's slave, Delano could not fathom the depression
from which he was only sporadically aroused to play his role of
tyrant-patriarch; when the Spaniard is restored to actual mastery,
the American is completely mystified by his melancholy.

Don Benito's recital of the events that had taken place on
board the *San Dominick* is presented in the form of a legal
deposition. Its archaic language and rigid conventions are appropriate both to the aristocratic character of the narrator and to
the substance of his statement: Members of the master class for-
mally prosecuted slave insurrectionists in the Old World and the
New for centuries.[9] The Spaniard's fragmented testimony traces
a torturous sequence of violent revolt, broken agreements, white
deception and black terror, climaxing in his participation in the
elaborate masquerade to deceive the American, and culminating
in the battle to capture the slaveship, the re-enslavement of the
blacks, and the recital of their crimes. Throughout, Don Benito
characterizes Delano as "the generous Captain" and depicts the
slaves as inherently cruel. He sees Babo, the insurrectionist leader,
as the quintessence of evil, "the plotter from first to last." He
cannot even confront him at the trial. Incapable of living with
his perception of the reality of evil, and—unlike the American—
unable to ignore it, the captain of the slaveship dies, blighted by
what he calls the shadow of the Negro.

The third figure of the triad, Babo, the prototypical black
slave, is unseen and unheard. His view of the Spaniard and the
American, his response to slavery, his perception of reality, of
good and evil, are known only through the commentaries of
his enemies. We see him through Delano's eyes as a configuration
of features which we later learn are carefully painted masks.
Throughout Don Benito's deposition, the slave is envisioned as
the faceless image of evil. We look at him directly only after his
execution when, his body burned, his head is stuck on a pole in
the city square, a practice—designed, like the display of Aranda's
skeleton, to terrorize—which was observed not only in Lima, but

also in Santo Domingo and in Southampton County, Virginia.
We never hear the sound of his voice. Before the plot is discovered,
he disguises his tones. Afterwards, he is silent.

The peculiar structure of "Benito Cereno" articulates this
deliberate omission. The center of the tale includes three sections:
the events on board the *San Dominick* as observed by the American, their origins and consequences as chronicled by the Spaniard,
and a dialogue between American and Spaniard in which an
attempt is made to determine their meaning. The immediate perceptions of the black man, his subsequent narration, and his final
interpretation are all omitted. But a complete understanding of
the characters and events and their significance—of appearance
and reality, of good and evil—is impossible if this third view-
point is unexpressed. Without the black perspective, ambiguity
is inevitable.

The crucial nature of this omission is underscored both by
Delano's confessed lack of awareness in the first section, and by
the form of Don Benito's narrative in the second. We strike
through the confusion of the American's conflicting perceptions
to encounter only one side of a legal argument. Melville's comment here is studiously ambiguous:

> If the Deposition have [sic] served as the key to fit into the
> lock of the complications which precede it, then, as a
> vault whose door has been flung back, the San Dominick's
> hull lies open today. (138)

But keys and locks, when presented earlier in the narrative,
proved false symbols. Nor does the dialogue between the two
captains satisfactorily disclose the meaning of events, although
it does serve further to reveal their own characters. When Delano,
who perceives black masters and white slaves as white masters
and black slaves, discovers the deception, he mechanically reverses the pattern to conform to his original notion, and believes
the puzzle solved. Complacently confident of the beneficence of

Providence and the efficacy of his own "good nature, compassion
and charity," he points to the brilliant sun, sea, and sky, and
heartily advises the Spaniard to forget what he has known. Don
Benito, who when enslaved was forced to play the role of master,
when restored to actual mastery is obsessed by the ambiguity of
appearances and the reality of evil. Unable to obliterate his
memory of the past or to confront the present, he perceives only
the shadow of the black man.

Melville frames these central sections of "Benito Cereno"
with short introductory and concluding passages. The problem
of the ambiguity of appearances is figured by the initial grayness
with which he shrouds our view; but at the conclusion, this
ominous cast has been illumined, and with clarity and precision
we see a rigid mosaic of intense blacks and whites. Babo's black
head fixed on a pike confronts us in the glare of the Plaza; we
follow its blank gaze across the square beyond Aranda's grave;
across the bridge up the hill beyond Don Benito's grave; and
beyond. Our final vision reveals not Delano's bright sky or Don
Benito's vague shadow, but the decapitated head of the black
man, eyes staring, tongue silent.

In "Benito Cereno" Melville used the standard literary versions of slavery and the black man, displayed their falseness, and
destroyed them. Although he did not attempt to render the black
man's living face or to sound the tones of his authentic voice,
Melville's tale, like the slave narratives, reveals the stereotyped
faces worn by black characters in our fiction to be masks. The
structure of his story, sometimes criticized as inept, brilliantly
articulates a complex vision. Melville did not pretend to speak
for the black man, but he dramatized the perception that his
voice had not been heard. After "Benito Cereno" the masks again
became the conventions of our literature. It would take a long
time for America to produce another literary artist who would
be able to expose them as lies, and still longer to create a writer
who would be able to speak the truth.

NOTES—CHAPTER X

1. Herman Melville, "Benito Cereno," *Putnam's Monthly: A Magazine of Literature, Science and Art*, XXXIV (October, November, December 1855). References in my text are to Herman Melville, *Piazza Tales*, ed. Egbert S. Oliver (New York, 1948).
2. Marion G. McDougall, *Fugitive Slaves (1619-1865)*, Publications of the Society for the Collegiate Instruction of Women, Fay House Monographs, No. 3 (Boston, 1891), discusses the Latimer Case, pp. 39, 40; the Sims Case, pp. 44, 45; and the Burns Case, pp. 45-46. Also see Wendell Phillips, *Speeches, Lectures and Letters* (Boston, 1884), p. 62. Charles H. Foster, "Something in Emblems," *New England Quarterly*, XXXIV (March 1961), 3-35, suggests that sections of *Moby-Dick* are a commentary on Justice Shaw's role. For Garrison's action see *Documents of Upheaval* . . . , ed. Truman Nelson (New York, 1966), p. 216. Thoreau's speech, "Slavery in Massachusetts," was excerpted in *The Liberator*, July 21, 1854. See *Writings*, IV (Boston and New York, 1906), pp. 388-408.
3. Olmsted, whose interest in slavery had led him to undertake a four-teen-month walking tour of the South in 1852, and whose commitment to preventing the spread of slavery had involved him in raising funds to supply guns for Kansas freesoilers and to support free colonies in western Texas, edited *Putnam's* for the publishers Dix and Edwards from May, 1855 until early in 1856. Later that year, the firm brought out his first account of his Southern tour, and Melville's *Piazza Tales*.

For *Putnam's* antislavery position, see Donald E. Liedel, "The Anti-Slavery Novel, 1836-1861," unpubl. diss. (Michigan, 1961), pp. 128-31; and Frank Luther Mott, *A History of American Magazines*, 4 vols. (Cambridge, Mass., 1957), II, 137-40, 426-27.
4. The quotation is from *The Diary of Philip Hone, 1828-1851*, ed. Bayard Tuckerman, 2 vols. (New York, 1951), I, 378.

For an account of the *Amistad* uprising, see McDougall, p. 27. Although doubtless aware of the wide publicity surrounding the insurrection and its leader Cinque, it is debatable whether Melville ever saw the ship. In August, when the mystery craft appeared, he was on the high seas bound from Liverpool; he did not dock in New York harbor until September 30. It is suggestive, however, that a gothic sketch, "The Death Craft," perhaps written by Melville, was published in the Lansingburgh *Democratic Press* on November 16. At the time of the Creole mutiny Melville was in the Pacific. Seven months later, he and his friend Greene themselves rebelled, jumping ship in the Marquesas. See Jay Leyda, *The Melville Log* . . . , 2 vols. (New York, 1951), I, 92-95, 129ff.

The heroism of Madison Washington, leader of the *Creole* mutiny, inspired Frederick Douglass to attempt a short story which in point of view provides an interesting comment on "Benito Cereno." See "The Heroic Slave," *Autographs for Freedom,* ed. Julia Griffiths (Boston and Cleveland, 1853).

5. Harold H. Scudder, "Melville's *Benito Cereno* and Captain Delano's Voyages," *PMLA,* XLIII (June 1928), 502-32, identifies Melville's source.

Though he notes the discrepancy in dates, Scudder dismisses it as "perhaps accidental rather than intentional." Recently, H. Bruce Franklin, *The Wake of the Gods* . . . (Stanford, Calif., 1963), pp. 136-52, has suggested the significance of the change in date, but many critics, evidently more familiar with ecclesiastical than with secular history, have neglected this change and ignored the social and historical implications of the new name for the Spanish ship, and have focussed instead on its religious significance.

For a discussion of the religious motif in "Benito Cereno," see Rosalie Feltenstein, "Melville's *Benito Cereno,*" *American Literature,* XIX (November 1947), 245-55; and Stanley T. Williams, " 'Follow Your Leader': Melville's 'Benito Cereno'," *Virginia Quarterly,* XXIII (Winter 1947), 61-76; and, more recently, William Bysshe Stein, "The Moral Axis of *Benito Cereno,*" *Accent,* XV (Summer 1955), 221-33; and John Albert Bernstein, *"Benito Cereno* and the Spanish Inquisition," *Nineteenth-Century Fiction,* XVI (March 1962), 345-50.

In addition to all of Melville's other associations with bachelordom, he doubtless was familiar with the history of Peter Faneuil, donor of the famous Boston public hall and market. A bachelor who inherited his bachelor uncle's wealth after an older nephew married and was disinherited, Faneuil made a fortune in the slave trade with his ship named the *Jolly Bachelor.* For the bachelor motif, see Richard H. Fogle, "Benito Cereno," *Melville's Shorter Tales* (Norman, Okla., 1960), pp. 116-47; and Max Putzel, "The Source and Symbols of Melville's "Benito Cereno,' " *American Literature,* XXXIV (May 1962), 191-206.

6. For this conception of the figures of the Yankee and the Cavalier—though not for its application to "Benito Cereno"—I am indebted to William R. Taylor, *Cavalier and Yankee: The Old South and American National Character* (New York, 1961). The theme of the Old World versus the New World in "Benito Cereno" is discussed in Richard Chase, *Herman Melville: A Critical Study* (New York, 1949), pp. 143-59; and Fogle, pp. 116-47.

7. The standard critical view of "Benito Cereno" is that the theme of the ambiguity of evil is crucial to the story but that the conception of the black man and the moral problem of slavery are not. See, for example, Feltenstein; Williams; Lewis Mumford, *Herman Melville* (New York, 1929), pp. 244-47; Chase, pp. 143-59; and Yvor Wintors, "Herman Melville and the Problems of Moral Navigation," *In Defense of Reason* (Denver, 1937; 1947), pp. 200-34; and, more recently, Barry Phillips, " 'The Good Captain': A Reading of 'Benito Cereno,' " *Texas Studies in Literature and Language,* IV (Summer 1962), 188-97; and John Seelye, *Melville: The Ironic Diagram* (Evanston, 1970). Newton Arvin,

Herman Melville (New York, 1950), pp. 238ff., suggests that this is why "Benito Cereno" is a failure, and F. O. Matthiessen, *American Renaissance* (New York, 1941), pp. 507-08, judged the work "comparatively superficial" precisely because it raises, and then does not deal with, the moral problem of black slavery.

Another group of critics, however, finds the theme of black slavery central, and believes the story essentially antislavery in attitude. First enunciated by Sterling Brown, *The Negro in American Fiction* (Washington, D.C., 1937), pp. 12-13, this position is developed by Charles I. Glicksberg, "Melville and the Negro Problem," *Phylon,* XI (Autumn 1950), 207-15; by Joseph Schiffman, "Critical Problems in Melville's Benito Cereno," *Modern Language Quarterly,* XI (September 1950), 317-24; and by Warren D'Azevedo, "Revolt on the San Dominick," *Phylon,* XVIII (June 1956), 129-40. In contrast, Sidney Kaplan, "Herman Melville and the American National Sin," *Journal of Negro History,* XLI (October 1956), 31-38; and XLII (January 1957), 11-37, regretfully seconds the conclusions of John Howard Lawson, *The Hidden Heritage* (New York, 1950), pp. 430-31, who had found it "propaganda for slavery."

A number of analyses, disputing this conclusion, suggest that the tale does not necessarily endorse any of the attitudes it presents. See, for example, Allen Guttmann, "The Enduring Innocence of Captain Amasa Delano," *Boston University Studies in English,* V (Spring 1961), 35-45. Also see Leslie Fiedler, *Love and Death in the American Novel* (Cleveland, 1960, 1964), pp. 382-84; R. W. B. Lewis, "Introduction," *Herman Melville,* Laurel ed. (New York, 1962), pp. 20-23; Klaus Ensslen, "Melville's *Benito Cereno,*" *Kleine Baitrage zur Amerikanischen Literaturgeschichte,* ed. Hans Galinsky and Hans-Joachim Lang (Heidelberg, 1961), pp. 27-33; and, more recently, David D. Galloway, "Herman Melville's Benito Cereno: An Anatomy," *Texas Studies in Literature and Language,* 9 (1967), 239-52; Theodore Gross, "Herman Melville: The Nature of Authority," *Columbia Quarterly,* 16 (1968), 397-412; Margaret M. Vanderhaar, "A Re-examination of 'Benito Cereno,'" *American Literature,* XV (May 1968), 179-91; Eleanor Simpson, "Melville and the Negro," *American Literature,* XLI (March 1969), 19-38; and Scott Donaldson, "The Dark Truth of *The Piazza Tales,*" *PMLA,* LXXXV (October 1970), 1082-86.

8. See Thomas F. Gossett, *Race: The History of an Idea in America* (Dallas, 1963). Kenneth S. Lynn relates the Sambo stereotype to "Benito Cereno" in *Mark Twain and Southwestern Humor* (Boston, 1959).

9. Critics disagree about the depositions. Leon Howard, *Herman Melville: a Biography* (Berkeley, 1951), pp. 218-23; and Geoffrey Stone, *Melville* (New York, 1949), pp. 217-21, criticize their inclusion and suggest that Melville should have worked up his source more completely. Fogle, concurring with Williams, suggests that the documents explain everything. Guttman and Lewis argue that their form implies the falsity of the content.

CHRONOLOGY

1776   Declaration of Independence passed after deletion of section condemning Crown for establishing slave trade and slavery.

1777   Abolition of slavery in Vermont.

1780   Gradual abolition of slavery in Pennsylvania. Dartmouth, Massachusetts, blacks protest taxation without representation.

1783   Abolition of slavery in Massachusetts and New Hampshire.

1784   Gradual abolition of slavery in Connecticut and Rhode Island. Jefferson, *Notes on Virginia*.

1787   Northwest Ordinance prohibits slavery in Northwest Territory. Free African Society organized in Philadelphia.

1789   Constitution of the United States adopted.

1791   Slaves revolt in Santo Domingo (twelve years later, black republic of Haiti secured). Bill of Rights takes effect.

1792   Antislavery societies organized in all states from Massachusetts to Virginia.

1793   First Federal fugitive slave law passed.

1799   Gradual abolition of slavery in New York.

1800   Gabriel Plot, Virginia.

1804   Abolition of slavery in New Jersey. Slave insurrection on the ship *Tryal*.

1808   Federal law forbidding African slave trade goes into effect.

1816 American Colonization Society organized. Tucker, *Letters from Virginia.*
1817 Paulding, *Letters from the South.*
1820 Missouri Compromise. *Emancipator,* first Southern abolitionist newspaper.
1821 Liberia founded.
1822 Denmark Vesey Conspiracy, South Carolina.
1824 Abolition of slavery in Central America. Tucker, *The Valley of Shenandoah.*
1827 *Freedom's Journal,* first Afro-American newspaper.
1829 Walker's *Appeal.* Abolition of slavery in Mexico.
1830 First national Negro convention.
1831 Nat Turner insurrection, Virginia. Virginia legislature debates emancipation. Garrison's *Liberator* established. Abolition of slavery in Bolivia. Gray, *Confessions of Nat Turner.*
1832 New England Anti-Slavery Society organized. Nullification Ordinance passed in South Carolina. Paulding, *Westward Ho!* Kennedy, *Swallow Barn.*
1833 American Anti-Slavery Society organized. British government enacts bill abolishing slavery throughout Empire.
1834 Lane Seminary debates.
1835 Garrison mobbed in Boston. Anti-black, anti-abolitionist riots in New York. Murrell Affair in Mississippi. Post Office sacked for antislavery mail in Charleston. Amos Dresser, Lane student, whipped in Nashville. Paulding, *Letters from the South,* revised edition. Simms, *The Yemasee.* Beaumont, *Marie.*
1836 Congress passes gag law against antislavery petitions. Birney mobbed in Cincinnati. Paulding, *Slavery in the United States.* Hildreth, *Archy Moore.*
1837 Elijah Lovejoy murdered at Alton, Illinois. Simms, review of Harriet Martineau, *Society in America.*
1839 Slave insurrection on the ship *Amistad. American Slavery As It Is.*
1840 American and Foreign Anti-Slavery Society formed in consequence of abolitionist schism. Liberty Party organized. Hildreth, *Despotism in America.*

1841   Slave insurrection on the ship *Creole*.

1842   Fugitive slave case: Latimer. Abolition of slavery in Uruguay. Child, "The Quadroons."

1843   Garnet, "Address."

1844   Garrison advances slogan, "No union with slaveholders." Slave plot, Cuba. Placido executed.

1845   Douglass, *Narrative*. Clarke, *Narrative* (revised and republished, 1846).

1846-1848   Mexican War.

1847   Douglass establishes *The North Star*. Liberia declared an independent republic. Brown, *Narrative* (republished, 1849).

1848   Slave insurrection on the ship *Pearl*. Free Soil Party founded.

1849   Paulding, *The Puritan and His Daughter*. Henson, *Life* (revised and republished, 1858, 1879).

1850   Fugitive Slave Law and Compromise of 1850.

1851   Fugitive slave case: Shadrach rescued. Fugitive slave case: Sims returned to slavery. Fugitive slave case: Christiana Affair. Abolition of slavery in Colombia. Kennedy, *Swallow Barn*, revised edition.

1852   Brown, *Three Years in Europe* (revised and retitled *The American Fugitive*, 1855). Delany, *The Condition, Emigration, and Destiny of the Colored People of the United States, Politically Considered*. Simms, *The Pro-Slavery Argument*. Stowe, *Uncle Tom's Cabin*. Simms, *The Sword and the Distaff* (retitled *Woodcraft*, 1854). Hildreth, *The White Slave*.

1853   Abolition of slavery in Argentina. Brown, *Clotel*. Stowe, *Key to Uncle Tom's Cabin*.

1854   Fugitive slave case: Burns returned to slavery. Garrison burns Constitution. Kansas-Nebraska Act. Republican Party formed. Abolition of slavery in Venezuela.

1855   Abolition of slavery in Peru, leaving Western Hemisphere free except for Cuba, Brazil, and the United States. Douglass, *My Bondage and My Freedom* (revised and expanded as *Life and Times*, 1882, 1892). Melville, "Benito Cereno."

1856   Lawrence, Kansas sacked. Sumner caned on floor of Senate. Stowe, *Dred.*
1857   Dred Scott decision.
1858   Convention at Chatham, Canada West.
1859   *Clothilde,* last African slave ship, docks in Alabama. John Brown raids Harper's Ferry. Delany begins serialization of *Blake* (complete text published 1861-1862).
1860   South Carolina secedes. Craft, *Running a Thousand Miles.* Brown, *Miralda* (revision of *Clotel;* reissued as *Clotelle,* 1864, 1867).
1861   Lincoln inaugurated. Fort Sumter fired upon. Delany, *Official Report of the Niger Valley Exploring Party.*
1862   Abolition of slavery in District of Columbia. Union Army accepts black troops.
1863   Emancipation Proclamation.

SELECTED BIBLIOGRAPHY

Where possible, current republications of nineteenth-century materials are included in this bibliography. Because of limited space, nineteenth-century journal articles are omitted.

Abzug, Robert H. "The Influence of Garrisonian Abolitionists' Fears of Slave Violence on the Antislavery Argument, 1829-40." *Journal of Negro History,* LV (January, 1970).

Adams, John R. *Harriet Beecher Stowe.* New York, 1963.

Aderman, Ralph M. "James Kirke Paulding on Literature and the West," *American Literature,* XXVII (March, 1955).

——. "James Kirke Paulding as Social Critic." *Papers on English Language and Literature,* I (Summer, 1965).

Adkins, Nelson F. "A Study of James K. Paulding's *Westward Ho!" American Collector,* III (1927).

American Anti-Slavery Society. *American Slavery As It Is: Testimony of a Thousand Witnesses.* 1839. Republ. New York, 1968.

Aptheker, Herbert. *American Negro Slave Revolts.* 1952. Republ. New York, 1967.

——. *Nat Turner's Slave Rebellion.* New York, 1966.

——, ed. *A Documentary History of the Negro People in the United States,* 2 vols. New York, 1951. Republ. 1962.

Arvin, Newton. *Herman Melville.* New York, 1950.

Bailey, Thomas P. *Race Orthodoxy in the South*. New York, 1914.

Baldwin, James. "Everybody's Protest Novel," *Partisan Review*, VI (1949).

Barnes, Gilbert Hobbs. *The Antislavery Impulse 1830-1844*. 1933. Republ. New York, 1964.

Beaumont, Gustave de. *Marie, or Slavery in the United States*, trans. Barbara Chapman. Stanford, Calif., 1958.

Bennett, Lerone, Jr. *Before the Mayflower: A History of the Negro in America 1619-1964*. Rev. ed. Baltimore, 1966.

Bernstein, John Albert. "*Benito Cereno* and the Spanish Inquisition." *Nineteenth Century Fiction*, XVI (March, 1962).

Bohner, Charles H. *John Pendleton Kennedy, Gentleman from Baltimore*, Baltimore, 1961.

———. "*Swallow Barn*: John Pendleton Kennedy's Chronicle of Virginia Society." *Virginia Magazine of History and Biography*, LXVIII (1960).

Bone, Robert. *The Negro Novel in America*. Rev. ed. New Haven and London, 1965.

Bontemps, Arna. Introduction to *The Book of Negro Folklore*, ed. Langston Hughes and Arna Bontemps. New York, 1958.

———. "The Negro Contribution to American Letters," *The American Negro Reference Book*, ed. John P. Davis. Englewood Cliffs, N.J., 1966.

———. "The Slave Narrative: An American Genre." *Great Slave Narratives*, ed. Arna Bontemps. Boston, 1969.

Botkin, B. A., ed. *Lay My Burden Down: A Folk History of Slavery*. Chicago, 1945.

Braithwaite, William. "The Negro in Literature," *The Crisis*, XXVIII (September, 1924).

Brawley, Benjamin. "The Negro in American Fiction." *The Dial*, LX (May, 1916).

———. "The Negro in American Literature." *The Bookman*, LVI (September, 1922).

———, ed. *Early Negro American Writers*. Chapel Hill, 1935.

Brooks, Van Wyck. *The World of Washington Irving*. Philadelphia, 1944.

Brown, Herbert Ross. *The Sentimental Novel in America, 1789-1860*. Durham, N. C., 1940.

[Brown, Josephine]. *Biography of an American Bondman: By His Daughter*. Boston, 1856.

Brown, Sterling A. "The American Race Problem as Reflected in American Literature." *Journal of Negro Education,* VIII (July, 1939).

————. "Athletics and the Arts." Howard University, *The Integration of the Negro into American Society*, ed. E. Franklin Frazier. Washington, D.C., 1951.

————. "A Century of Negro Portraiture in American Literature." *Massachusetts Review*, VII (1966).

————. *The Negro in American Fiction*. Bronze Booklet No. 6. Washington, D.C., 1937. Republ. New York, 1969.

————. "Negro Character as Seen by White Authors." *Journal of Negro Education*, II (April, 1933).

————. "Negro Folk Expression." *Phylon*, XI (1950).

————, Arthur P. Davis, and Ulysses Lee, eds. *The Negro Caravan: Writings by American Negroes*. New York, 1941.

Brown, William Wells. *Clotel; or, the President's Daughter: a Narrative of Slave Life in the United States. With a Sketch of the Author's Life*. London, 1853. Republ. New York, 1969.

Revised and retitled *Miranda; or, the Beautiful Quadroon. A Romance of American Slavery. Founded on Fact. Weekly Anglo-African*, November 30, 1860-March 16, 1861.

Revised and retitled *Clotelle: A Tale of the Southern States*. Boston, 1864. Republ. with an introduction by Maxwell Whiteman, Philadelphia, 1955.

Revised and retitled *Clotelle; or, the Colored Heroine*. Boston, 1867. Republ. Miami, 1969.

————. *A Description of William Wells Brown's Original Panoramic Views of the Scenes in the Life of an American Slave.* . . . London, n.d.

————. *Narrative of William W. Brown, a Fugitive Slave, Written by Himself*. Boston, 1847. Preface by J. C. Hathaway. Republ. in *Puttin On Ole Massa*, ed. Gilbert Osofsky. New York, 1969.

Revised and retitled *Narrative of William W. Brown, an American Slave, Written by Himself*. London, 1849.

————. *Three Years in Europe: or, Places I Have Seen and People I Have Met . . . With a Memoir of the Author, by William Farmer, Esq.* London and Edinburgh, 1852.

Revised and retitled *The American Fugitive in Europe. Sketches of Places and People Abroad. With a Memoir of the Author.* Boston, Cleveland, and New York, 1855. Republ. Freeport, N.Y., 1970.

Buck, Paul H. *The Road to Reunion, 1865-1900.* Boston, 1937.

Bullock, Penelope. "The Mulatto in American Fiction." *Phylon,* VI (1945).

Burch, Charles E. "Negro Characters in the Novels of William Gilmore Simms." *The Southern Workman,* LII (April, 1923).

Butcher, Margaret Just. *The Negro in American Culture, Based on Materials Left by Alain Locke.* 1956. Republ. New York, 1965.

Campbell, Stanley W. *The Slave Catchers: Enforcement of the Fugitive Slave Law, 1850-1860.* Chapel Hill, 1970.

Cappon, Lester J., ed. *The Adams-Jefferson Letters.* 2 vols. Chapel Hill, 1959.

Cardwell, Guy A. "The Plantation House: An Analogical Image." *Southern Literary Journal,* II (Fall, 1969).

Cash, W. J. *The Mind of the South.* New York, 1941.

Chametzky, Jules and Sidney Kaplan, eds. *Black and White in American Culture.* New York, 1971.

Channing, Steven A. *Crisis of Fear: Secession in South Carolina.* New York, 1970.

Chapman, Charles E. *A History of the Cuban Republic.* 1927. Republ. New York, 1969.

Chase, Richard. *The American Novel and Its Tradition.* Garden City, N.Y., 1957.

————. *Herman Melville: A Critical Study.* New York, 1949.

Child, Lydia Maria. "The Quadroons." *Fact and Fiction: A Collection of Stories.* New York, 1846.

Clarke, Lewis. *Narrative of the Sufferings of Lewis Clarke, During a Captivity of More than Twenty-five Years, Among the Algerines of Kentucky, One of the So-called Christian States of North America. Dictated by Himself.* Boston, 1845.

————, and Milton Clarke. *Narratives of the Sufferings of Lewis and Milton Clarke, Sons of a Soldier of the Revolution, During a Captivity of More than Twenty Years Among the Slaveholders of Kentucky, One of the So-called Christian States of North America. Dictated by Themselves.* Boston, 1846. Republ. New York, 1969.

Clasby, Nancy T. "Frederick Douglass's 'Narrative': A Content Analysis." *College Language Association Journal,* XIV (March, 1971).

Cohen, William. "Thomas Jefferson and the Problem of Slavery." *Journal of American History,* LVI (December, 1969).

Cohn, Jan. "The Negro Character in Northern Magazine Fiction of the 1860's." *New England Quarterly,* XLIII (December, 1970).

Conklin, W. T. "Paulding's Prose Treatment of Types and Frontier Lore Before Cooper." *Studies in English,* University of Texas Publications No. 3926 (July, 1939).

Conrad, Earl. *The Invention of the Negro.* New York, 1966.

Cowie, Alexander. *The Rise of the American Novel.* New York, 1948.

Craft, William and Ellen. *Running a Thousand Miles for Freedom: or, The Escape of William and Ellen Craft from Slavery.* London, 1860. Republ. in *Great Slave Narratives,* ed. Arna Bontemps, Boston, 1969.

Crozier, Alice. *The Novels of Harriet Beecher Stowe.* New York, 1969.

Davis, David Brion. *The Problem of Slavery in Western Culture.* Ithaca, N.Y., 1966.

————. *The Slave Power Conspiracy and the Paranoid Style.* Baton Rouge, 1969.

————, ed. *The Fear of Conspiracy: Images of Un-American Subversion From the Revolution to the Present.* Ithaca, N.Y., 1971.

Davis, Richard Beale. *Intellectual Life in Jefferson's Virginia 1790-1830.* Chapel Hill, 1964.

————. "The 'Virginia Novel' Before *Swallow Barn.*" *Virginia Magazine of History and Biography,* LXXI (July, 1963).

D'Azevedo, Warren. "Revolt on the San Dominick." *Phylon,* XVII (June, 1956).

Delany, Martin Robison. *Blake; or the Huts of America.* Boston, 1970.

————. *The Condition, Emigration, and Destiny of the Colored People of the United States, Politically Considered.* Philadelphia, 1852. Republ. New York, 1969.

————. *Official Report of the Niger Valley Exploring Party.* New York, 1861. Republ. in M. R. Delany and Robert Campbell, *Search For a Place; Black Separatism and Africa, 1860,* with an introduction by Howard H. Bell, Ann Arbor, 1969.

Detweiler, Philip F. "Congressional Debate on Slavery and the Declaration of Independence, 1819-1821," *American Historical Review,* LXIII (April, 1958).

Donaldson, Scott. "The Dark Truth of *The Piazza Tales.*" *PMLA,* LXXXV (October, 1970).

Douglass, Frederick. *Life and Times of Frederick Douglass, Written By Himself.* Hartford, Conn., 1881. Republ. with an introduction by George L. Ruffin, Hartford Conn., 1882. Rev. ed. Boston, 1892. Rev. ed. republ. with a foreword by Alain Locke, Centenary Memorial Subscribers ed., New York, 1941. Rev. ed. republ. with an introduction by Rayford W. Logan, New York, 1962.

————. *My Bondage and My Freedom.* New York and Auburn, 1855. Republ. New York, 1968.

————. *Narrative of the Life of an American Slave. Written by Himself.* Boston, 1845. Republ. with an introduction by Benjamin Quarles, Cambridge, 1960.

Drewry, William Sidney. *Slave Insurrections in Virginia (1830-1865).* Washington, D.C., 1900.

Duberman, Martin, ed. *The Antislavery Vanguard: New Essays on the Abolitionists.* Princeton, 1965.

DuBois, W. E. B. *John Brown.* Philadelphia, 1909. Republ. New York, 1962.

————. "The Negro in Literature and Art." *Annals of the American Academy of Political and Social Science,* XLIX (1913).

————. *The Souls of Black Folk.* Chicago, 1903.

Duff, John B., and Peter M. Mitchell, eds. *The Nat Turner Rebellion: The Historical Event and the Modern Controversy.* New York, 1971.

Dumond, Dwight Lowell. *Antislavery: The Crusade for Freedom in America.* Ann Arbor, 1961.

Duvall, S. P. C. "William Gilmore Simm's Review of Mrs. Stowe." *American Literature,* XXX (1958).

————. *"Uncle Tom's Cabin:* The Sinister Side of the Patriarchy." *New England Quarterly,* XXXVI (March, 1963).

Eaton, Clement, *The Freedom-of-Thought Struggle in the Old South.* Rev. ed. New York, 1964.

————. "The Romantic Mind." *The Mind of the Old South.* Baton Rouge, 1964.

Einsslen, Klaus. "Melville's *Benito Cereno.*" *Kleine Beitrage zur Amerikanischen Literaturgeschichte,* ed. Hans Galinsky and Hans-Joachim Lang. Heidelberg, 1961.

Elkins, Stanley M. *Slavery: A Problem in American Institutional and Intellectual Life.* Chicago, 1959.

Ellison, Ralph. *Shadow and Act.* New York, 1966.

Emerson, Donald E. *Richard Hildreth.* The Johns Hopkins University Studies in Historical and Political Science. Series LXIV, No. 2. Baltimore, 1946.

Farrison, William Edward. *William Wells Brown: Author and Reformer.* Chicago, 1969.

Feldstein, Stanley. *Once a Slave: The Slave's View of Slavery.* New York, 1970.

Feltenstein, Rosalie. "Melville's *Benito Cereno.*" *American Literature,* XIX (1947).

Fiedler, Leslie. *Love and Death in the American Novel.* 1960. Republ. Cleveland, 1964.

————. "Negro and Jew: Encounter in America." *No! In Thunder: Essays on Myth and Literature.* Boston, 1960.

Fields, Annie. *Life and Letters of Harriet Beecher Stowe.* Boston and New York, 1899.

Floan, Howard V. *The South in Northern Eyes 1831-1861.* Austin, 1958.

Fogle, Richard H. *Melville's Shorter Tales.* Norman, Okla, 1960.

Foner, Philip S. *Frederick Douglass.* 1950. Republ. New York, 1964.

————, ed. *The Life and Writings of Frederick Douglass.* 4 vols. New York, 1950.

Foster, Charles H. *The Rungless Ladder.* Durham, N. C., 1954.

————. "Something in Emblems." *New England Quarterly,* XXXIV (March, 1961).

Franklin, H. Bruce. *The Wake of the Gods.* Stanford, Calif., 1963.

Franklin, John Hope. *From Slavery to Freedom.* 2nd ed. New York, 1967.

Frederickson, George M. *The Black Image in the White Mind: The Debate on Afro-American Character and Destiny, 1817-1914.* New York, 1971.

Friedland, Louis S. "Richard Hildreth's Minor Works." *Papers,* Bibliographic Society of America, XL (1945-46).

Furnas, J. C. *Goodbye to Uncle Tom.* New York, 1956.

Gaines, Francis Pendleton. "The Racial Bar Sinister in American Romance." *South Atlantic Quarterly,* XXV (1926).

————. *The Southern Plantation: a Study in the Development and the Accuracy of a Tradition.* New York, 1925.

Galloway, David D. "Herman Melville's Benito Cereno: An Anatomy." *Texas Studies in Literature and Language,* IX (1967).

Glicksberg, Charles I. "Melville and the Negro Problem." *Phylon,* XI (1950).

Gloster, Hugh M. *Negro Voices in American Fiction.* Chapel Hill, 1948.

Goldman, Hannah S. "The Tragic Gift: the Serf and Slave Intellectual in Russian and American Fiction." *Phylon,* XXIV (1963).

Gossett, Thomas F. *Race: the History of an Idea in America.* 1963. Republ. New York, 1965.

Graham, Pearl M. "Thomas Jefferson and Sally Hemings." *Journal of Negro History,* XLIV (April, 1961).

Gray, Thomas R. *The Confessions of Nat Turner, the Leader of the Late Insurrection in Southampton, Va. As fully and voluntarily made to Thomas R. Gray, In the prison where he was confined, and acknowledged by him to be such when read before the Court of Southampton; with the certificate, under seal of the Court, convened at Jerusalem, Nov. 5, 1831, for his trial.* . . . Baltimore, 1831. Republ. in Aptheker, *Nat Turner's Slave Rebellion.* New York, 1966.

Gross, Seymour L. "Introduction: Stereotype to Archetype: the Negro in American Literary Criticism." *Images of the Negro in American Literature,* ed. Seymour L. Gross and John Edward Hardy. Chicago and London, 1966.

————, and Eileen Bender. "History, Politics and Literature: The Myth of Nat Turner." *American Quarterly,* XXIII (October, 1971).

Gross, Theodore. "Herman Melville: The Nature of Authority." *Columbia Quarterly,* XVI (1968).

Guttman, Allen. "The Enduring Innocence of Captain Amasa Delano." *Boston University Studies in English,* V (Spring, 1961).

Gysin, Brion. *To Master, a Long Goodnight.* New York, 1948.

Hawke, David. *A Transaction of Free Men: the Birth and Cause of the Declaration of Independence.* New York, 1964.

Hazard, Lucy Lockwood. *The Frontier in American Literature.* New York, 1927.

Helderman, Leonard C. "A Social Scientist of the Old South." *Journal of Southern History,* II (May, 1936).

Henson, Josiah. *The Life of Josiah Henson, Formerly a Slave, Now an Inhabitant of Canada, as Narrated by Himself.* Boston, 1849.

Revised and retitled *Truth Stranger than Fiction: Father Henson's Story of His Own Life.* Boston and Cleveland, 1858. Republ. New York, 1962.

Revised and retitled *Truth Is Stranger Than Fiction: An Autobiography of the Rev. Josiah Henson.* . . . Boston, 1879.

Herold, Amos L. *James Kirke Paulding, Versatile American.* New York, 1926.

Herring, Hubert. *A History of Latin America.* New York, 1955.

Higginson, Thomas Wentworth. *Travellers and Outlaws: Episodes in American History.* Boston and New York, 1889. Republ. as *Black Rebellion,* New York, 1969.

Higham, John W. "The Changing Loyalties of William Gilmore Simms." *Journal of Southern History,* IX (May, 1943).

[Hildreth, Richard]. *Despotism in America; or, an Inquiry into the Nature and Results of the Slave-Holding System in the United States. By the Author of "Archy Moore."* 2nd ed. Boston and New York, 1840. 3rd ed. Boston, Cleveland, London, 1854. Republ. Clifton, N.J., 1969.

————. "Uncle Tom, The White Slave, Ida May and the New York Evening Post." Boston *Evening Telegraph,* November 13, 1854.

————. *The Slave, or Memoirs of Archy Moore.* 2 vols. Boston, 1836. Republ. New York, 1969.

Revised and retitled *The White Slave; or, Memoirs of a Fugitive.* Boston and Milwaukee, 1852. Republ. London, 1852; New York, 1969.

Hill, Herbert, ed. *Anger and Beyond: The Negro Writer in the United States.* New York, 1966.

Hinton, Richard. *John Brown and His Men.* New York, 1894.

Holman, C. Hugh. "The Influence of Scott and Cooper on Simms." *American Literature,* XXIII (1951).

————. "William Gilmore Simms' Picture of the Revolution as a Civil Conflict." *Journal of Southern History,* XV (1949).

Hone, Philip. *The Diary of Philip Hone, 1828-1851,* ed. Bayard Tuckerman. 2 vols. New York, 1889.

Howard, Leon. *Herman Melville: a Biography.* Berkeley, 1951.

Howells, William Dean. *Literary Friends and Acquaintance: a Personal Retrospect of American Authorship.* New York and London, 1901.

Hubbell, Jay B. *The South in American Literature, 1607-1900.* Durham, 1954.

————. *Southern Life in Fiction.* Athens, Ga., 1960.

————. *Virginia Life in Fiction.* Dallas, 1922.

Hudson, Benjamin F. "Another View of 'Uncle Tom.' " *Phylon,* XXIV (1963).

Hughes, Langston. "To Negro Writers." *American Writers Congress,* ed. Henry Hart. New York, 1935.

Jackson, Blyden. "An Essay on Criticism." *Phylon,* II (1950).

————. "A Golden Mean for the Negro Novel." *College Language Association Journal,* II (1959).

————. "The Negro's Image of His Universe as Reflected in His Fiction." *College Language Association Journal,* IV (1960).

————. "The Negro's Negro in Negro Literature." *Michigan Quarterly Review,* IV (1965).

Jackson, Esther Merle. "A 'Tragic Sense' of the Negro Experience." *Freedomways,* VII (1967).

Jackson, Margaret Young. "An Investigation of Biographies and Autobiographies of American Slaves Published Between 1840 and 1860. . . ." Dissertation. Cornell University, 1954.

Jefferson, Thomas. *Notes on Virginia. The Works of Thomas Jefferson. . . . ,* ed. Paul Leicester Ford. Federal edition. 12 vols. New York and London, 1904-5.

Johnson, F. Roy. *The Nat Turner Slave Insurrection.* Murfreesboro, N.C., 1966.

Jordan, Winthrop D. *White Over Black: American Attitudes Toward the Negro, 1550-1812.* Chapel Hill, 1968.

Jorgenson, Chester E. *Uncle Tom's Cabin as Book and Legend.* Detroit, 1952.

Kaplan, Sidney. "Herman Melville and the American National Sin." *Journal of Negro History,* XLI (October, 1956); XLII (January, 1957).

Kelly, Alfred. "Richard Hildreth." *The Marcus Jernegan Essays in American Historiography by his Former Students at the University of Chicago,* ed. William T. Hutchinson, Chicago, 1937.

[Kennedy, John Pendleton]. *Swallow Barn, or a Sojourn in the Old Dominion.* 2 vols. Philadelphia, 1832. 2nd ed. New York, 1851. Republ. with an introduction by Jay B. Hubbell, American Authors Series, New York, 1929 and 1962.

Killens, John Oliver, ed. *The Trial Record of Denmark Vesey.* Boston, 1969.

Klein, Herbert S. *Slavery in the Americas: A Comparative Study of Virginia and Cuba.* Chicago, 1967.

Lader, Lawrence. *The Bold Brahmins: New England's War Against Slavery, 1831-1863.* New York, 1961.

Lane, Ann, ed. *The Debate Over Slavery: Stanley Elkins and His Critics*. Urbana, 1971.

Lash, John S. "On Negro Literature." *Phylon,* X (1945).

Lawson, John Howard. *The Hidden Heritage*. New York, 1950.

Levy, Leonard William. *Jefferson and Civil Liberties: the Darker Side*. Cambridge, 1963.

Lewis, R. W. B. "Introduction," *Herman Melville*. New York, 1962.

Leyda, Jay. *The Melville Log: A Documentary Life of Herman Melville 1819-1891*. 2 vols. New York, 1951.

Liedel, Donald E. "The Antislavery Novel, 1836-1861." Dissertation. University of Michigan, 1961.

Litwack, Leon F. *North of Slavery: the Negro in the Free States 1790-1860*. 1961. Republ. Chicago and London, 1965.

Lively, Robert A. *Fiction Fights the Civil War*. Chapel Hill, 1957.

Locke, Alain. "Of Native Sons: Real and Otherwise." *Opportunity,* XIX (January, 1941); (February, 1941).

————, ed. *The Negro in America*. Chicago, 1933.

————. "The Negro Minority in American Literature." *The English Journal,* XXXV (June, 1946).

————. "The Negro's Contribution to American Culture." *Journal of Negro Education,* VIII (July, 1939).

Logan, Rayford W., ed. *Memoirs of a Monticello Slave: as dictated to Charles Campbell in the 1840's by Isaac, one of Thomas Jefferson's Slaves*. Charlottesville, 1951.

Loggins, Vernon. *The Negro Author: His Development in America to 1900*. 1931. Republ. Port Washington, N.Y., 1964.

Long, George, George R. Porter, and George Tucker, eds. *America and the West Indies Geographically Described*. London, 1841.

Lyman, Jane Louise. "Jefferson and Negro Slavery." *Journal of Negro Education,* XVI (Winter, 1947).

Lynn, Kenneth S. *Mark Twain and Southwestern Humor*. Boston, 1959.

————. "Mrs. Stowe and the American Imagination." *New Republic,* June 29, 1963.

Mabee, Carleton. *Black Freedom: The Nonviolent Abolitionists from 1830 Through the Civil War*. New York, 1970.

McColley, Robert. *Slavery and Jeffersonian Virginia.* Urbana, 1964.

McDougall, Marion Gleason. *Fugitive Slaves (1619-1865).* Publications of the Society for the Collegiate Instruction of Women, Fay House Monographs, No. 3. Boston, 1891. Republ. Freeport, N.Y., 1971.

McDowell, Tremaine. "The Negro in the Southern Novel Prior to 1850." *Journal of English and Germanic Philology,* XXV (1926).

McIlwaine, Shields. *The Southern Poor-White from Lubberland to Tobacco Road.* Norman, Okla., 1939.

McLean, Robert Colin. *George Tucker, Moral Philosopher and Man of Letters.* Chapel Hill, 1961.

Malone, Dumas. *Jefferson and His Time.* 3 vols. Boston, 1948-62.

Martineau, Harriet. *Society in America.* 3 vols. London, 1837. Republ. New York, 1969.

Marx, Leo. *The Machine in the Garden.* New York, 1964.

Matthiessen, F. O. *American Renaissance: Art and Expression in the Age of Emerson and Whitman.* New York, London, Toronto, 1941.

Maurice, Arthur B. "Famous Novels and their Contemporary Critics, I: *Uncle Tom's Cabin.*" *Bookman,* XVII (1903).

Melville, Herman. *The Letters of Herman Melville,* ed. Merrell R. Davis and William H. Gilman. New Haven, 1960.

————. *The Piazza Tales.* New York, 1856. Egbert S. Oliver, ed. New York, 1948.

Moffitt, Cecil L. "Simms's Porgy as National Hero." *American Literature,* XXXVI (1956).

Moore, Jack B. "Images of the Negro in Early American Short Fiction." *Mississippi Quarterly, XXII (Winter,* 1968-69).

Morris, J. Allen. "The Stories of William Gilmore Simms." *American Literature,* XIV (1942).

Mott, Frank Luther. *Golden Multitudes: The Story of Best Sellers in the United States.* New York, 1947.

————. *A History of American Magazines.* 4 vols. Cambridge, Mass., 1957.

Mumford, Lewis. *Herman Melville.* New York, 1929.

Nelson, John H. *The Negro Character in American Literature. Bulletin of University of Kansas Humanistic Studies,* IV, No. 1. Lawrence, Kan., 1926.

Nelson, Truman, ed. *Documents of Upheaval: Selections from William Lloyd Garrison's The Liberator, 1831-1865.* New York, 1966.

Nicholas, Herbert G. "Uncle Tom's Cabin, 1852-1952." *Georgia Review,* VIII (Summer, 1954).

Nichols, Charles Harold. "The Origins of Uncle Tom's Cabin." *Phylon,* XIX (1958).

———. "Slave Narratives and the Plantation Legend." *Phylon,* X (1949).

———. "A Study of the Slave Narrative." Dissertation. Brown University, 1948.

———. *Many Thousand Gone.* Leiden, 1963; Bloomington, Ind., 1969.

Nilon, Charles Hampton. "Some Aspects of the Treatment of Negro Characters by Five Representative American Novelists: Cooper, Melville, Tourgee, Glasgow, Faulkner." Dissertation. University of Wisconsin, 1952.

Nye, Russel Blaine. *A Baker's Dozen: Thirteen Unusual Americans.* Lansing, Mich., 1956.

Osofsky, Gilbert. "The Significance of Slave Narratives." *Puttin' On Ole Massa,* ed. Gilbert Osofsky. New York, 1969.

Papashvily, Helen Waite. *All the Happy Endings.* New York, 1956.

Parks, Edd Winfield. *Ante-Bellum Southern Literary Critics.* Athens, Ga., 1962.

———. *William Gilmore Simms as Literary Critic.* Athens, Ga., 1961.

Parrington, Vernon L. *Main Currents in American Thought.* 3 vols. 1927-1930. Republ. New York, 1954.

Paulding, James Kirke. "The Conspiracy of Fanaticism." *Democratic Review,* XXVI (May, 1850).

———. "Fugitive Slaves." *Democratic Review,* XXVII (July, 1850).

[Paulding, James Kirke]. *Letters from the South, Written during an Excursion in the Summer of 1816. By the Author of John*

Bull and Brother Jonathan &c. &c. 2 vols. New York, 1817. Republ. New York, 1972.

    Revised and retitled *Letters from the South: By a Northern Man.* 2nd ed. New York, 1835.

Paulding, James Kirke. *The Letters of James Kirke Paulding,* ed. Ralph M. Alderman. Madison, Wisc., 1962.

————. *The Puritan and his Daughter.* New York, 1849.

————. *Slavery in the United States.* New York, 1836. Republ. New York, 1968.

————. *Westward Ho!* 2 vols. New York, 1832. Republ. New York, 1968.

Paulding, William I. *Literary Life of James K. Paulding.* New York, 1867.

Phillips, Barry. " 'The Good Captain': A Reading of 'Benito Cereno'." *Texas Studies in Literature and Language,* IV (Summer, 1962).

Phillips, Wendell. *Speeches, Lectures, and Letters.* Boston and New York, 1884.

Pierson, George Wilson. *Tocqueville and Beaumont in America.* New York, 1938.

Quarles, Benjamin. *Black Abolitionists.* New York, 1969.

————. *Frederick Douglass.* Washington, D.C., 1948.

————. *The Negro in the Making of America.* New York, 1967.

Ratner, Lorman. *Powder Keg; Northern Opposition to the Antislavery Movement: 1831-1840.* New York, 1968.

Redding, J. Saunders. *To Make a Poet Black.* Chapel Hill, 1939.

Richards, Leonard L. *"Gentlemen of Property and Standing": Anti-Abolition Mobs in Jacksonian America.* New York, 1970.

Ridgely, J. V. *John Pendleton Kennedy.* New York, 1966.

————. *William Gilmore Simms.* New York, 1962.

————. *"Woodcraft:* Simms's First Answer to *Uncle Tom's Cabin." American Literature,* XXXI (1960).

Rollin, Frank A., pseud. [Whipper, Francis E. Rollin]. *Life and Public Services of Martin R. Delany.* Boston, 1868, 1883.

Roper, Laura Wood. " 'Mr. Law' and *Putnam's Monthly Magazine:* a Note on a Phase in the Career of Frederick Law Olmstead." *American Literature,* XXVI (1954).

Rose, Alan Henry. "The Image of the Negro in the Pre-Civil-War Novels of John Pendleton Kennedy and William Gilmore Simms." *Journal of American Studies,* IV (February, 1971).

Rosenberger, Francis Coleman, ed. *The Jefferson Reader: A Treasury of Writings About Thomas Jefferson.* New York, 1953.

Rourke, Constance. *American Humor: a Study of the National Character.* New York, 1931.

———. "Tradition for a Negro Literature." *The Roots of American Culture.* New York, 1942.

———. *Trumpets of Jubilee.* 1927. Republ. New York, 1963.

Ruchames, Louis, ed. *The Abolitionists: A Collection of Their Writings.* 1963. Republ. New York, 1964.

———. "The Sources of Racial Thought in Colonial America." *Journal of Negro History,* 52 (1967).

Savage, W. Sherman. *The Controversy over the Distribution of Abolitionist Literature 1830-1860.* Washington, D.C., 1938.

Schiffman, Joseph. "Critical Problems in Melville's *Benito Cereno.*" *Modern Language Quarterly,* XI (September, 1950).

Schlesinger, Arthur M., Jr. "The Problem of Richard Hildreth." *New England Quarterly,* XIII (June, 1940).

Scudder, Harold H. "Melville's *Benito Cereno* and Captain Delano's Voyages." *PMLA,* XLII (June, 1928).

Seelye, John. *Melville: The Ironic Diagram.* Evanston, Ill., 1970.

Sheldon, Austin J. "African Realistic Commentary on Cultural Hierarchy and Racistic Sentimentalism in *The Yemasee.*" *Phylon,* XXV (1964).

Simms, Henry H. "A Critical Analysis of Abolition Literature 1830-1840." *Journal of Southern History,* VI (1940).

Simms, William Gilmore. *The Letters of William Gilmore Simms,* ed. Mary C. Simms Oliphant, Alfred Taylor Odell, and T. C. Duncan Eaves. Introduction by Donald Davidson. Biographical sketch by Alexander S. Salley. 5 vols. Columbia, S. C., 1952-56.

———. [A South Carolinian]. "Miss Martineau on Slavery." *Southern Literary Messenger,* III (November, 1837).

———. "The Morals of Slavery." In Chancellor Harper, Gov.

Hammond, Dr. Simms, and Prof. Dew, *The Pro-Slavery Argument*. Charleston, 1852. Republ. New York, 1968.

[Simms, William Gilmore]. Review of Harriet Beecher Stowe, *A Key to Uncle Tom's Cabin.* . . . *Southern Quarterly Review* (July, 1853).

Simms, William Gilmore. *The Sword and the Distaff*. Charleston, 1852.

Revised and retitled *Woodcraft; or, Hawks about the Dovecote.* . . . New York, 1854. Rev. ed. republ. New York, 1961; Lexington, Mass., 1968.

————. *Views and Reviews in American Literature, History and Fiction*. First series. Ed. with an introduction by C. Hugh Holman. Cambridge, Mass., 1962.

————. *The Yemasee*. 2 vols. New York, 1835. Republ. New York, 1962. Rev. ed. New York, 1853; republ. Alexander Cowie, ed. American Fiction Series. New York and Cincinnati, 1937; Boston, 1962.

Simpson, Eleanor. "Melville and the Negro." *American Literature*, XLI (March, 1969).

Smith, Helena M. "No-Nation Bastards." *Studies in the Humanities*, I (March, 1969).

Smith, Henry Nash. *Virgin Land: The American West as Symbol and Myth*. Cambridge, Mass., 1950.

Stampp, Kenneth M. *The Peculiar Institution: Slavery in the Ante-Bellum South*. New York, 1956.

Starling, Marion Wilson. "The Slave Narrative: Its Place in American Literary History." Dissertation. New York University, 1946.

Starobin, Robert S. *Industrial Slavery in the Old South*. New York, 1970.

Stein, William Bysshe. "The Moral Axis of *Benito Cereno*." *Accent*, XV (Summer, 1955).

Sterling, Dorothy. *The Making of an Afro-American: Martin Robison Delany, 1812-1885*. Garden City, N.Y., 1971.

Stone, Geoffrey. *Melville*. New York, 1949.

Stowe, Charles Edward and Lyman Beecher Stowe. *Harriet Beecher Stowe: The Story of Her Life*. Boston and New York, 1911.

Stowe, Harriet Beecher. *Dred: A Tale of the Great Dismal Swamp.*
2 vols. Boston, 1856. Vols. III, IV of *The Writings of Harriet
Beecher Stowe.* Riverside ed. 16 vols. Cambridge, Mass.,
1896. Republ. New York, 1970.

————. *A Key to Uncle Tom's Cabin, presenting the original
facts and documents upon which the story is founded, together with corroborative statements verifying the truth of
the work.* London, 1853. Vol. IV of *The Writings.* Republ.
New York, 1968.

————. *Uncle Tom's Cabin.* . . . Boston, 1852. Vols. I, II of *The
Writings.* Republ. with an introduction by Kenneth S. Lynn,
Cambridge, Mass., 1962; this ed. reviewed in *The Times Lit-
erary Supplement,* October 4, 1963.

Strout, Cushing. "*Uncle Tom's Cabin* and the Portent of Mil-
lenium." *Yale Review,* 57 (1968).

Stuckey, Sterling. "Through the Prism of Folklore: The Black
Ethos in Slavery." *Massachusetts Review,* IX (Summer, 1968).

Tandy, Jeanette Reid. "Pro-Slavery Propaganda in American Fiction of the Fifties." *South Atlantic Quarterly,* XXI (1922).

Taylor, William R. *Cavalier and Yankee: The Old South and the
American National Character.* 1961. Republ. Garden City,
N.Y., 1963.

Tragle, Henry Irving. *The Southampton Slave Revolt of 1831: A
Compilation of Source Material.* Amherst, 1971.

Trent, William P. *William Gilmore Simms.* American Men of
Letters Series. Cambridge, Mass., 1892.

Tucker, George. "Autobiography of George Tucker." *Bermuda
Historical Quarterly,* XVIII (1961).

————. *History of the United States from their Colonization to
the End of the Twenty-Sixth Congress, in 1841.* 4 vols. Philadelphia, 1856-58.

————. *Letter to a Member of the General Assembly of Virginia,
on the Subject of the Late Conspiracy of the Slaves with a
Proposal for Their Colonization.* Baltimore, 1801.

[Tucker, George]. *Letters from Virginia. Translated from the
French.* Baltimore, 1816.

Tucker, George. *The Valley of Shenandoah.* 2 vols. in 1. New
York, 1824. Republ. Chapel Hill, 1970.

Tucker, St. George. *A Dissertation on Slavery: with a Proposal for the Gradual Abolition of it, in the State of Virginia.* New York, 1861.

Tuckerman, Henry T. *The Life of John Pendleton Kennedy.* New York, 1871.

Turner, Arlin. "James Kirke Paulding and Timothy Flint." *Mississippi Valley Historical Review,* XXXIV (June, 1947).

Turner, Lorenzo Dow. *Anti-Slavery Sentiment in American Literature Prior to 1865.* Washington, D.C., 1929.

Turner, Lucy Mae. "The Nat Turner Family, 1831 to 1954." *Negro History Bulletin,* XVIII (March, April, 1955).

Tuveson, Ernest Lee. *Redeemer Nation: The Idea of America's Millennial Role.* Chicago, 1968.

Uhler, John Earle. "Kennedy's Novels and his Posthumous Works." *American Literature,* III (January, 1932).

Ullman, Victor. *Martin R. Delany, the Beginnings of Black Nationalism.* Boston, 1971.

Vanderhaar, Margaret M., "A Re-examination of 'Benito Cereno'." *American Literature,* XV (May, 1968).

Wagenknecht, Edward. *Harriet Beecher Stowe. The Known and the Unknown.* New York, 1965.

Walker, David. *David Walker's Appeal, in Four Articles; together with a Preamble, to the Coloured Citizens of the World, but in particular, and very expressly, to those of the United States of America.* Boston, 1829. 3rd ed. Boston, 1830. Republ. Charles M. Wiltse, ed. New York, 1965.

Ward, John William. "*Uncle Tom's Cabin,* as a Matter of Historical Fact." *Columbia University Forum,* IX (Winter, 1966).

Warner, Samuel G. *Authentic and Impartial Narrative of the Tragical Scene Which Was Witnessed in Southampton County (Virginia) on Monday the 22nd of August Last, when fifty-five of its inhabitants (mostly women and children) were inhumanly MASSACRED BY THE BLACKS!* . . . New York, 1831.

Watkins, Floyd C. *James Kirke Paulding, Humorist and Critic of American Life.* Nashville, 1951.

————. "James Kirke Paulding and the South." *American Quarterly,* V (1953).

————. "The Political Career of James Kirke Paulding." *Emory University Quarterly,* VI (1950).

Weld, Theodore Dwight, Angelina Grimké Weld, and Sarah Grimké. *Letters of Theodore Dwight Weld, Angelina Grimké Weld and Sarah Grimké 1822-1844,* ed. Gilbert H. Barnes and Dwight L. Dumond. 2 vols. New York and London, 1934.

Welsh, John R. "William Gilmore Simms, Critic of the South." *Journal of Southern History,* XXVI (1960).

Williams, Stanley T. "Follow Your Leader: Melville's *Benito Cereno.*" *Virginia Quarterly,* XXIII (Winter, 1947).

Wilson, Edmund. *Patriotic Gore: Studies in the Literature of the Civil War.* 1962. Republ. New York, 1966.

Wilson, Forrest. *Crusader in Crinoline: the Life of Harriet Beecher Stowe.* Philadelphia, London, New York, 1941.

Wilson, Janet. "The Early Anti-Slavery Propaganda." *More Books,* Boston Public Library, XIX (November, December, 1944); XX (February, 1945).

Winters, Yvor. "Herman Melville and the Problems of Moral Navigation." *In Defense of Reason.* 1937. Republ. Denver, 1947.

Woodson, Carter G., ed. *The Mind of the Negro as Reflected in Letters Written During the Crisis 1800-1860.* Washington, D.C., 1926.

[Woodson, Carter G.?] "Thomas Jefferson's Thoughts on the Negro." *Journal of Negro History,* III (January, 1918).

Woodward, C. Vann. "The Anti-Slavery Myth." *American Scholar,* XXXI (Spring, 1962).

Wright, Lyle H. "Propaganda in Early American Fiction." *Papers.* Bibliographical Society of America, XXXIII (1939).

Wright, Richard. "The Literature of the Negro in the United States." *White Man, Listen!* 1957. Republ. Garden City, N.Y., 1964.

Yellin, Jean Fagan. "The Negro in Pre-Civil War Literature." Dissertation. University of Illinois, 1969.

Zanger, Jules. "The 'Tragic Octoroon' in Pre-Civil War Fiction." *American Quarterly,* XVIII (Spring, 1966).

INDEX

Abolitionist fiction, 83-86; 87-181; Beaumont, Gustave de, *Marie,* 89-90; Brown, William Wells, *Clotel,* 171-74; Brown, William Wells, *Clotelle,* 175-76; Brown, William Wells, *Miralda,* 174-75; Child, Lydia Maria, "The Quadroons," 172; Hildreth, Richard, *Archy Moore,* 91-103; Hildreth, Richard, *Archy Moore* 1852 edition, *The White Slave,* 109-16; Stowe, Harriet Beecher, *Dred,* 143-46; Stowe, Harriet Beecher, *Uncle Tom's Cabin,* 130-40; black and mulatto characters in, 84-86, 184-85; and colonization, 84; and Delany, *Blake,* 198, 202-03, 206; French, 89; and insurrectionist fiction, 184; and Jefferson, *Notes on Virginia,* 3, 4, 84; and Melville, "Benito Cereno," 219; and plantation fiction, 84-85; and race, 84-86; and the sentimental novel, 85; and slave narratives, 85; slavery in, 84; tone, 84

Abolitionists: and non-violence, 121-22; and political action, 108; and race prejudice, 154-55; violence against, 100-01, 109, 123-25, 156-57, 194

Adams, John Quincy, 217

Afro-American writers. *See* Allen, William G.; Banneker, Benjamin; Brown, William Wells; Clarke, Lewis and Milton; Craft, William and Ellen; Delany, Martin Robison; Douglass, Frederick; Garnet, Henry Highland; Henson, Josiah; Nell, William C.; Placido; Smith, James McCune; Walker, David

Allen, William G., 139

American Antislavery Society, *American Slavery As It Is,* 140-42

American Colonization Society, 84, 196

American Peace Society, 170

American Revolution, 5, 24, 28, 33, 39, 52, 53, 58, 59, 63, 70, 71, 76, 93, 128

American Quarterly, 67

Amistad, 216-17

Anderson, Alexander, 14

Anglo-African Magazine, 193, 206

Annexation: of Cuba, 195; of Texas, 107

The Anti-Slavery Advocate, 171

Antislavery arguments: American Antislavery Society, *American Slavery As It Is,* 140-42; Delany, *Condition, Elevation, Emigration and Destiny . . . ,* 195-96; Hildreth, *Despotism in America,* 104-07; Jefferson, *Notes on Virginia,* 3-13; Martineau, *Society in America,* 67-68; Stowe, *Key to Uncle Tom's Cabin,* 142-43; Tucker, George, *Letters . . . on . . . the*